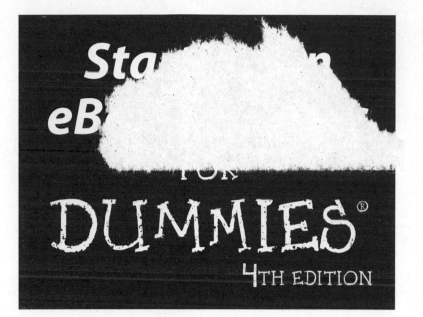

Sta...
eB...
FOR
DUMMIES®
4TH EDITION

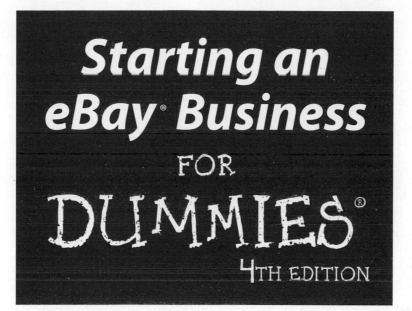

Starting an eBay® Business

FOR

DUMMIES®

4TH EDITION

by Marsha Collier

WILEY

Wiley Publishing, Inc.

Starting an eBay® Business For Dummies®, 4th Edition

Published by
Wiley Publishing, Inc.
111 River Street
Hoboken, NJ 07030-5774
www.wiley.com

For general information on our other products and services, please contact our Customer Care Department within the U.S. at 877-762-2974, outside the U.S. at 317-572-3993, or fax 317-572-4002.

For technical support, please visit www.wiley.com/techsupport.

Wiley also publishes its books in a variety of electronic formats. Some content that appears in print may not be available in electronic books.

Library of Congress Control Number: 2011924114

ISBN: 978-1-118-00467-8

Manufactured in the United States of America

10 9 8 7 6 5 4 3 2 1

WILEY

About the Author

Marsha Collier spends a good deal of time online. She loves buying and selling on eBay as well as meeting online denizens from around the world. As a columnist, author of the bestselling *Dummies* books on eBay, and a radio host, she shares her knowledge of the online world with millions. Her *eBay For Dummies* was published in special versions for the United Kingdom, Canada, Germany, China, France, Spain, and Australia. Currently, she has 30 books in print on her favorite subject — eBay. She also authored the popular book *The Ultimate Online Customer Service Guide: How to Connect with Your Customers to Sell More!*

Before her eBay career took off, Marsha owned and operated her own marketing and advertising firm, a company that won numerous awards and earned her "Small Business of the Year" accolades from several organizations. She got started online during the Internet's early years and quickly mastered the art of making friends online.

Marsha is one of the foremost eBay experts and educators in the world and the top-selling eBay author. In 1999, Marsha created the first edition of *eBay For Dummies,* the bestselling book for eBay beginners. Then she followed up the success of the first book with *Starting an eBay Business For Dummies,* a book targeting individuals interested in making e-commerce their full-time profession. That book became an instant nationwide hit, making several notable bestseller lists. These books are updated regularly to keep up with site and market changes.

Marsha's books have sold more than 1,000,000 copies (including the special editions in foreign countries.

Along with her writing, Marsha is an experienced e-commerce educator. She was the lead instructor at eBay University (teaching seminars all over the United States), as well as a regular presenter at the eBay Live national convention since its inception. Marsha also hosted "Make Your Fortune Online," a PBS special on online business that premiered in 2005. The show was the basis for her PBS premium five-DVD set, "Your Online Business Plan." In 2006, she was invited to address the Innovations Conference in Singapore to present the ideas of e-commerce to a new market.

In 2008, she was dubbed one of 20 influential iCitizens in Kelly Mooney's *The Open Brand: When Push Comes to Pull in a Web Made World,* and was invited to speak at a leading e-commerce conference attended by Coca-Cola, Hewlett Packard, Procter & Gamble, Victoria's Secret, and leading e-commerce leaders.

She hosts Computer & Technology Radio on KTRB 860 AM in San Francisco as well as on the Web at www.computerandtechnologyradio.com. She also makes regular appearances on television, radio, and in print to discuss customer needs and online commerce.

Marsha currently resides in Los Angeles. She can be reached via her Web site, www.marshacollier.com.

Dedication

This book is dedicated to the eBay entrepreneurs who have a zest for knowledge and the "stick-to-it-iveness" to follow through on their projects and stare success straight in the eye. It's dedicated also to those who are convinced that get-rich-quick schemes don't work and that, in the long run, hard work and loving what you do get the job done and lead to financial achievement and contentment.

Good luck in your endeavors. I know this book will help you get started.

Author's Acknowledgments

Updating a book like this is a challenge. Lots of people have helped, but the lion's share of assistance comes from the encouragement that I receive from the eBay community and those I've met when "doing it eBay."

Thank you to the eBay sellers referred to in this book for helping me show how eBay can reach out to the world: Jody Rogers and Asad Bangash (Beachcombers!), Robin Le Vine (Bubblefast), Dan Glasure (Dan's Train Depot), John Lawson (3rdPowerOutlet), Stephen Kline (GalleryNow), Robert McMahan (McMahanPhoto), Jeff Stannard (Melrose Stamp), and Clarissa Parashar (PerpetualVogue).

Then, of course, I want to thank the upper crust at Wiley. My publisher, Andy Cummings, and my acquisitions editor, Steven Hayes, have tried to reach "out of the box" with some of my crazy ideas.

In this book, I had an amazing editor: Barry Childs-Helton helped me upgrade this edition to make it even better. As always, thanks to Patti Louise Ruby, my technical editor and dear friend. This is the eighth book of mine that she's worked on as tech editor; I just can't think of a smarter person to go to for bouncing off ideas.

Publisher's Acknowledgments

We're proud of this book; please send us your comments at http://dummies.custhelp.com. For other comments, please contact our Customer Care Department within the U.S. at 877-762-2974, outside the U.S. at 317-572-3993, or fax 317-572-4002.

Some of the people who helped bring this book to market include the following:

Acquisitions and Editorial

Project Editor: Susan Pink

Acquisitions Editor: Steven Hayes

Copy Editor: Barry Childs-Helton

Technical Editor: Patti Louise Ruby

Editorial Manager: Jodi Jensen

Editorial Assistant: Amanda Graham

Sr. Editorial Assistant: Cherie Case

Cartoons: Rich Tennant
   (www.the5thwave.com)

Composition Services

Project Coordinator: Katherine Crocker

Layout and Graphics: Andrea Hornberger, Corrie Socolovitch, Christin Swinford

Proofreader: ConText Editorial Services, Inc.

Indexer: BIM Indexing & Proofreading Services

Publishing and Editorial for Technology Dummies

   Richard Swadley, Vice President and Executive Group Publisher

   Andy Cummings, Vice President and Publisher

   Mary Bednarek, Executive Acquisitions Director

   Mary C. Corder, Editorial Director

Publishing for Consumer Dummies

   Diane Graves Steele, Vice President and Publisher

Composition Services

   Debbie Stailey, Director of Composition Services

Contents at a Glance

Table of Contents

Introduction

You're here! You've made it! Welcome to the fourth edition of the best-selling book on eBay business: *Starting an eBay Business For Dummies*. This is the book you need to make that leap from casual seller to online mogul. You've probably been on eBay for a while and have seen that there really is a huge opportunity to make a part- or full-time living online. This book will serve as your manual to get organized and get your eBay business launched. Here you'll find the essential information — from how to handle your selling time more efficiently to stocking your store to the *real* way to set up your books and daily operations.

I give you all the details about running a successful eBay business. I pass along not only my own experiences from 11 years of selling on eBay and thousands of interactions with eBay sellers but also timesaving and moneysaving tips and lots of eBay secrets. There's even information on how to use social media to boost your sales!

I've made a successful living while working out of my home for what seems like a lifetime (those corporate-newspaper years fade farther into the background as time passes), and I share my personal experiences to show that you too can run a successful home business. I started my own marketing and advertising business so I could be at home and near my daughter. She's a big-time executive now (don't start counting the years — it's not polite), and I devote my time to selling on eBay (I'm a PowerSeller), running my Web sites, and participating on Twitter and Facebook. Through perseverance and dedication, my small homegrown business financed my home and my daughter's upbringing, private school, and college education. I know that the only limits to my eBay business are time constraints. With the information in this book and some hard work, you too can expand to be an online success.

One thing that I can't guarantee is how much money you can earn. I've discovered — perhaps the hard way — that it takes a good deal of discipline to run a home business. Don't look for shortcuts — the time you spend and the amount of devotion you give your business will be the measure of your success.

About This Book

Profits await! If you've read *eBay For Dummies,* you have the basics. You've probably picked up this book because you've heard stories about people making big money online, and you're interested in getting your piece of the pie.

Do you have a full-time job, but you'd like to sell on eBay part-time? eBay can easily supplement your income for the better things in life. Perhaps you're looking to make a career change, and jumping into an eBay business with both feet is just what you have in mind. If so, this is the book for you.

I've watched eBay change from a homey community of friendly collectors to a Wall Street giant with tens of thousands of categories of items and more than 393 million registered users worldwide. What are *you* waiting for? There's no time like the present to get started on your new career. Thousands of people around the world are setting up businesses online, and now is your time to take the leap of faith to begin a profitable enterprise. eBay gives you the tools, the customers, and the venue to market your wares. All you need is a bit of direction.

Starting an eBay Business For Dummies picks up where my *eBay For Dummies* leaves off. The tips I include here give you the opportunity to improve your eBay moneymaking ability, and can possibly turn an eBay novice into a professional running a booming eBay business. I also show the experienced user the prudent way to turn haphazard selling into an organized business. I've combined the fine points of eBay with real business and marketing tools to help you complete the journey from part-time seller to online entrepreneur.

In this book, you find the answers to some important questions as I take you through the following lessons:

- Reviewing what you know and introducing some of the finer points of eBay auctions

- Sprucing up your auctions to attract more bidders

- Dealing with customers and their needs

- Setting up your business in a professional manner

- Deciding how to handle inventory (and where to find it)

- Using social media to build your customer base

- Getting your online store up and running

- Figuring out what you need to be in an eBay business . . . for *real*

What You're Not to Do

If you use this book the way you'd use a cookbook, jumping around from recipe to recipe (or chapter to chapter), you'll be able to find answers to particular questions. Or read the book from beginning to end if you'd like. Either way, be sure to keep the book handy to answer future questions as they come to you — there's a concise index.

Foolish Assumptions

Because you're reading this, I assume you're getting serious about selling on eBay and want to find out the fine points of just how to do that. Or perhaps you want to know how much time and effort are involved in an eBay business so you can make an informed decision on whether to give it a go.

If I have you figured out, and you've decided that it's time to get serious, here are some other foolish assumptions I've made about you:

✔ You have a computer and an Internet connection.

✔ You've bought and sold on eBay and are familiar with how it works.

✔ You have an existing small business or you'd like to start one.

✔ You like the idea of not having to work set hours.

✔ You feel that working from home in jeans and a T-shirt is a great idea.

I must stop here and say that it would really help (especially if your transactions on eBay total fewer than 100) if you read my beginning book, *eBay For Dummies,* 6th Edition or my *eBay For Seniors For Dummies* (in large print) to get familiar with the basics you need to get started selling successfully.

If you can say yes to my foolish assumptions, you're off and running! Take a few moments to read the following section to get a feel for how I've put this book together.

How This Book Is Organized

This book has five parts. Each part stands on its own, which means you can read Chapter 12 after reading Chapter 8 and maybe skip Chapter 13 altogether (but I know you won't because that's where I discuss the money!).

Part 1: Getting Serious about eBay

Reviewing what you know is always a great place to start. Considering the way eBay constantly changes, you'll probably find a little review worthwhile. So in Part I, I delve into the finer points of eBay. Perhaps you'll discover a thing or two you didn't know — or had forgotten.

Setting up your eBay Store is important; in this part, I show you, step by step, the best way to do it — and give you tips to figure out when the timing is right for you to open your store.

Part 11: Setting Up Shop

You need to decide what type of business you plan to run and what type of inventory you'll sell. Here's where I discuss how to find merchandise and the best way to sell it. I also give you the lowdown on some other places you can sell.

You'll also find out how to research items — before you buy them to sell — so you'll know for how much (or whether) they'll sell on eBay.

I also discuss the importance of having your own Web site and using social media for online sales.

Part 111: Business 1s Business — Time to Get Serious

In Part III, I discuss exactly how to use available online and offline tools, implement auction-management software, jazz up your auctions, and handle shipping efficiently and effectively. Because working with customers and collecting payments are important, too, you'll find that information here as well.

Most importantly, you also find out how to get free shipping material for your business delivered to your door, get your postal carrier to pick up your boxes at no charge, and insure your packages without standing in line at the post office.

Part IV: Your eBay Back Office

Setting up your eBay business as a real business entity involves some moderately nasty paperwork hassles and red tape — but this part will help you get through the maze. I fill in the essential blanks in Part IV and show you how to set up your bookkeeping. This is the place where you'll find a checklist of the items you'll need to run your online business.

You also need to know how to set up your home business space and how to store your stuff. I cover that here — plus bunches more!

Part V: The Part of Tens

You can't write a *For Dummies* book without including the traditional Part of Tens. So, in an untraditional manner, here are ten real-life stories of successful (and happy) people selling on eBay. You also find out about ten places to move your merchandise (if you want to sell elsewhere).

Appendices

I include a not-quite-random collection of terms in Appendix A, the glossary. You're probably already familiar with many of these words from having seen them pop up on eBay, but others will be new to you. Refer to the glossary often as you peruse other parts of the book. Appendix B shows you how to set up a network at home.

Icons Used in This Book

All *For Dummies* books have cute little icons. I certainly wouldn't want to ruin your reading experience and leave them out. So I selected a few and use them sparingly throughout the book. Be sure to take heed when you see them.

Here I share some of the interesting stories I've picked up from eBay sellers over the years. Because I believe that knowledge is enhanced through learning from the successes and mistakes of others, I include these little auction factoids for the insight they offer. After all, if someone else has learned from a unique trick, you can benefit by taking heed.

If there's something I need to interject — okay, something I'm jumping up and down to tell you but it won't fit directly into the text — I indicate it by placing this Tip icon in front of the paragraph. You'll know the tip to follow will be right on target!

Do you really know people who tie string around their fingers to remember something? Me neither; but this icon gives me the opportunity to give you a brief reminder. Kinda like a sticky yellow Post-it note.

I like this picture of the bomb device that Wile E. Coyote slam-dunks in the cartoons. In that vein, if you don't heed the warning indicated by the small petard (hey, Shakespeare knew about old-fashioned bombs), you may end up "hoist by your own petard," or made a victim of your own foolishness.

Where to Go from Here

Time to hunker down and delve into the book. If you have time, just turn the page and start from the beginning. If you're anxious and already have some questions you want answered, check out the handy index at the end of the book and research your query.

Take this information and study it. Success on eBay awaits you. I can't wait to hear your success stories if I meet you at an eBay event or at a book signing in your town.

My goal is to help you reach your goals. Feel free to visit my Web site: www. coolebaytools.com. That way you can stay up to date.

For more about me (and to contact me), visit www.marshacollier.com. To contact me with a brief note, you can find me on Twitter (@MarshaCollier) almost every day. Join me on Facebook, too, at www.facebook.com/ MarshaCollierFanPage, where I share even more (perhaps I overshare?). I respond there, too.

Please send me suggestions, additions, and comments. I want to hear from you and hope to update this book with your words of wisdom. (Humorous war stories are also gratefully accepted!). Please know that I read every e-mail I get, but I just can't answer every one. Know that your comments are truly appreciated and mean a lot to me.

Part I
Getting Serious about eBay

The 5th Wave   By Rich Tennant

©RICHTENNANT

"So, someone's using your eBay ID to buy stylish clothes, opera tickets, and exercise equipment. In what way would this qualify as 'identity theft?'"

In this part . . .

When we've been doing something for a while (such as selling on eBay), often we forget some of the basics. eBay continually makes improvements, and some of its features are like hidden gems in a diamond mine. In this first part, I delve into the finer points of eBay with you. Perhaps you'll discover a thing or two you didn't know or had forgotten.

Chapter 1

Launching Your Business on eBay

In This Chapter

▶ Getting serious about your business

▶ Making decisions about what to sell

▶ Having what it takes to make a living online

▶ Running your business efficiently

So you've decided to step up to the plate and start that eBay business. You should first decide how much time you have to devote. I suggest that you don't quit your day job (yet). Instead, start expanding your sales in baby steps. You can sell part-time and still be a business — and have a nice chunk of extra income. A large portion of sellers, even eBay PowerSellers (those who gross more than $1,000 a month in sales), work on eBay only part-time.

eBay sellers come from all walks of life. A good number of stay-at-home moms are selling on eBay. And so many retirees find eBay a great place to supplement their income that I wouldn't be surprised if AARP creates a special eBay arm. If you're pulled out of your normal work routine and faced with a new lifestyle, you can easily make the transition to selling on eBay.

In this chapter, I talk about planning just how much time you'll be able to devote to your eBay business — and how to budget that time. I also talk about figuring out what to sell. Your eBay business won't grow overnight, but with dedication and persistence, you may just form your own online empire.

I recently received an e-mail from someone who read my book *eBay For Dummies,* and with a head full of enthusiasm, listed more than 100 items for sale. Unfortunately, she failed miserably — so much so that she immediately gave up on the idea of making money on eBay. I know you may get excited to start, but use baby steps. Even with all the advice in this book, you may make mistakes. Baby steps are the way to long-term success.

Getting Down to Bidness (Er, Business)

Before launching any business, including an eBay business, you need to set your priorities. And to be successful at that business, you must apply some clear level of discipline.

I won't bore you with the now-legendary story of how Pierre Omidyar started eBay to help fulfill his girlfriend's Pez dispenser habit, blah, blah, blah. I *will* tell you that he started AuctionWeb.com (the original eBay Web site) with a laptop, a regular Internet service provider (ISP), and an old school desk. He and his buddy Jeff Skoll (a Stanford MBA) ran AuctionWeb 24 hours a day, 7 days a week, all by themselves. When I began using the service, I had a lot of questions — and I always got prompt, friendly answers to my e-mails. When the site started attracting more traffic, Pierre's ISP began to complain about all the traffic and raised his monthly fees. To cover the higher costs, Pierre and Jeff began charging 25 cents to list an auction. Pierre was so busy running the site that the envelopes full of checks began to pile up — he didn't even have time to open the mail.

When Pierre incorporated eBay AuctionWeb in 1997 with his partner Jeff, they were each drawing a salary of $25,000. Their first office consisted of one room, and they had one part-time employee to handle the payments. They started small and grew. Now eBay is a respected, worldwide corporation, employing thousands of people and trading on the NASDAQ Exchange.

Budgeting your time: eBay as a part-time moneymaker

A part-time eBay business can be very profitable. One thing I stress in this book, however, is that the more time and energy you spend on your eBay business, the more money you can make. That said, let's examine the lowest possible level of time you should devote to your business.

Maybe you enjoy finding miscellaneous items to sell on eBay. You can find these items randomly in your day-to-day life. So let's suppose that you could spend at least a few hours (maybe two to three) a day on eBay. Now you must include the time it takes to write up your auctions. If you're selling only one type of item, allow about ten minutes to write your auction, photograph the item (or scan it), and upload it to eBay or a photo-hosting site.

The amount of time required to perform these tasks varies from person to person, and will improve according to your level of expertise. Regardless, every task in your eBay auction business takes time — and you must budget for that time. See the sidebar "Some handy eBay timesaving tips" for pointers.

Some handy eBay timesaving tips

Crunched for time? The following are some eBay features you're sure to find handy:

✔ **HTML templates:** In Chapter 11, I give you some basic HTML templates for attractive auctions (and show you how to find more). These HTML templates cut your auction design time to a few minutes. Most experienced eBay sellers use preset templates to speed up the task of listing auctions, and this should be your goal.

✔ **The Turbo Lister program (free):** When you want to list a bunch of auctions at once, I recommend using the eBay Turbo Lister program. I estimate that Turbo Lister enables you to put together and upload 10 auctions in just 15 minutes. In Chapter 9, I run down the details on how to use this very cool tool.

✔ **The Selling Manager (free) and Selling Manager Pro (free with Premium or Anchor Stores or $15.99 per month) programs:** These eBay subscription programs can help you speed up the nuts and bolts of an ongoing eBay business when you're selling many items a week (more on the Selling Manager program in Chapter 9).

✔ **Relisting (or Sell Similar) feature:** When you sell the same item time after time, you can use Turbo Lister (it archives your listings so you can repeat them) or the handy eBay relisting or Sell Similar feature. When your listing ends on eBay, links pop up offering to relist your listing or to Sell Similar. If you want to sell a different item with a similar HTML format to the one that just ended, simply select the Sell Similar option, and cut and paste the new title and description into the Sell Your Item page of your new listing. Use the Relist feature *only* when an item hasn't sold the first time, so it will qualify for a listing fee credit when it sells. Use Sell Similar to relist the same item after it fails to sell a second time.

✔ **Auction management software:** See the "Software you can use" section in this chapter and also see Chapter 9, where I detail various programs to integrate into your eBay business.

Okay, even if you can take great photos and write brilliant descriptions, cashmere sweaters won't sell for as much in the heat of summer as they do in winter. Doing your research can take up a good deal of time when you're selling a varied group of items. Only you can decide how much time you can afford to spend researching going rates for items on eBay.

You also have to consider how much time it takes to shop for your merchandise. You may have to travel to dealers, go to auctions, or spend time online discovering new ways to find your auction merchandise. Many sellers set aside a full day each week for this undertaking. Your merchandise is what makes you money, so don't skimp on the time you spend identifying products.

Here's a list of various tasks you must perform when doing business on eBay:

✔ Photograph the item.

✔ Upload the images to eBay when you list — or before listing to your ISP or third-party hosting service.

✔ Pack and weigh the item to determine the shipping cost.

✔ Choose a listing title with popular keywords.

✔ Write a concise and creative description.

✔ List the item for sale on eBay.

✔ Answer bidder questions.

✔ Send an end-of-listing e-mail (you can automate this task through Selling Manager Pro).

✔ Carry out bookkeeping and banking.

✔ Address the label and affix postage.

✔ Ship the item safely and securely.

Time yourself to see how long it takes to accomplish each of these tasks. The time varies when you list multiple items, so think of the figures that you come up with as your *baseline,* a minimum amount of time that you must set aside. This information can help you decide how many hours per week or month you need to devote to running your part-time eBay business.

Jumping in with both feet: Making eBay a full-time job

As you can see in the list in the preceding section, the tasks required for your eBay business can be time-consuming. But careful planning and scheduling can turn your business into an online empire.

The best way to go full time on eBay is to first run your business part time for a few months to iron out the wrinkles. After you become comfortable with eBay as a business (and decide that you enjoy both selling and customer relations), you're ready to make the transition to full-time seller. The minimum gross monthly sales for a Bronze-level PowerSeller total $1,000. If you plan your time efficiently, you can easily attain this goal. Head to Chapter 3 for more information on the PowerSeller program.

Running a full-time business on eBay is the perfect option for working parents who prefer staying at home with their children, retirees looking for a way to supplement their income, or those who'd just rather do something else than work for a boss. Read some real-life profiles of happy full-time sellers in Chapter 18.

See Figure 1-1 for an example of the eBay home page, the first stop for most visitors to eBay. Note how eBay makes an effort to reflect its members' sales promotions to help market the items it puts up for sale, as well as assure them of buyer protection.

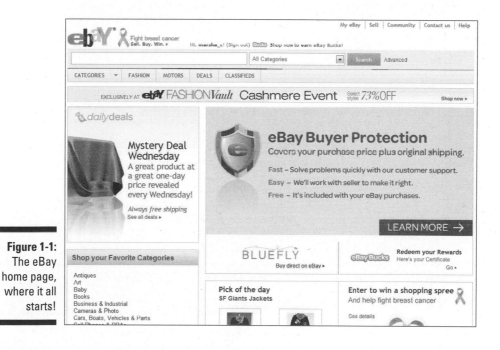

Figure 1-1: The eBay home page, where it all starts!

Deciding What to Sell

What should I sell? That is *the* million-dollar question! In your quest for merchandise, you're bound to hear about soft goods and hard goods. *Soft,* or nondurable, goods are generally textile products, such as clothing, fabrics, and bedding. *Hard* goods are computer equipment, housewares, and anything else that's basically nondisposable.

Following are just a few points to consider when you're deciding what to sell:

✔ **Shipping costs:** Some differences exist between shipping hard and soft goods. Soft goods can fold up and be packed in standard box sizes, available from the United States Postal Service (USPS), or (better yet) in bubble or Tyvek envelopes for much lower shipping costs. Most hard goods come in their own boxes, which may or may not be individually shippable. You'll also need to use Styrofoam peanuts or bubble cushioning (or double-package the item) if it's in an odd-size box. See Chapter 17 for the lowdown on shipping and packing.

✔ **Other shipping considerations:** Do you *want* to handle large boxes and deal with the hassles of shipping them?

✔ **Do you enjoy dealing with your products?** I would have been out of the eBay game years ago if I were forced to sell auto parts — no matter how big the profits. Enjoying what you sell makes you an expert and a top-drawer seller.

✔ **Possible storage problems:** Do you have the room to store enough merchandise to keep you going? Soft goods can take up considerably less space than hard goods.

You don't always have to buy your items in bulk to make money on eBay. The first things you sell might be items you find in your garage or attic. To find out about some other fun ways to acquire goods to sell, check out the next section.

Turning your hobby into a business

C'mon, you have a hobby; everyone does! Did you collect stamps or coins as a kid? Play with Barbie dolls? Maybe your hobby is cars? Did you inherit a bunch of antiques? Been collecting Hummel figurines for a few years? eBay has a market for almost anything.

You can't possibly be an expert on everything (but you knew that). You do need to keep up to date on the market for your items. Following more than four or five basic item groups may divert your attention from selling.

Selling within a particular category or two can be a good idea for repeat business. Should you decide to major in miscellany and sell anything and everything, you may not realize the highest possible prices for your items unless you thoroughly research them. This can be okay if you have the time to do the homework — and a source that permits you to buy items at dirt-cheap prices.

Collectibles: Big business on eBay

Pierre Omidyar started eBay with the idea to trade collectible Pez dispensers. eBay now lists more than 40 main categories of collectibles (see Figure 1-2), and those categories are divided into thousands of categories, subcategories, and sub-subcategories. Almost anything that you'd want to collect is here, from advertising memorabilia to Girl Scout pins to Zippo lighters!

Figure 1-2: The eBay Collectibles hub page with links to hundreds of categories.

If you have a collection of your own, eBay is a great way to find rare items. Because your collection is something dear to your heart, and you've studied it on and off for years, you could probably call yourself an expert. Bingo — you're an expert at something! I recommend that you hone your skills to find things in your area of expertise at discount prices (you're liking this more and more, aren't you?) and then sell them on eBay for a profit. Start small and start with something you know.

If there's one thing you know, it's fashion!

Are you one of those people who just knows how to put together a great outfit? Do you find bargains at Goodwill, but people think you've spent hundreds on your garb? Do you know where to get in-season closeouts before anyone else does? Looks like you've found your market (see Figure 1-3).

Figure 1-3:
eBay area
for clothing,
shoes, and
accessories.

Buy as many of those stylish designer wrap dresses (you-know-whose at you-know-where) as you can, and set them up on the mannequin you've bought to model your fashions for eBay photos. (For more on setting up fashion photos on eBay, check out Chapter 11.) Within a week, you just may be doubling your money — 'cause sweetie-darling, who knows fashion better than you?

If a ball, a wheel, or competition is involved — it's for you

I don't want to preach in generalities, but I think I'm pretty safe in saying that most guys like sports. Guys like to watch sports, play sports, and look good while they're doing it. I see that as opening up venues for a profitable empire on eBay. I don't want to leave out all the women who excel and participate in sports. Women may have even more discriminating needs for their sporting endeavors! I know I do. My golf game stinks — but I do make a point to at least look good when I go out there, with respectable equipment and a fabulous outfit.

eBay has an amazing market going on right now for exercise equipment, and I don't even want to go into how much fishing equipment is selling on eBay. And the last time I looked, golf clubs alone totaled more than 121,000 listings! What a bonanza! New stuff, used stuff — it's all selling on eBay. It's enough to put your local pro shop out of business — or perhaps put you *in* business.

Including the whole family in the business

Sometimes just the idea of a part-time business can throw you into a tizzy. After all, don't you have enough to do? School, work, soccer, kids glued to the TV — you might sometimes feel as if you have no time left for family. Well, the importance of family time is what brought me to eBay in the first place: I was working long hours in my own business, and at the end of the day, when my daughter Susan wanted to go shopping for some Hello Kitty toy or a Barbie doll, I was just too tired. (Can you relate?)

I'd heard about AuctionWeb (eBay's original site name) from a friend, and had bought some things online for my own collections. (Okay, you got me; I collected *Star Trek* stuff — call me a geek with a capital *G*.) I'd also browsed around the site and found some popular toys selling for reasonable prices. So one evening I introduced Susan to AuctionWeb, and life has never been the same. We'd go to toy stores together, right when they opened on Saturday morning, so we'd get first dibs on shipments of the hottest, newest toys. She'd go to the dolls and I'd go to the action figures. We'd buy several, go home, and post them for sale on eBay. We made money, yes, but the best part was our toy runs. They will always remain a special memory.

Susan has since graduated from college (she majored in business and marketing — must have been inspired by our eBay enterprise), but she still calls home when she finds a hot CD or closeouts of a top-selling item. We still purchase and list items together. The family that eBays together . . . always does.

My short trip down memory lane has a point: A family business can succeed, and everyone can enjoy it. (Take a look at some of the family sellers I profile in Chapter 18.) I was in charge of the financing and the packing while Susan looked up ZIP codes on the Internet and put pins in a four-foot-by-five-foot map showing every city that we bought from or sold to. She learned some excellent lessons in marketing, advertising, and geography, all in one swoop.

Toys, books, and music — oh MY!

Having children in your home brings you closer to the latest trends than you could ever imagine. I remember sitting at a Starbucks a couple of years ago, watching some dads and their sons poring over notebooks full of Pokémon cards. (Actually, the kids were off playing somewhere and the dads were coveting the cards.)

And what about *Star Wars*? *Star Trek*? *G.I. Joe*? Can you say "action figures?" (If guys have them, they're not dolls — they're action figures.) If you have access to the latest and greatest toys, buy them up and sell them to those who can't find them in their neck of the woods.

If your home is like mine, books pile up by the tens! Old educational books that your children have outgrown (even college textbooks) can be turned into a profit. Remember that not every book is a classic that needs to be part of your library forever. Let another family get the pleasure of sharing children's tales!

If anything piles up faster than books, CDs and DVDs do. Could be somehow that old lambada or macarena music doesn't hold the magic it once did. Or maybe those Care Bears cartoons don't mesmerize the kids the way they used to. You can get rid of your own items and find plenty of stock at garage sales. Buy them cheap and make a couple of dollars.

Selling children's clothes

When I recently checked eBay for the number of listings of baby and toddler clothes up for sale, I found more than 253,000 in the Boys: Clothing (Newborn-5T) category — and the bidding was hot and heavy. For stay-at-home parents, selling infant and children's clothing is a super way to pick up extra income.

If you've had a baby, you know all too well that friends and relatives shower new moms with lots of cute outfits. If you're lucky, your baby gets to wear one or two of them (maybe only for a special picture) before outgrowing them. These adorable portrait outfits can earn you a profit on eBay. Many parents, with children a few steps behind yours, are looking for bargain clothing on eBay — a profitable hand-me-down community. As your children grow up (and out of their old clothes), earn some money while helping out another parent.

Bringing your existing business to eBay

Do you already have an existing business? eBay isn't only a marketplace where you're able to unload slow or out-of-season merchandise. You can also set up your store right on eBay (see Figure 1-4). An eBay Store allows you to list a fixed-price item at a reduced fee and keep the item online until it's sold. When you run your regular auctions for special items, they will have a link to your store, thereby drawing in new shoppers to see your store merchandise.

Here are a few ways you can expand your current business with eBay:

✔ **Open a second store on eBay:** How many people run stores that sell every item, every time? If you're a brick-and-mortar retailer, you've probably made a buying mistake or two. Many times the item that *isn't* selling in your store *is* selling like hotcakes in similar stores elsewhere in the country. eBay gives you the venue to sell those extra items to make room for more of what sells at your home base.

Perhaps you just need to raise some cash quickly. eBay has tens of thousands of categories in which you can liquidate regular stock or specialty items. (For a caveat on what's verboten, check out Chapter 4.)

✔ **Sell by mail order:** If you've been selling by mail order, what's been holding you back from selling on eBay? It costs you far less to list your item on eBay than to run an ad in any publication. Plus, on eBay, you get built-in buyers from every walk of life and all over the world. If you can sell your item legally through the mail, it *will* sell through eBay.

✔ **Sell property:** Licensed real estate agents, take note: Plenty of land, homes, and condos are selling on eBay right now. List your properties online so that you can draw from a nationwide audience. When you offer listings on the Web, you're bound to get more action. Give it a whirl and read more about selling real estate on eBay in Chapter 2.

You won't find a cheaper landlord than eBay. Jump over to Chapter 5 if you really can't wait for more information about how to set up your eBay Store.

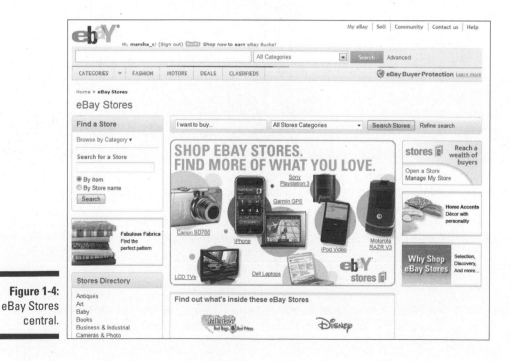

Figure 1-4:
eBay Stores
central.

Getting What It Takes to Sell

I've heard many sellers-to-be say they want to start a business on eBay so they can relax. Since when is running any business a way to relax? Granted, you don't need a whole lot of money to get started on eBay and you won't have a boss breathing down your neck. But to run a successful eBay business, you need drive, determination, and your conscience to guide you, as well as a few solid tools, such as a computer and an Internet connection. In this section, I give you the lowdown on these things and more.

Computer hardware

First, you're gonna need a computer. In my basic assumptions about you (see the book's introduction), I figure that you have one and know how to use it. Your computer doesn't have to be the latest, fastest, and best available. It does help if your computer has a good deal of memory to process your Web browsing and image touchups. One of my eBay listing computers is an antique notebook that runs on Windows XP, an absolute turtle next to my new 4.3-GHz model. But combined with a high-speed Internet connection, my little machine enables me to manage many eBay listings easily.

Having a computer that will read all sorts of camera data cards is a time-saver. Instead of having to hardwire your camera and download images, you can just zip in the memory card and copy the pictures to your hard drive.

One thing to keep in mind is that hard drives are getting cheaper by the minute. The bigger your hard drive, the more space you'll have to store images for your auctions. (Individual pictures shouldn't take up much space because each should be 100K max.) Make sure that you set up a sensible filing system by using folders and subfolders.

Check out Chapter 11, where I talk more about the other stuff you might need, such as a scanner and a digital camera.

Connecting to the Internet

If you've been on eBay for any length of time, you know that your Internet connection turns into an appendage of your body. If your connection is down or you can't log on due to a power outage, you can't function; maybe, instead, you flounder around babbling to yourself. I understand because I've been there. If you're selling in earnest, I recommend pulling the plug on your dial-up connection and shelling out for a speedier option unless you have no choice.

Before investing in any broadband connection, visit `www.broadband reports.com` (see Figure 1-5) and read the reviews of Internet service providers (ISPs) in your area. Users post their experiences with the many providers across the country, so you can get a good idea of what's in store in your neighborhood in the connection arena. The site also has more testing tools than you can imagine — and will test the speed of your (or your friend's) Internet connection at no charge.

Figure 1-5:
The results of the free speed test of my cable connection.

Dial-up connections

If you absolutely must use a dial-up connection, avail yourself of the many free trials that different ISPs offer to see which one gives your computer the fastest connection. After you find the fastest, be sure that it's reliable and has at least a 99 percent uptime rate.

Thirty-five percent of the United States still logs on to the Internet with a dial-up connection, so what can be so wrong about a dial-up connection? Well, this type of connection is painfully slow; a listing with lots of images can take *minutes* to load. The average eBay users want to browse many listings and won't wait while your images load; they'll just go to the next listing.

To make the best use of your time when running your auctions and conducting research, you need to blast through the Internet. You need to answer e-mail, load images, and conduct your business without waiting around for snail's-pace connections. Although a modem is supposed to link up at 56K, FCC regulations state that it can't connect any faster than 53K. In practice, the highest-speed connection I've ever experienced on dial-up was 44K.

DSL

A confusing bunch of digital subscriber line (DSL) flavors (ADSL, IDSL, SDSL, and more) are available these days, ranging from reasonably priced to out of sight. DSL, when it works as advertised, is fast and reliable.

A DSL line depends on the reliability of your telephone service: Crackling or unreliable phone lines can be a barrier to using DSL.

The main problem with a DSL connection is that your home or office needs to be no farther than 18,000 feet from your local telephone switch. The service runs from as little as $12.95 to as much as $100 a month, and it might cost even more if you get DSL through a *booster* that boosts the signal to a location farther away than the minimum 18,000-foot distance.

True DSL service can give you a connection as fast as 1.5 MB-per-second download. (IDSL is only 144K.)

I had DSL for about a year and was initially blown away by the speed. Unfortunately, every time it rained (it *does* rain occasionally in Southern California), my service went out. I had to call time after time to get the line serviced. Sadly, this is a well-known drawback of DSL. Your local telephone company (*telco* in DSL-speak) owns your home or office phone lines. Because DSL goes over plain old telephone service (POTS), your DSL provider has to negotiate connection problems with the folks at your telephone company. As you might guess, one company often blames the other for your problems.

A friend of mine tried to get around this issue by getting DSL from the local phone company, which sounded great to me. It turned out to be not so great; it seems that the local phone companies tend to form other companies to handle high-speed connections. So even though the two companies are technically the same, the two will still argue about who is responsible for your problems. Broadband with this much difficulty can be too much trouble.

Digital cable

Eureka — I think I've found the mother lode of connections: cable. If you can get digital cable television, you can probably get a blazingly fast cable Internet connection. Your cable company is probably replacing old cable lines with newfangled digital fiber-optic lines. These new lines can carry a crisp HD digital TV signal *and* an Internet connection as well. Fiber-optic lines have plenty of room to carry even more stuff (including telephone service), and I'm sure it won't be long before cable companies have some hot new services to sell us.

My digital cable Internet connection is generally fast and reliable. I can download 2 megabytes of data in only *8 seconds* (compared to almost 7 minutes with a dial-up connection). So far, the service has been very reliable, and I've experienced little downtime. For around $40 a month, I consider my cable connection well worth the investment.

As far as the myth about more users on the line degrading the speed, a cable connection is more than capable of a 10 megabit-per-second (Mbps) transfer. That's already about 10 times faster than DSL. It would take a whole lot of degrading to noticeably slow down your connection.

Choosing your eBay user ID

"What's in a name?" goes the old quote. On eBay, there's a whole lot in your name! When you choose your eBay user ID, it becomes your name — your identity — to all those who transact with you online. They don't know who you are; they know you only by the name they read in the seller's or bidder's spot.

Ever wonder why you don't see many banks named *Joe and Fred's Savings and Loan*? Even if Joe is the president and Fred is the chairman of the board, the casual attitude portrayed by their given names doesn't instill much confidence in the stability of the bank. *Joe and Fred* might be a better name for a plumbing-supply company — or a great name for guys who sell plumbing tools on eBay! Joe and Fred strike me as the kind of friendly, trustworthy guys who might know something about plumbing.

Does your retail business have a name? If you don't have your own business (yet), have you always known what you'd call it if you did? Your opportunity to set up your business can start with a good, solid, respectable-sounding business name. If you don't like respectable (it's too staid for you), go for trendy. Who knew what a Verizon was? Or a Cingular? Or a Bubblefast, which is one of my favorite eBay shipping suppliers?

Are you selling flamingo-themed items? How about `pink_flamingos` for your selling identity? Be creative; *you* know what best describes your product.

Stay away from negative-sounding names. If you really can't think up a good user ID, using your own name is fine.

You've no doubt seen a bunch of lousy user IDs out there — you know, names that scream "unprofessional" or "bad self-image." Here are a few examples of what not to use: `ISellJunk`, `trashforsale`, `mystuffisgarbage`.

The lowdown on user IDs

When choosing your user ID, keep the following points in mind:

✔ Your ID must contain at least two characters.

✔ It doesn't matter if you use uppercase; eBay displays your ID in all-lowercase letters.

✔ You may use letters, numbers, and any symbol except @, ´, <, >, and &.

✔ You can't use an implied or distinct URL or e-mail address as your user ID.

✔ You can't use the word *eBay* in your user ID; that privilege is reserved for eBay employees.

✔ Your ID can't be the letter *e* followed by numbers (not sure why anyone would want to do that anyway).

✔ Spaces aren't allowed; if you want to use two words, you can separate them with underscores (press Shift and hyphen to type the underscore character) or hyphens. You can't use consecutive underscores.

✔ Don't use a brand or a trademarked name unless you own it.

✔ Do I have to tell you this? Don't use a name that's hateful or obscene; eBay (and the community) just won't permit it.

eBay protects and does not reveal your e-mail address unless you're in a transaction with another member. If another user wants to contact you, he or she can do so by clicking the Contact Seller link on the item page. The e-mail will be sent to you through eBay's e-mail system.

If you decide to change your user ID; don't do it too often. Customers recognize you by name and you may miss some repeat sales by changing it. Besides, eBay places a special icon next to your user ID to show others that you've changed it. This icon will stick with you for 30 days. Your feedback profile (permanent record) follows you to your new ID.

Finding your eBay feedback

The number that eBay lists next to your name is your *feedback rating*; see Figure 1-6 for my rating. Anyone on the Internet has only to click this number to know how you do business on eBay — and what other eBay users think of you. At the top of every user's feedback page is an excellent snapshot of all your eBay transactions for the past year, as well as detailed one- through five-star ratings. For the lowdown on feedback, go to Chapter 3.

Feedback Profile

marsha_c (7210 ⭐) me 📋

Positive Feedback (last 12 months): 100%
[How is Feedback Percentage calculated?]
Member since: Jan-04-97 in United States

This member is a **Top-rated seller**
- Consistently receives highest buyers' ratings
- Ships items quickly
- Has earned a track record of excellent service

» Learn more

Recent Feedback Ratings (last 12 months)

	1 month	6 months	12 months
Positive	26	144	340
Neutral	0	0	0
Negative	0	0	0

Detailed Seller Ratings (last 12 months)

Criteria	Average rating	Number of ratings
Item as described	★★★★★	250
Communication	★★★★★	250
Shipping time	★★★★★	250
Shipping and handling charges	★★★★★	258

Member Quick Links
View your Seller Dashboard
View items for sale
View seller's Store
View more options ▾

| Feedback as a seller | Feedback as a buyer | **All Feedback** | Feedback left for others |

8,065 Feedback received (viewing 1-25)   Revised Feedback: 0

Period: All

Feedback	From / Price	Date / Time
Fast Shipping. A +++++++++++++++++ Seller, THANKS!!!!!	Buyer: nrlit558 (305 ⭐)	Oct-19-10 07:24

Figure 1-6:
My eBay feedback rating.

If you're serious about this business thing and your feedback rating isn't as high as you'd like it to be, go online and buy some stuff. Even though eBay now distinguishes between buyer and seller feedback, the numbers will still grow. Feedback should always be posted for both buyers and sellers. Every positive feedback increases your rating by +1; a negative decreases it by –1. To get a high rating, you'd better be racking up those positives.

Making Your Auctions Run More Smoothly

In this section, I discuss a few more niceties that you'll need to round out your eBay home base. The following tools are important, but you must decide which ones you'll use. Some people prefer a totally automated office; others prefer to do things the old-fashioned way. One of my favorite eBay PowerSellers works with file folders, a handwritten ledger book, and hand-written labels. If it makes you happy, do it your way. I'm going to suggest a few options that will ease the pain of paperwork.

Software you can use

These days, software is available to accomplish just about anything. It would seem fitting that an all-encompassing software package exists that can help you with your auction, right? Well, maybe. It depends on how much you want your software to do and how much of your business you want to control fully. In this section, I describe some software examples that you might find useful.

Auction management

Auction management software can be a very good thing. It can automate tasks and make your record keeping easy. You can keep track of inventory, launch auctions, and print labels using one program. Unfortunately, most of these programs can be daunting when you first look at them (and even when you take a second look).

You have choices to make regarding the software: How much are you willing to spend for the software, and do you want to keep your inventory and information online? Maintaining your listing information online enables you to run your business from anywhere; you just log on and see your inventory. Online management software is tempting and professional, and may be worth your time and money.

A good many sellers prefer to keep their auction information on their own computers. This method is convenient and allows sellers to add a closer, more personal touch to their auctions and correspondence. Some folks say that keeping information local, on their own computers, is more suited to the small-time seller. I think it's a matter of preference.

In Chapter 9, I discuss the wide selection of management software available, including Vendio, Channel Advisor, Auction Wizard 2000, and the eBay-owned Selling Manager products.

HTML software

You may want to try some basic HTML software to practice your ad layouts. I tell you where to find some templates in Chapter 11, but you'll want to preview your auctions before you launch them. You might also enjoy my book *eBay Listings That Sell For Dummies* (co-authored with eBay tech maven Patti Louise Ruby). Half the book is on HTML, and the other half helps you perfect your photography.

You can use a full-blown Web page software package, to check out how your auction will look, or you may want to keep it simple. The simplest way is to use eBay's intuitive listing tool, which works in the same way as many word-processing programs to format text. (For more information, turn to Chapter 11.)

Spreadsheets and bookkeeping

Many sellers keep their information in a simple spreadsheet program such as Excel. The program has all the functionality you need to handle inventory management and sales info.

For bookkeeping, I like QuickBooks, which is as complete as it gets. It's straightforward and professional, and it no longer requires you to have a basic knowledge of accounting. It also integrates with spreadsheets. In Chapter 16, I discuss QuickBooks in some detail.

Collecting the cash

Credit card payments are the way to go for the bulk of your sales. Often credit cards make the difference between a sale and no sale. People are getting savvy (and more comfortable) about using their credit cards online because they're becoming better informed about the security of online transactions and certain guarantees against fraud. So although you might truly love money orders, let's be realistic: You need to take credit cards as well. In this section, I discuss another decision you need to make: Do you want your own private merchant account or would you rather run your credit card sales through an online payment service? For more about these options, read on.

Online payment services

Until you hit the big time, you should save yourself a bucket of trouble and go with the services of an online payment service such as the eBay-owned PayPal. PayPal offers excellent services, and its rates are on a sliding scale, according to your monthly dollar volume. Online payment services accept credit cards for you. They charge you a small fee and process the transaction with the credit card company. Payment for the sold item is deposited in your designated bank account. Unless your sales go into tens of thousands of dollars a month, an online payment service is far more economical than having your own merchant account. For more about these services and accounts, see Chapter 13.

Your own merchant account

As you may or may not know (depending on the amount of spam in your e-mail), thousands of merchant credit card brokers guarantee they can set you up so that you can take credit cards yourself. These people are merely middlemen. You have to pay for their services, either in an application fee or as part of a hefty percentage, or by buying processing software. Some of these brokers are dependable businesses; others are nothing more than hustlers. If you have decent credit, you don't need these guys: Go straight to your bank!

Your bank knows your financial standing and creditworthiness better than anybody. It's the best place to start to get your own *merchant account,* an account in which your business accepts credit card payments directly from your buyers. You pay a small percentage to the bank, but it's considerably less than what you pay to an online payment service. Some banks don't offer merchant accounts for Internet transactions because ultimately the bank is responsible for the merchandise related to the account if you fail to deliver the goods. Remember that your credit history and time with the bank play a part in whether you can get a merchant account.

The costs involved in opening a merchant account can vary, but you'll need between $300 and $2,000 to get started. Here are some of the possible costs you may face:

- ✔ A monthly processing fee if you don't reach the monthly minimum set by your bank
- ✔ The discount rate (your bank's cut) of 15–45 cents per transaction
- ✔ About $700 for software that processes your transaction costs
- ✔ A monthly gateway fee of as much as $40 (an online connection to process charges)

This is quite an investment in time and effort. In Chapter 13, I get into the details of a merchant account and explain exactly where all these costs go.

Home base: Your Web site

eBay offers you a free page — the About Me page — that's the most important link to your business on eBay; see Chapter 3 for more information. The About Me page is part of your eBay Store if you have one. You can insert a link on your About Me page that takes bidders to your listings. In addition, you can link to your own Web site from the About Me page!

If you don't have your own Web site, I recommend that you get one, especially if you're serious about running an online business. Check out Chapter 8, where I provide some tips on finding a Web host and a simple way to put up your own Web site.

You can keep a list of your complete inventory of items on your Web site and also list them in your eBay Store as their selling season comes around. (Remember that there's no listing or Final Value fee when you have repeat customers on your Web site.)

Setting up your shop

Office and storage space are must-haves if you plan to get big. Many a business was started at the kitchen table (that's how Pierre started eBay), but to be serious with a business, you must draw definite lines between your home life and your online ventures. Concentrating when you have a lot of noise in the background is difficult, so when I say draw a line, I mean a physical line as well as an environmental one.

Your dedicated office

You must first separate the family from the hub of your business. Many eBay sellers use a spare bedroom. (I started my home business in a 10-by-12-foot room.) As time progresses and your business grows, you might have to move. I chose to sacrifice my detached two-car garage. I guess I could have made it into a one-car garage, but I decided to take over the whole thing instead.

Here's what I did: Zoning laws in Southern California require me to have a garage, so I put a false office wall in the back so that the garage door could open normally. I used that area for extra storage. My garage had been wired (for some guy who was going to use big-time power tools, I suppose) and had its own breaker box. I hired an electrician to come in and place outlets around my office and had a large window cut into the wall overlooking my backyard (to remove the claustrophobic feeling and for ventilation). I now had a window and electricity.

The phone man came by and brought a line into the garage; a friend installed double jacks all around to accommodate the two phone lines. I picked out some reasonably priced paneling, and hired workmen to install it and (while they were at it) to drop a paneled ceiling with florescent lights. Finally, I bought furniture from my local Goodwill store. Presto-chango — I had successfully transformed what was once a dark, musty garage into a bright, gleaming 18-by-20-foot *private* office. And here I successfully ran my advertising and marketing business for more than ten years.

You, too, have adjustments and decisions to make, just as I did, because you're going to need office space and storage space, too.

One PowerSeller I know moved all the junk out of his basement and set up shop down there. He now has three computers and employs his wife and a part-time *lister* (who puts his items up on eBay) to run the show. His basement office is networked and is as professional as any office.

Your eBay room

If you're able to set up an office similar to mine, your storage space should be covered for a while. For a real business, a closet just won't do, even though most sellers begin their eBay careers with an "eBay closet." Seclude your stuff from your pets and family by moving it into another room. You'll also have to get shelving and more supplies to organize things. I talk more about these everyday (but crucial) matters in Chapter 17.

Chapter 2

The Finer Points of eBay Selling

At first glance, eBay is this behemoth Web site with millions of listings that seems way too large for any novice to possibly master. On the surface, that's right. eBay is always growing and changing to meet the demands of its users. Under all the cosmetic changes, however, you always come back to the basics. eBay is still a traditional trading site: a community of buyers and sellers who follow rules and policies, making eBay a safe place to trade.

As anything expands, it must compartmentalize to be manageable. The folks at eBay have done this most handily. The original basic eight categories now number in the thousands. The category breakdown is far clearer and more concise than originally conceived. When a new trend begins, the eBay tech gurus evaluate the market and, when necessary, add new categories.

All this growth has forced eBay to expand. Aside from the traditional eBay auctions, you'll now find fixed-price listings, private auctions, restricted auctions, and more. Whoa, that's confusing! In this chapter, I explain the eBay features by reviewing the ways you can transact your business on eBay. Armed with this knowledge, you can succeed with your listings — sooner than later.

Finding Where to Sell Your Stuff

The Internet is crowded with e-commerce sites selling everything possible. Many major portals also include auctions as part of their business. But the majority of buyers and sellers go to eBay. Why? Because eBay is the largest, attracting more buyers and sellers than any other site on the Web. More computers and electronics are sold on eBay than at Buy.com; more used cars are sold on eBay than in many states. Even name-brand manufacturers have opened outlets on eBay to sell directly to their customers. You can expand your business on a few other sites; check out Chapters 8 and 18 for some ideas.

Whether you're selling auto parts, toys, fine art, or land, eBay can work for you. But first, you have to find your niche. Sounds easy enough. After all, deciding where to put your stuff for sale is straightforward, right? Not necessarily. The task is complicated by the inclusion of thousands of categories on the eBay category-overview page, shown in Figure 2-1. To see these item counts, click the link in the lower-right corner of the page.

Figure 2-1: Just a portion of the vast eBay category-overview page.

All Categories

Search

☐ Search titles & descriptions

Browse Categories

Category	Format	Listings	Location	
All Categories ▾	All Items ▾	All Active ▾	Available on: eBay.com ▾	Show

◉ Show number of items in category   ○ Show category numbers

Antiques (731724)
Antiquities (20524)
Architectural & Garden (37957)
Asian Antiques (85988)
Books & Manuscripts (17093)
Decorative Arts (97728)
Ethnographic (18190)
Furniture (38964)
Home & Hearth (3032)
Linens & Textiles (Pre-1930) (29093)
Maps, Atlases & Globes (76083)
Maritime (9003)
Mercantile, Trades & Factories (2433)
Musical Instruments (Pre-1930) (884)
Periods & Styles (17837)
Primitives (36891)
Restoration & Care (183)
Rugs & Carpets (37276)
Science & Medicine (Pre-1930) (7099)
Sewing (Pre-1930) (6834)
Silver (154489)
Reproduction Antiques (20655)
Other (13488)
See all Antiques categories...

Art (1618541)
Direct from the Artist (166735)
Art from Dealers & Resellers (1428619)

Computers & Networking (6075433)
Apple Desktops (3685)
Apple Laptops & Notebooks (6792)
PC Desktops (61937)
PC Laptops & Netbooks (75672)
iPads & Tablets (3862)
Computer Components (948801)
Computer Accessories (2510332)
Drives & Storage (464582)
iPad & Tablet Accessories (16927)
Keyboards, Mice & Input (162351)
Monitors & Projectors (67361)
Networking & Communications (581343)
Printers (45605)
Printer Parts, Supplies & Accs (715221)
Scanners (10251)
Servers (45621)
Software (183659)
Technology Books & Resources (37530)
Vintage Computing (24965)
Wholesale Lots (5313)
Other (103623)
See all Computers & Networking categories...

Crafts (2776749)
Art Supplies (84169)
Beads & Jewelry Making (456518)
Glass & Mosaics (30752)

Musical Instruments (813278)
Accordion & Concertina (2762)
Brass (10853)
Electronic Instruments (18391)
Equipment (19338)
Guitar (277780)
Harmonica (5793)
Instruction Books, CDs & Video (33218)
Percussion (55393)
Piano & Organ (10243)
Pro Audio Equipment (140818)
Sheet Music & Song Books (157005)
String (43345)
Woodwind (30000)
Wholesale Lots (491)
Other (7848)
See all Musical Instruments categories...

Pet Supplies (630291)
Aquarium & Fish (80824)
Bird Supplies (24864)
Cat Supplies (34287)
Dog Supplies (455903)
Horse Supplies (8802)
Reptile Supplies (7441)
Small Animal Supplies (10086)
Wholesale Lots (875)
Other (7209)

Consider the example of a Harry Potter toy. Harry Potter toys are hugely popular, with the continuing saga in both the books and the movies. (***Note:*** You can replace "Harry Potter" with whatever the big pop-culture trend is when you read this book.) The easy choice is to list the item under Toys & Hobbies⇨TV, Movie, Character Toys⇨Harry Potter. But what about the category Collectibles⇨Fantasy, Mythical & Magic⇨Harry Potter? This is the point where you must decide whether to list in two categories and pay double (see the review of extra charges in Chapter 10) or count on the fact that your beautifully keyword–infested item title will drive prospective buyers who use the search engine directly to your item.

Throughout this book, I mention the use of keywords. *Keywords* are single words that are used to describe the content of the online listing or Web page. Search engines use them to find your eBay listing or to classify your Web pages when they come up in a specific search.

eBay supplies you with a great tool that grabs your attention with a question: *What do you want to sell today?* That link is the first step in listing your item for sale. After clicking *Sell an item* in the upper navigation menu, you land on the Welcome Sellers, List Your Item page. Click the List Your Item box. On the next page, you see a form where you can type a UPC, an ISBN, or a few keywords that describe your item. After you click the Search button, the next page presents the categories where items that match your keywords are listed, as shown in Figure 2-2.

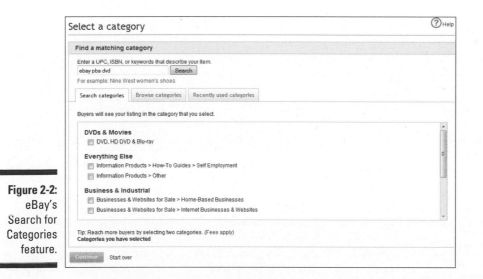

Figure 2-2: eBay's Search for Categories feature.

Perhaps you aren't selling Harry Potter toys. Suppose you're selling a DVD of the movie *The Red Violin*. Would listing it in DVD & Movies⇨DVD be the right choice? Or would you reach an untapped audience of category browsers in the Music⇨Musical Instruments⇨String⇨Violin?

Selling in two categories

Some sellers feel they get more punch by listing in two categories. (I don't, but that's just me.) However, eBay does not allow you to list in two categories if you choose one of the following categories. It you try to choose a second category along with one of these, eBay won't allow you to list in the second category.

✔ Adult items: Adult-oriented items cannot be listed in any category outside eBay's Adult Only section. But you can list your item in any two subcategories within that section.

✔ Business & Industrial⇨Capital Equipment.

✔ DVD, HD DVD & Blu-ray.

✔ Electronics⇨GPS Navigation⇨GPS Systems.

✔ Electronics⇨iPod & MP3 Players.

✔ Listings with variations: Some categories on eBay permit you to list variations of an item (see later in this chapter). If you select a second category that doesn't allow variations, you won't be able to create a listing with variations.

✔ Motor vehicles.

✔ Real estate.

I once came across a lovely small book featuring the fashions of 1960s fashion icon Emilio Pucci. Do you think such a book should be listed in Books⇨ Non-Fiction? I tried that category twice; even after lowering my price, I couldn't sell the book there. Then inspiration hit! I listed the book at my original starting price ($9.99) in this category: Clothing, Shoes & Accessories⇨ Vintage⇨Women's Clothing⇨1965–76 (Mod, Hippie, Disco). I had amazingly good luck by going directly to the fans of '60s fashion. So much luck, in fact (the book sold for close to $40), that I found an inexpensive source for the book, bought a case, and listed them one at a time (so they would seem exclusive and I would continue to get the higher bids). During 18 months, I bought and sold several dozen until I could no longer get a supply!

The popularity of categories varies from time to time. News stories, the time of year, hot trends, or whether Paris Hilton makes a comment about something can change a category's popularity in a nanosecond. How can you possibly know the best category for your item? Research your items regularly using my favorite tool: the awesome eBay search engine. (Visit Chapter 7 for more about using the search engine.) Searching for *completed listings*, I check items that have sold for the highest prices and see which category they were listed in. After you've found the right category for the item you're listing, give it a try. Just be sure to throw in a wildcard occasionally by trying alternatives.

After you've been selling a particular item for a while — and doing well with it — selling it in a different but related category can boost your sales. A little research now and then into where people are buying can go a long way to increasing your eBay sales.

Automotive? Go eBay Motors

Anything and everything automotive can go in the eBay Motors category (see Figure 2-3), and it will sell like giant tires at a monster truck rally. Following are just a few of the car-related items that fit in this category.

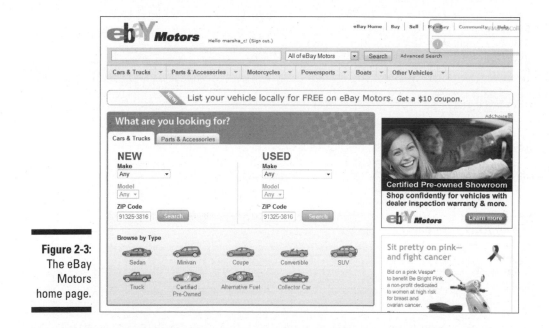

Car parts

Have used car parts? eBay has an enormous market in used car parts. One seller I know goes to police impound sales and buys complete wrecks for close to nothing — just to save valuable parts that he can resell on eBay for big money. (Have you priced replacing your bumper lately? Yeow!)

New car parts are in demand, too. So if you catch a sale at your local auto-parts store when it's blasting out door handles for a 1967 Corvette (a vehicle for which it's hard to find parts), it wouldn't hurt to pick up a few. Sooner or later, someone's bound to search eBay looking for them. If you're lucky enough to catch a trend, you'll make a healthy profit.

Cars

Yes, you can sell (entire) cars on eBay. In fact, car sales (used and new) have skyrocketed online thanks to the thousands of people who find eBay a trusted place to buy and sell used vehicles every day. Check out Figure 2-4 for an example of a used-car auction. Selling vehicles on eBay is a natural business for you if you have access to good used cars, work as a mechanic, or have a contact at a dealership that lets you sell cars on eBay for a commission or on consignment. (For the ins and outs of consignment selling, check out Chapter 6.)

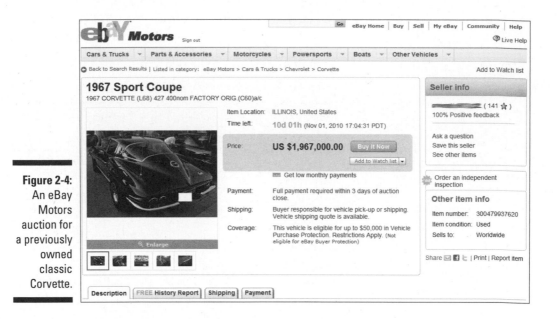

Figure 2-4: An eBay Motors auction for a previously owned classic Corvette.

eBay Motors and its partners offer useful tools to complete your sale. eBay Motors features Free Vehicle Purchase Protection up to $50,000, one-click access to vehicle history reports, vehicle inspection and escrow services, and vehicle shipping quotes from GigaMoves (an eBay company). Access eBay Motors and its services from the eBay home page or go directly to www.ebaymotors.com.

Here are just a few things to keep in mind if you plan to sell cars on eBay:

✔ Selling a car on eBay Motors is a bit different from selling on regular eBay, mainly in the fees area. Take a look at Table 2-1 for the significant differences. In Chapter 10, I include a table of all basic eBay.com fees for listings, options, and final values.

✔ To sell a vehicle on eBay Motors, you must enter all the details, the options, and the Vehicle Identification Number (VIN) on the Sell Your Item page. This way, prospective buyers can access a vehicle history report.

✔ Although many people who have found the vehicle of their dreams on eBay are more than happy to take a one-way flight to the vehicle location and drive it home, shipping a vehicle is a reasonably priced alternative. You can make arrangements to ship a car quickly and simply. In Table 2-2, I list some sample costs for shipping cars around the country, based on mileage.

✔ If your reserve isn't met in an eBay Motors auction, you may still offer the vehicle to the high bidder through the Second Chance option. (More information on that later in this chapter.) You may also reduce your reserve during the auction if you feel you've set your target price too high.

Table 2-1	eBay Motors Fees on the First 4 Listings in a 12-Month Period *		
Category	*Listing Fee*	*Successful Listing Fee, Final Bid $2,000 or less*	*Successful Listing Fee, Final Bid $2,000.01 or more*
Cars & Trucks, RVs & Campers, and Commercial Trucks	$0	$60	$125
Motorcycles, Powersports, Trailers and Boats	$0	$60	$125
Powersports vehicles under 50cc	$0	$10	$10
All other vehicles (trucks, trailers, planes, boats, etc.)	$0	$60	$125
Reserve price in listing (refundable if the vehicle sells)	$7	Based on reserve price	

* Should you decide to list more than four vehicles a year on eBay, it's clear that you are acting as a dealer. eBay rearranges its charges to make the selling climate easier for dealers.

Table 2-2	Estimated Costs for Shipping a Car
Mileage	*Terminal-to-Terminal Cost*
Under 750	$350 to $650
751 to 1,000	$450 to $750

(continued)

Table 2-2 *(continued)*

Mileage	Terminal-to-Terminal Cost
1,000 to 1,500	$550 to $850
1,501 to 2,000	$650 to $950
2,001 to 2,500	$750 to $1,100
2,501 and over	$850 to $1,150

An item that you've listed on eBay Motors will appear in any search, whether potential buyers conduct a regular search on eBay.com or execute their search in eBay Motors.

Real estate: Not quite an auction

eBay Real Estate isn't quite an auction. Because of the wide variety of laws governing the sale of real estate, eBay auctions of real property aren't legally binding offers to buy and sell. Putting your real estate up on eBay is an excellent way to advertise and attract potential buyers. When the auction ends, however, neither party is obligated (as they are in other eBay auctions) to complete the transaction — because it's for real estate. The buyer and seller must get together to consummate the deal.

Nonetheless, eBay Real Estate sales are popular, and the gross sales are growing by leaps and bounds. You don't have to be a professional real estate agent to use this category, although that kind of pro experience may help when it comes to closing the deal. If you know land and your local real estate laws, eBay gives you the perfect venue to subdivide those 160 acres in Wyoming that Uncle Regis left you in his will.

For less than the cost of a newspaper ad, you can sell your home, condo, land, or even timeshare on eBay Real Estate in the auction format (see Figure 2-5). You can also choose to list your property in an ad format, accepting not bids but *inquiries* from prospective buyers from around the world. On the Create Your Listing form, you must specify certain information about your piece of real estate (as illustrated in Figure 2-5) for it to appear in the eBay Real Estate category (shown in Figure 2-6).

Figure 2-5:
Item specifics for selling a timeshare.

To enable your item to appear in the TimeShares Product Finder search results, enter the Item Specifics below.

* Seller State of Residence
California

Property Address

* State/Province   City
Florida   Miami

Zip/Postal Code

Resort Name   Type
                           Beach/Ocean

Week #   Demand Color Code
                           Red - high

Number of Bedrooms   Number of Bathrooms
3   2

Sq Footage (Sq. ft.)
2,000

Maintenance Fees (dollars)
$524

☑ Allow users to see a map for this location
☑ Allow users to see a neighborhood profile for this location

Figure 2-6:
eBay Real Estate home page.

Categories within Real Estate

Commercial   Residential
State/Province   State/Province
Florida   Florida
New York   Michigan
Pennsylvania   Ohio
Tennessee   Pennsylvania

Type   Sale Type
Hotel/Motel   Existing Homes
Office   Foreclosed Homes
Restaurant   New Homes
Retail
                           Number of Bedrooms
Land   1
                           2
Manufactured Homes   3
                           4

                           Number of Bathrooms
                           1
                           2
                           2.5
                           3

                           Timeshares for Sale

                           Other Real Estate

LOOKING TO BUY OR SELL REAL ESTATE?
Learn how to sell property on eBay. Get up-to-speed on real estate rules.

Get "For Sale" signs for your real estate. Learn more ▸

Popular Searches
land
house
texas
florida
cabin

Related Neighborhoods
Loans
187 members
42 posts

In Tables 2-3 and 2-4, I provide a listing of fees that you can expect to encounter on eBay Real Estate.

Table 2-3	eBay Real Estate Timeshare, Land, and Manufactured Home Listing Fees
Listing Type	**Fee Amount**
1-, 3-, 5-, 7-, or 10-day auction or Fixed Price	$35
30-day auction or Fixed Price	$50
30-day classified ad	$150
90-day classified ad	$300
Reserve less than $200 (refundable if reserve is met)	$2
Reserve $200 or more	1% (up to $50)
Final value fee	$35

Table 2-4	eBay Real Estate Residential, Commercial, and Other
Listing Type	**Fee Amount**
1-, 3-, 5-, 7-, or 10-day auction or Fixed Price	$100
30-day auction or Fixed Price	$150
30-day classified ad	$150
90-day classified ad	$300
Reserve $200 or more (refundable if reserve is met)	1% (up to $50)
Final Value fee	None

Fixed-Price and Store Sales on eBay

To compete with other e-commerce sites, eBay includes a *fixed-price sales* option. You put an item up for sale at a fixed price, and buyers pay the price that you're asking. Simple as that. Sellers are doing a great job at it, too.

You can also find fixed-price sales at eBay Stores. Each eBay Store is run by an eBay auction seller. eBay Store items appear in regular eBay searches, but you can find the Stores hub on eBay — accessible in the following ways:

- ✔ By clicking the Stores link on the bottom of the eBay home page
- ✔ By going straight to www.ebaystores.com from the Web

Potential buyers will be able to access your items from anywhere on the eBay site. The cost of an eBay Store (see Tables 2-5, 2-6, 2-7, and 2-8) compares favorably to any of the Web's megasite stores.

Table 2-5	eBay Store Subscription Fees
Store Level	*Monthly Fee*
Basic	$15.95
Premium	$49.95
Anchor	$299.95

See Chapter 5 for a breakdown on the differences between Store levels.

Table 2-6	eBay Store Owners' Auction Fees*
Start or Reserve Price	*Insertion Fee*
$0.01 to $0.99	$0.10
$1.00 to $9.99	$0.25
$10.00 to $24.99 price	$0.50
$25.00 to $49.99	$0.75
$50.00 to $199.99	$1.00
$200.00 and above	$2.00

* Stores sellers are not eligible for the 100 free insertion fees per month on auction listings.

Table 2-7	eBay Store Owners' Auction Final Value Fees
Closing Price	*Final Value Fee*
$0.01 to $50.00	**8.75%** of the selling price
$50.01 to $1,000.00	**8.75%** of the first $50.00 ($4.38) **plus 4%** of the remaining selling price between $50.01 to $1,000.00
$1,000.01 and up	**8.75%** of the first $50.00 ($4.38) **plus 4%** of the next $50.01 to $1,000.00 ($38.00) **plus 2%** of the remaining selling price

Table 2-8	eBay Stores Fixed-price Fees per 30 Days	
Basic	*Premium*	*Anchor*
$0.20	$0.05	$0.03

Just as with auctions, fixed-price sales that are successful incur Final Value fees. The Final Value fees for eBay Stores sales are different from those that apply to Store auctions. See Table 2-9 for details.

For a complete overview on how to set up your own eBay Store, check out Chapter 5.

Table 2-9	eBay Stores Fixed-Price Final Value Fees			
Final Sale Price	Electronics	Clothing, Shoes and Accessories, Motor Parts & Accessories	Books, DVDs & Movies, Music, Video Games	All Other Categories
Item not sold	No fee	No fee	No fee	No fee
$0.99 to $50.00	**8%** of the final sale price	**12%** of the final sale price	**15%** of the final sale price	**12%** of the final sale price
$50.01 to $1,000.00	**8%** of the initial $50.00, plus **5%** of the remaining final sale price balance ($50.01 to $1,000.00)	**12%** of the initial $50.00, plus **9%** of the remaining final sale price balance ($50.01 to $1,000.00)	**15%** of the initial $50.00, plus **5%** of the remaining final sale price balance ($50.01 to $1,000.00)	**12%** of the initial $50.00, plus **6%** of the remaining final sale price balance ($50.01 to $1,000.00)
$1,001.01 or more	**8%** of the initial $50.00, plus **5%** of the next $50.01 to $1,000.00, plus **2%** of the remaining final sale price ($1,000.01 min final sale price)	**12%** of the initial $50.00, plus **9%** of the next $50.01 to $1,000.00, plus **2%** of the remaining final sale price ($1,000.01 min final sale price)	**15%** of the initial $50.00, plus **5%** of the next $50.01 to $1,000.00, plus **2%** of the remaining final sale price ($1,000.01 min final sale price)	**12%** of the initial $50.00, plus **6%** of the next $50.01 to $1,000.00, plus **2%** of the remaining final sale price ($1,000.01 min final sale price)

Types of eBay Auctions

An auction is an auction is an auction, right? Naw. eBay has four types of auctions for your selling pleasure. Most of the time you'll run traditional auctions, but other auctions have a place, too. After you've been selling on eBay for a while, you may find that one of the other types of auctions also suits your needs. Keep in mind that eBay was founded on the regular auction format — the allure of "winning" is what brings users back to the site. In this section, I go over these auctions to clarify what they are and when it's appropriate to use them.

Standard auctions

Auctions are the bread and butter of eBay. You can run a traditional auction for one, three, five, seven, or ten days; and when the auction closes, the highest bidder wins. I'm sure you've bid on several and I hope you've won a few. If you've tried selling, I suspect you've made some money running some of your own.

You begin the auction with an opening bid, and bidders bid up your opening price, competing with one another and building a healthy profit for you on your item.

If you'd like, you can set a *Buy It Now* option on your auction for an additional fee. By setting such fixed selling prices at the get-go, you give buyers the option of buying your item outright. This is attractive for many users of the eBay system. The Buy It Now price you post should be the price at which you'd be happy to sell the item.

Even with a Buy It Now option, people can still bid on your item — but the first bid changes the auction: After a bid is placed, the Buy It Now Option disappears, and the item proceeds in a regular auction for the duration you indicated when you placed the listing. (If the listing has a reserve price, Buy It Now goes away when the reserve is met. See Chapter 10 for more info on fees.)

Reserve-price auctions

In a *reserve-price auction,* you're able to set an undisclosed minimum price for which your item will sell, thereby giving yourself a safety net. Figure 2-7 shows an auction in which the reserve has not yet been met. Using a reserve-price auction protects the investment you have in an item. If, at the end of the auction, no bidder has met your undisclosed reserve price, you aren't obligated to sell the item, and the high bidder isn't required to purchase the item.

For example, if you have a rare coin to auction, you can start the bidding at a low price to attract bidders you hope will click your auction and read your infomercial-like description. If you start your bidding at too high a price, you might dissuade prospective bidders from even looking at your auction, and you won't tempt them even to bid. They may feel that the final selling price will be too high for their budgets.

Everyone on eBay is looking for a bargain or a truly rare item. If you can combine the mystical force of both of these needs in one auction, you have something special. The reserve-price auction enables you to attempt — and perhaps achieve — this feat.

Figure 2-7:
Note that
a reserve
hasn't been
met for this
auction.

The fees for a reserve-price auction are the same as those for a traditional auction with one exception. eBay charges between $2 and $50 for the privilege of running a reserve-price auction. If the reserve price is $200 or more, the reserve-price fee is 1 percent of the reserve price (with a maximum of $50).

The reserve-price auction is a safety net for the seller, but often an uncomfortable guessing game for the prospective bidder. To alleviate buyer anxiety, I recommend that you put reserve prices in the item's description. This allows bidders to decide whether the item will fit into their bidding budgets.

Restricted-access auctions

eBay won't allow certain items to be sold in nonrestricted categories, so you must list them in the Adult Only category on eBay. eBay makes it easy for the user to find (or avoid) these types of auctions by making this area accessible only after the user enters a password and agrees to the terms and conditions of the area.

Items in the Adult Only area are not accessible through the regular eBay title search, nor are they listed in Newly Listed Items to users of eBay who haven't verified their identities.

Anyone who participates in Adult Only auctions on eBay, whether as a bidder or a seller, must have a credit card on file on eBay for verification (see Figure 2-8).

Terms of use for Adult Only category

You must be 18 years of age or older to view items in this category. Materials in this category include graphic visual descriptions and depictions of nudity and sexual activity. Federal, state and local law may prohibit anyone under the age of 18 from viewing items listed in this category and/or possessing items listed for sale in this category.

In order to gain access to this category, you must agree to the following terms of use and indicate your agreement by clicking the "I agree" button at the bottom of this page:

- I am 18 years of age or older and a member of the eBay community, and I agree to comply with all aspects of the eBay User Agreement governing my use of the eBay website and the Adult Only category.
- I agree to provide eBay with a valid credit card in my name.
- I understand that listings in the Adult Only category depict and describe nudity and sexual activity, and I am knowingly and voluntarily seeking to access listings in this category.
- I will not permit any persons under the age of 18 to view the listings in this category or have access to the items listed for sale.
- I am solely responsible for my actions and will not hold eBay or its employees liable for any materials located in this category. I waive all claims against eBay relating to materials found in this category.
- I will exit this category immediately if I am in any way offended by the sexual nature of the items listed for sale.

By clicking the "I agree" button below, you agree to the above Terms of Use. If you do not agree with these Terms, please click "Cancel" below and you will be directed away from the Adult Only category.

I agree   Cancel

Figure 2-8:
You must agree to the legalities to enter the Adult Only category.

Do not attempt to slip an adult-only auction into a nonrestricted category. eBay doesn't have a sense of humor when it comes to this violation of policy and may relocate — or end — your auction. eBay might even suspend you from its site.

Private auctions

Bidders' names are often kept private when dealing in the expensive fine art world. Likewise, to protect the innocent, eBay *private auctions* don't place bidders' names on the auction listing. No one needs to know just how much you choose to pay for something, especially if the item is rare and you really want it.

As a seller, you have the option (at no extra charge) of listing your auction as a private auction. The option can be found in the How You're Selling portion of the Create Your Listing form. To find this option (should it be hidden), click Show/Hide Options in the top-right corner of the form, select Format⇨Private Listing.

The eBay search page features an area where you can conduct a bidder search. You — and everyone else, including your family — can find the items you've bid on. One December, my daughter told me that she didn't want a particular item — something that I had just bid on — for Christmas. My creative daughter had been regularly perusing my bidding action on eBay to see what I was buying for the holidays! Buying from private auctions might have kept my Santa shopping secret.

Not quite "adult" enough . . . ?

I was surprised to see a private auction listed on one of my favorite eBay seller's lists. She usually doesn't sell items like "Fringe Black BRA 36B SEXY SEXY SEXY," so I looked through this seller's past auctions. I saw that she didn't get any bids when she listed the bra in the restricted (Adult Only) area of eBay in the category Everything Else⇨Adult Only⇨Clothing, Shoes & Accessories. When she put the bra up for private auction in the category Clothing, Shoes & Accessories: Women's Clothing: Lingerie: Bras: General, she got five bidders and sold the item. I guess it wasn't sexy enough for the "adult" crowd!

The private auction is a useful tool for sellers who are selling bulk lots to other sellers. It maintains the privacy of the bidders, and customers can't do a bidder search to find out what sellers are paying for the loot they then plan to resell on eBay.

A great option for sales of items that are a bit racy — or perhaps for purchases of items that may reveal something about the bidder — the private auction can save you the potential embarrassment associated with buying (hypothetically, of course) a girdle or a tie that flips over to reveal a racy half-nude female on the back.

Although the private auction is a useful tool, it may intimidate the novice user. On the other hand, if your customer base comes from experienced eBay users, and you're selling an item that may benefit from being auctioned in secret, you might want to try this option.

Running Your Auction

The basic plan for running an auction is the same for everyone, except for decisions regarding the timing of the auction and the starting price. If you speak to 20 different eBay sellers, you'll probably get 20 different answers about effective starting bids and when to end your auction. Until you develop your own philosophy, I'd like to give you some ideas to help you make a sound decision.

You can successfully promote your auctions online and offline, and can legally offer your item to the next highest bidder if the auction winner doesn't come through with payment. I discuss a few of these ideas in this section.

Starting the bidding

The most generally accepted theory about starting bids is that setting the bidding too high scares away new bids. Also, as in the case of the reserve-price auction, if the bidding begins too high, novices might be afraid that the bidding will go up out of sight and they'll never win the auction.

Some sellers begin the bidding at the price they paid for the item, plus an additional amount to cover fees, thereby protecting their investment. This is a good tactic, especially if you bought the item at a price far below the current going rate on eBay.

To determine the current going value for your item, I recommend using the Completed Listings search, which I explain in Chapter 7. If you know that the item is selling on eBay for a certain price and that there is a demand for it, starting the bidding at a reasonably low level can be a great way to increase bidding and attract prospective bidders to read your auction.

My years of advertising experience have taught me a lot of marketing lessons. If an item is in demand, and people are actively buying, start the bidding low. Retail stores have done this for years with ads that feature prices starting at $9.99 or $14.98. Even television commercials advertising automobiles quote a low starting price. To get the car as shown in the ad, you may end up paying twice the quoted price.

When sellers know that they have an item that will sell, they begin their bidding as low as a dollar or even a penny. Because of the eBay *proxy bidding system* (which maintains your highest bid as secret, increasing it incrementally when you are bid against), it takes more bids (due to the smaller bidding increments) to bring the item up to the final selling price.

The downside is that new bidders who aren't familiar with the system may bid only the minimum required increment each time they bid. This can be frustrating, and they may quit bidding because it might take them several bids to top the current bid placed by someone who's familiar with the proxy-bid system. Very few of us know the proxy increments by heart, so (as a refresher) I give you the goods in Table 2-10.

Table 2-10	Proxy-Bidding Increments
Current High Bid	*Bid Increment*
$0.01 to $0.99	$0.05
$1.00 to $4.99	$0.25

(continued)

Table 2-10 *(continued)*

Current High Bid	Bid Increment
$5.00 to $24.99	$0.50
$25.00 to $99.99	$1.00
$100.00 to $249.99	$2.50
$250.00 to $499.99	$5.00
$500.00 to $999.99	$10.00
$1,000.00 to $2499.99	$25.00
$2,500.00 to $4999.99	$50.00
$5,000.00 and up	$100.00

Auction timing

Another debatable philosophy is auction timing. People are always asking me how long to run auctions and the best day to end an auction. You have to evaluate your item and decide the best plan:

 ✔ **One-day auction:** This format can be very successful if you have an item that's the hot ticket for the moment on eBay. I used this format when I sold some TV show memorabilia. The 24-hour auction opened at midday before the final episode and ended the next day — at a healthy profit!

 ✔ **Three-day auction:** If the item's price will shoot up right after you post it, as in the heyday of Beanie Babies, a three-day auction works just fine. And it's great for those last-minute holiday shoppers looking for hard-to-find items.

With the Buy It Now feature, you can pretty much accomplish the same thing. When you list your item for sale, set a price at which you will sell the item; this is your target price. This price can be any amount, and if someone is willing to pay, it sells. I recently sold an iPod that I received as a gift. I listed it with a $99 starting bid and a $180 Buy It Now price. It sold within two hours of posting the listing.

 ✔ **Five-day auction:** Five days will give you two days more than three and two days less than seven. That's about the size of it. If you just want an extended weekend auction, or if your item is a hot one, use it. Five-day auctions are useful during holiday rushes, when gift buying is the main reason for bidding.

✔ **Seven-day auction:** Tried-and-true advertising theory says that the longer you advertise your item, the more people will see it. On eBay, this means you have more opportunity for people to bid on it. The seven-day auction is a staple for the bulk of eBay vendors. Seven days is long enough to cover weekend browsers and short enough to keep the auction interesting.

✔ **Ten-day auction:** Many veteran eBay sellers swear by the ten-day auction. Sure, eBay charges you an extra 40 cents for the privilege, but the extra three days of exposure (it can encompass two weekends) can easily net you more than 40 cents in profits.

If you're selling an esoteric collectible that doesn't appear on eBay often, run a ten-day auction to give it maximum exposure. Start it on a Friday, so it will cover the aforementioned two weekends' worth of browsers.

Your auction closes exactly one, three, five, seven, or ten days — *to the minute* — after you start the auction. Be careful not to begin your auctions when you're up late at night and can't sleep: You don't want your auction to end at two in the morning when no one else is awake to bid on it. If you can't sleep, be productive and use Turbo Lister to prepare your listings ahead of time and upload them for future launching when the world is ready to shop.

The specific day you close your auction also is no longer as important as it was in the early days of eBay. Buyers browse the site 7 days a week, 24 hours a day. The weekdays and the weekends are full of browsers, so it's hard to guesstimate when your perfect buyer will be browsing. In Chapter 10, I show you how to combine your search-engine research with this special kind of statistical counter to help you identify the best closing time for your items. (See Chapter 7 for the details about using the search engine as a valuable research tool.) The best person to figure out the closing information for your auctions is you. Use the tools, and over time you'll work out a pattern that works best.

A definite time *not* to close your auctions? Experience has taught many sellers never to close an auction on a national holiday. Memorial Day, the Fourth of July, and Veteran's Day may be bonanza sales days for retail shops, but eBay auction items that close on these days go at bargain prices. I guess everyone is out shopping at the brick-and-mortar stores.

Pirates of the Caribbean, er, Carribean?

Just before the *Pirates of the Caribbean* movie premiered, Disneyland gave out exclusive movie posters to their visitors. My daughter, savvy eBayer that she is, snagged several copies to sell on the site. She listed them (one at a time) when the movie opened and couldn't get more than the starting bid, $9.99, for each of them.

When we searched eBay for *pirates poster,* we found that the same posters with a misspelled title, *Pirates of the Carribean*, were selling for as high as $30 each. We immediately changed her auctions to have the more popular (and misspelled) *Carribean* in the title and quickly saw those dollar signs! After selling out her initial stock, she found another seller who had ten for sale — in one auction — with the proper spelling in the title. She bought those as well (for $5 each) and sold them with misspelled titles on the site for between $15 and $27!

Marketing your sales

How do you let people know about your listings? What do you do if all one hundred million users on eBay happen to not be on the site the week that your items are up for sale? You advertise.

Many mailing lists and newsgroups permit self-promotion. Find a group that features your type of items and post a bit of promotion. This works best if you have your own e-commerce Web site. Your site, which should be the hub for your sales, can give you an identity and level of professionalism that makes your business more "official" in the eyes of buyers.

Social media have become big players in attracting buyers to your eBay listings, but we're not talking advertising here. It's more of a touchy-feely type of marketing. In Chapter 8, I detail the ins and outs of social media and marketing business sites on the Web.

When you have an eBay Store, eBay allows you to send a number of e-mails to customers who request to be on your mailing list. Also, eBay makes sure that your store (and its listings) will appear in searches on Google. Take a look at Figure 2-9, which shows my store in a Google search.

If you have an eBay Store, you will have access to some valuable marketing tools such as customer e-mail marketing, Markdown Manager, and branding. I address all these benefits in Chapter 5.

I'm guessing that you already know all about your About Me page, a handy tool when it comes to marketing your auctions. In Chapter 3, I discuss the values of the About Me page.

Figure 2-9:
My eBay
Store listed
on Google.

Here's a great way to market future listings: When you're sending items after making a sale on eBay, include a list of items that you'll be selling soon (along with your thank-you note, of course) — especially items that may appeal to that customer. If you schedule your auctions in advance, you're given the auction number before the item is listed.

Do not link your auction to your Web site. Doing so is against eBay policy because it can possibly divert sales away from the auction site. *Do* link your About Me page to your Web site. See the "Linking from your auctions" section, later in this chapter, to find out just what you can and cannot link to and from.

A second chance to buy (and sell)

The Second Chance feature on eBay helps sellers legitimize something that previously went on behind closed doors and in violation of eBay policy. When a winner doesn't complete a sale, or you have multiple units of the same item, or the reserve price wasn't met but you're willing to accept the highest bid that didn't meet the reserve, the Second Chance feature allows sellers to offer the item to the next highest bidders.

You must still go through the proper channels and file your Unpaid Item case with eBay (see Chapter 4). After doing that, you can then send a Second Chance offer to any underbidder no more than 60 days after the end of the auction. Your Final Value fee is based on the price you receive when the offer is accepted.

In the Second Chance offer scenario, the seller can leave two feedback messages: one for the winner (nonpaying bidder) and one for the person who bought the item through the Second Chance offer transaction.

The bidder to whom you proffer your Second Chance offer is covered by the eBay fraud-protection program.

Listing Violations

eBay does not actually sell merchandise. eBay is merely a venue that provides the location where others can put on a giant e-commerce party (in other words, sell stuff). To provide a safe and profitable venue for its sellers, eBay must govern the auctions that take place on its site. eBay makes the rules; you and I follow the rules. I like to think of eBay as the place that lets you hold your senior prom in its gym. When I was in school, my classmates and I had to follow the rules or see our prom cancelled. Same deal here: If we buyers and sellers don't agree to follow eBay's rules, a safe and trusted eBay community can't exist.

Listing policies

eBay has some hard-and-fast rules about listing your items. You must list your item in the appropriate category (that only makes sense), and I highlight here a few other rules that you should keep in mind when listing. What I discuss in this section isn't a definitive list of eBay listing policies and rules, but it will give you a good working sense of what to look out for. Take time to familiarize yourself with the User Agreement (which details all eBay policies and rules) at http://pages.ebay.com/help/policies/user-agreement.html. I recommend that you check the eBay User Agreement regularly for any policy changes.

Duplicate listings

Remember the old supply-and-demand theory from your economics class? When people list the same items repeatedly, they drive down the item's going price while ruining all the other sellers' opportunities to sell the item during that time frame.

eBay allows you five identical listings, no more, at any time. If you're going to list an item that many times, at least be sure to list it in different categories. That's a rule, but it also makes sense. Nothing drives down the price of an item faster than closing identical auctions, one after another, in the same category. eBay also requires that you list your auction in a category that's relevant to your item. (No fashion dolls among the car parts, please, or vice versa.)

If you have multiple copies of something, a better solution is to run a fixed-price listing for the total number of items you have for sale. Buyers may buy one item or many in one transaction.

Listings with variations

Certain categories on eBay allow you to list multiples of a single item with variations. For example, you may have just purchased a case of baby onesies (those one-piece wrap-around outfits that close with snaps — very popular with the parents of newborns and toddlers), and you have several sizes and colors to sell. If they're all of the same style, you can put them all in one listing as variations. Currently, listings with variations are only available in certain categories:

- ✔ Baby
- ✔ Clothing, Shoes & Accessories
- ✔ Crafts
- ✔ Health & Beauty
- ✔ Home & Garden and most subcategories
- ✔ Jewelry & Watches
- ✔ Pet Supplies
- ✔ Sporting Goods

Before you attempt to list an item with variations (eBay won't allow you to do this if the option is not available for the category in which you want to list your item), it's best to check the eBay *Category Look-Up Tool,* shown in Figure 2-10. You can find it by clicking the drop-down menu from the top Navigation bar by clicking Sell⇨Seller Information Center. Or type the following in your browser's address line:`http://pages.ebay.com/ sellerinformation/growing/variationtable.html`

When you list an item in any of these categories, you can indicate that you want to create a listing with variations. On the menu provided, select Yes, then click Continue, and then complete the steps in the List Your Variations tool.

Presale listings

If you're tempted to sell something that hasn't been delivered to you yet, well, as a rule . . . don't. eBay doesn't like it when you try to sell something that's not already in your hands (known as a *presale listing*). Doing so is a dangerous game to play anyway. In many situations, being the first seller to put a very popular item up for sale can get you some pretty high bids. And if you can *guarantee* in your auction description that the item will be available to ship within 30 days of the purchase or the auction closing, you can run a presale. However, I don't recommend even attempting a presale listing if you're not *completely* sure that you'll have the item in time.

Figure 2-10:
Click the top-level category from the top of the Look-Up Tool and see which subcategories currently support variation listings.

Growth Strategies

Choose a Topic
▸ Home
▸ Getting Started
▾ Growth Strategies

Learning Essentials
Tools & Stores
Best Practices
International Selling
eBay for Business
Resources

▸ Shipping
▸ PowerSeller Program

Multi-variation listings are now available in the following categories. Use the look up table below to find the category and subcategories with this listing feature. Go to the multi-variation page for more information on how multi-variation listings work and best practices.

Sporting Goods	Clothing Shoes & Accessories	Crafts	Home & Garden	Health & Beauty	Baby	Pet Supplies	Jewelry & Watches

◆ Bath & Body

Description
Bath Bombs & Fizzies
Bath Brushes & Sponges
Bath Oils
Bath Salts
Bath Sets & Kits
Body Butters
Body Powders

If you know that you'll have the item to ship — and it won't be lost on its way to you — you may list the item with the following requirement: You must state in your auction description that the item is a presale and will be shipped 30 days from the end of the listing or purchase. You'll also have to use a little HTML to do this because the text must be coded with an HTML font no smaller than font size 3. (For more about HTML, see Chapter 11.)

Before you set up such an auction, check out the Federal Trade Commission's 30-day rule covering these matters, which you can find at the following address: business.ftc.gov/documents/bus02-business-guide-mail-and-telephone-order-merchandise-rule.

Bonuses, giveaways, raffles, or prizes

Because eBay sells to every state in the United States, it must follow explicit laws governing giveaways and prizes. Each state has its own set of rules and regulations, so eBay doesn't allow individual sellers to come up with their own promotions. If your auction violates this rule, eBay might end it.

Keyword spamming

Keyword spamming is when you add words, usually brand names, to your auction description that don't describe what you're selling (for example, describing that little black dress as Givenchy-style when Givenchy has nothing to do with it). Sellers use keyword spamming to pull viewers to their auctions after viewers have searched for the brand name. To attract attention to their listings, some sellers use *not* or *like* along with the brand name, such as *like Givenchy*.

AUCTION ANECDOTE

Preselling: Not worth the hassle

A seller I once knew presold Beanie Babies on eBay. She had a regular source that supplied her when the new toys came out, so she fell into a complacent attitude about listing presales. Then her supplier didn't get the shipment. Motivated by the need to protect her feedback rating (and by the fear that she'd be accused of fraud), she ran all over town desperately trying to get the Beanies she needed to fill her orders. Those particular Beanies were so rare that she ended up spending several hundred dollars more than what she had originally sold the toys for, just to keep her customers happy.

Keyword spamming actually causes your auction to fall under "potentially infringing" items for sale on eBay. Keyword spamming is a listing violation, and I mention it here because it affects all listings. The wording you choose when you run this kind of auction manipulates the eBay search engine and prospective bidders. For a complete discussion of keyword spamming, see Chapter 4.

Linking from your auctions

Few issues set sellers to arguing more than the rules on linking. In your auction item description, you *can* use the following links:

- One link to an additional page that gives further information about the item you're selling.

- A link that opens an e-mail window on the prospective buyer's browser so the buyer can send you an e-mail.

- Links to more photo images of the item you're selling.

- Links to your other auctions on eBay and your eBay Store listings.

- One link to your About Me page, in addition to the link next to your user ID that eBay provides.

- Links to vendors' sites that help you with your auctions. eBay considers listing services, software, and payment services to be third-party vendors. You can legally link to them as long as the HTML font is no larger than size 3; if you're using a logo, it must be no larger than 88 x 33 pixels. Most third-party vendors are well aware of these restrictions. They don't want their credits pulled from eBay, so the information they supply as a link generally falls within eBay's parameters.

In your auction description, you *cannot* link to the following:

- ✔ A page that offers to sell, trade, or purchase merchandise outside the eBay site.
- ✔ Any area on the Internet that offers merchandise considered illegal on eBay. (See Chapter 4 for information on illegal items.)
- ✔ Any site that encourages eBay bidders to place their bids outside eBay.
- ✔ Sites that solicit eBay user IDs and passwords.

Linking from your About Me page

eBay rules on your About Me page are pretty much the same as they are on the rest of the site. Because eBay gives you this page for self-promotion, *you* may link to your own business Web site from it (e-commerce or otherwise). Be sure not to link to *other* trading sites or to sites that offer the same merchandise for the same or a lower price. Read more about the About Me page dos and don'ts in Chapter 3.

Chapter 3

Cool eBay Tools

*e*Bay offers you an amazing variety of tools. But because the site is constantly changing, many users fail to notice when new tools appear on the system. I must admit that I have fallen victim to the "Oh, I didn't know I could do that" syndrome. When I poke around eBay and find a new cool tool or neat shortcut, it's always an eye-opener!

eBay users frequently share with me some nugget of information that has helped them along the way. And now I share these nuggets with you.

To stay on top of upcoming changes on eBay, you can subscribe to the Announcements e-mail. eBay tends to fill these missives with lots of promotional folderol, but a quick once over will keep you abreast of the many changes before they occur on the site. To sign up for this e-mail, mouse over (hold your cursor still for a moment over) Community on the navigation bar in the upper part of most eBay pages, and, from the drop-down menu that appears, click Announcements. On the resulting Announcements page, click the link to receive this information by e-mail (or through an RSS feed).

Aside from the tools I tell you about in this chapter, the most important shortcut I can give you is to remind you that when you sign in, but before you start your business on eBay, select the Keep Me Signed In for Today check box. This permits you to close your window during the day and reopen it later without having to sign in again. Just keep these pointers in mind:

✔ As on other sites, your computer will maintain your sign-in information for a 24-hour period (or until you sign out).

✔ If you're on a public computer, leave the check box deselected for security's sake.

✔ If you have more than one user ID or share a computer with other people, be sure to sign out when you're finished.

In addition to the gems that eBay users uncover, eBay has some incredibly useful features; here are two of my favorites:

- ✔ My eBay allows you to customize eBay for your home page.
- ✔ The About Me page lets you tell the story of your business to the world as well as find out (with a click of the mouse) about the people you plan to buy from.

To get the lowdown on these and other favorite cool eBay tools, read on.

My eBay

The first tool eBay gives you is your My eBay page. Every time you sign on to the site, this page will pop up on your screen with a cheery `My eBay — Hello, marsha_c` (substitute your user ID for mine), followed by your current feedback rating. The My eBay page is the perfect tool for running a small eBay business. It's no longer a step-by-step list of what you're bidding on and selling; it's an out-and-out Swiss Army knife of eBay tools.

Access the My eBay page by clicking the My eBay button in the eBay navigation links, which appear at the top of every eBay page. You'll see that if you mouse over one of the five selections, a drop-down menu appears. You can go directly to the main pages by clicking the navigation bar. But if you know that you want to go to one of the specialized areas, you can mouse over and click the individual links. A sample is shown in Figure 3-1.

Figure 3-1:
The eBay navigation bar appears at the top of every eBay page; each link has a drop-down menu.

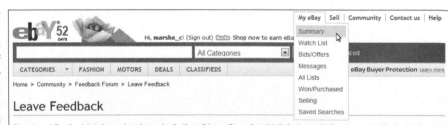

When you arrive at your My eBay page, you see a summary of the business that you have in progress on the site (see Figure 3-2). Each comment has a link so you can investigate the progress of each transaction.

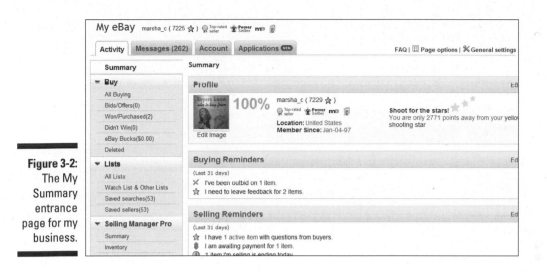

Figure 3-2:
The My
Summary
entrance
page for my
business.

Most My eBay areas are divided into several areas (Summary, Buy, Lists, Sell, and the Resolution Center), which you can visit by clicking links in the My eBay Views area on the left side of the page. The top link of each My eBay area presents you with a summary of the activity in that area. The links below the top link take you to specific data, without making you scroll through a long page.

Even if you subscribe to eBay's Selling Manager later (after you get your feet wet), you might want to check back to this page from time to time. You'll see information here you won't see anywhere else, such as Total Views, as in Figure 3-3 below.

Figure 3-3:
Note the
Views count
and note
from eBay
in the Active
Selling area.

At the bottom of My eBay Views is another area with Shortcuts to services and to answers you may need while doing business at eBay. You also see a box showing the icons that eBay uses on the My eBay pages, as shown in Figure 3-4.

Figure 3-4: Icons used on the My eBay and Selling Manager pages.

🔑	Auction Format		Item Shipped
	Fixed Price Format		Left Feedback
	Best Offer Format		Feedback Received
	Classified ad Format		Payment was refunded
	Second chance offer		Item Partially Paid
	Checkout complete	Σ	Request Total
$	Item Paid		Relisted

On the left side of each of the Views is a mini-size tote board, giving you a snapshot of your financial business dealings. In the Buying area, it displays the number of items you're bidding on and the dollar amount of all your winning bids. In the Selling area, you see the number of items and the dollar amounts bid (see Figure 3-5).

Totals	Edit ▾
Selling totals	
Current	
Listed	19
Will sell	0
Bids	0
Amount	$0.00
Sold (last 31 days)	
Listed	40
Sold	54
Amount	$1,658.46
Payments (last 31 days)	
Received	$1,558.46
Not received	$100.00
Total sales:	**$1,658.46**

Figure 3-5: My Selling Totals tote board.

Buy: All Buying

Here it is: All Buying is the hub for keeping track of your bids, your wins, items you're watching, and any items you didn't win. Although you plan to sell more than you buy at eBay, I'm sure you'll occasionally find something to buy only to turn around and resell. I've found many a bargain item at eBay that I've resold immediately at a profit. Plus, I purchase much of my shipping supplies on eBay.

Bids/Offers

When you place a bid, eBay registers it automatically in the All Buying: Bids/Offers area; Figure 3-6 shows an example.

Figure 3-6: Keeping track of your bidding on My eBay.

If you're shopping on eBay, make the bidding page a daily stop so you can see the status of your bids:

- ✔ Bid amounts in green indicate that you're the high bidder in the auction.

- ✔ Bid amounts in red indicate that your bid is losing. If you decide to increase your bid, simply click the auction title to go to the auction.

- ✔ The My Max Bid column reminds you of the amount of your highest bid; if you see a bid that's getting close to surpassing your own, you'll know it's time to throw in another bid (or throw in the towel).

- ✔ The Buying Totals box, on the left side of the Buy: All Buying page, lists the current dollar amount you're spending and the number of items you're currently winning in pending auctions. You'll see the total amount you've bid — and a separate total representing auctions you've won.

- ✔ As auctions on which you've bid end, they transfer automatically to the Won and Didn't Win pages, depending on whether your bidding process met with success or failure.

You can make notations on your bidding or item-watching — for example, to help you organize your gift giving. (See the note I added in Figure 3-7.) Click to place a check mark next to the item you want to annotate, click the Add Note button, and then add the information.

Figure 3-7:
My holiday
gift notation
on my bid.

		WristWrap Gel Grip Leather Weight Lifting Gloves S Blk **Your max bid:** $9.01	1	$8.99	$3.99	13h 19m	**View seller's other items** More actions ▾
		Eye Pillow Aromatherapy/Yoga /Organic Lavender&Flax RED **Your max bid:** $10.01 Holiday gift for Heather	1	$7.99	Free	18h 42m	**View seller's other items** More actions ▾
		Cartier love bracelet **Your max bid:** $51.28	7	$51.00	Free	4d 17h	**View seller's other items** More actions ▾

[Add note] [Add to list]

Won/Purchased

Clicking the Won/Purchased link in the bidding area displays all the items you've won or bought as far back as the last 60 days. The Won/Purchased page is a great place to keep track of items that you're waiting to receive from sellers. It's also a convenient way to keep track of your expenditures, should you be buying for resale. Helpful features on this page include the following:

- ✔ **Check box:** Click this box to add a check mark, and you can indicate that you'd like to add a note to your record, add the item to a list, or delete it.

- ✔ **Seller's user ID:** It always helps to remember the seller's name, and this link sends you to the seller's Member Profile (feedback page) where you can send an e-mail to the seller.

- ✔ **Listing title:** A link to the item. I always use this when an item arrives so I can be sure that the item I received is exactly as advertised.

- ✔ **Item sale date:** A convenient way to see whether your item is slow in shipping. After a week, it doesn't hurt to drop the seller an e-mail to check on the item's shipping status.

- ✔ **Sale price** and **shipping cost:** These help you keep track of the money you've spent. You use them with the totals in your tote board.

- ✔ **Actions:** This drop-down menu displays commands that differ according to the status of your transaction. You can click a link to pay for the item through PayPal, view the payment status on paid items, mark the item paid if you've already paid through methods other than PayPal, or leave feedback after you've received the item and are satisfied that it's what you ordered.

- ✔ **Icons:** At the end of each item's listing you can find a list of icons that appear dimmed until the selected action is taken. (Refer to Figure 3-4 for the 411 on what these icons represent.)

Sell: All Selling

eBay provides some smooth management tools on your Selling page. You can track items you currently have up for auction and items you've sold. It's a quick way to get a snapshot of the dollar value of your auctions as they proceed. Although this page isn't an ideal source of marketing information (detailed counters are best — see Chapter 9), it's a pretty good way to tell at a glance how your items are faring.

All Selling: Active

When you click the Active link, you see the page shown in Figure 3-8, where you can keep an eye on your store items, your fixed-price sales, and the progress of your auctions. You can see how many bids your auctions have, whether your reserve prices have been met, and how long before your listings close. By clicking an item title, you can visit the listing to make sure your pictures are appearing or to check your counter.

Figure 3-8: My Active Items area at My eBay.

Many people watch auctions and don't bid until the last minute, so you may not see a lot of bidding activity on your page. The Watchers feature can give you important information on the progress of your items.

The auctions that appear in green have received one or more bids (and met any reserve prices you've set). Auctions in red haven't received any bids, or the set reserve price hasn't been met. Fixed-price (or store listings) aren't color-coded; they appear in black.

TIP

The tech crew is always adding more features to these pages. Occasionally, go to the top-right corner of these pages and click the General Settings link. Here you can see a chart of additional options that you may display on the page. They vary depending on the page.

All Selling: Sold

Click the Sold link in the Sell: All Selling Views area and you'll come to the items you've sold. The Items on this page keeps your sales in a concise place, as shown in Figure 3-9. You can use it in lieu of fancy auction management software until you're selling lots of items (although eBay's Selling Manager does a fabulous job at this). If you're selling hundreds of items, your list will probably be too long to monitor individual auctions, but you can view the total current price of the items that will sell.

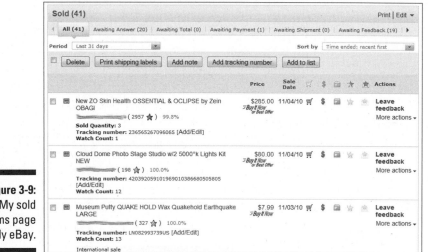

Figure 3-9:
My sold items page in My eBay.

TIP

If you're selling more than 20 items a week, consider using eBay's Selling Manager to give you a more complete auction-management solution. (See Chapter 9 for the lowdown on how to make this tool work for you.)

The Sold page has the following features, which I'm sure you'll find helpful in completing your transactions:

✔ **Check box:** Click here to add a personal note to your record, print shipping labels right from eBay, add tracking numbers (more on printing labels in Chapter 14), or remove an item from a list.

✔ **Buyer's user ID** and **feedback rating:** The eBay ID of the winner of the sale. Click it to go to the user's Member Profile, where you can use eBay's e-mail sever to contact the buyer.

✔ **Sold Quantity:** If the sale was for multiple items, you see the number of items displayed here.

✔ **Watch Count:** Here you find out how many people have marked your item to watch on their my eBay pages at the time of the sale.

✔ **Item title:** A direct link to the listing. If it's an auction, you can click this link to see the other bidders — especially useful, should you want to make a Second Chance offer.

✔ **Sale price:** The final selling price for your item.

✔ **Sale date:** Keep an eye on the end date so you can be sure you get your payment and ship out as agreed.

✔ **Action:** Here's where you find a hidden drop-down menu that works with the icons to the right and offers links to various actions you can take. Some of the more popular options are:

- **Mark as payment received:** If the customer hasn't paid using PayPal, indicate the method of payment (*after* you receive it).

- **View PayPal transaction:** See a copy of the payment receipt if the buyer paid using PayPal.

- **Print shipping label:** You can print a shipping label from here. (See Chapter 14 for professional options.)

- **Leave feedback:** Leave feedback with a single click after you've heard that the item arrived safely and your customer is happy. For more information on leaving feedback, check out the section "Feedback: Your permanent record," later in this chapter.

- **Mark as shipped:** After you've shipped the item, click here to indicate that it's on the way.

- **Second Chance offer:** Make a Second Chance offer to one of your underbidders if you have multiple items for sale.

- **Relist:** Here you can relist your item on the site.

✔ **Icons:** My eBay has several icons that appear dimmed until you perform an action with the Action command. You may also click the icons at the top of the list to sort your listings by actions completed (although most sellers prefer to keep the listings in the default chronological order). You can see whether a buyer has reached these stages of the process:

- **Shopping cart:** The buyer has completed checkout (supplying a shipping address and planned payment method).

- **Dollar sign:** The buyer has paid using PayPal, or you've used the drop-down menu to indicate that the buyer has paid with a different form of payment (such as a money order or a personal check).

- **Shipping box:** The item has shipped.

- **Star:** You've left feedback.

• **Comment bubble:** The buyer has left feedback. A plus sign (+) indicates a positive comment, and a minus sign (–) indicates a negative comment.

Lists: All Lists

If you want to keep track of items (say you've set up a Christmas gift list) and have an interest in a few categories, look no farther than the My eBay All Lists. This feature gives you some links for checking out what's hot and what's not. The Lists pages help you track trends and find some bargains to resell at eBay.

List: Watch List

Have you ever seen an item that made you think, "I don't want to bid on this or buy just now, but I'd like to buy it if it's a bargain"? Clicking the Watch List link from the My eBay Lists box will bring you to the Watch List page (see Figure 3-10), one of the most powerful features of the My eBay area. This page lists each item with a countdown (time-left) timer, so you know exactly when the auction or listing will close. (When an auction on your Watch List gets close to ending, you can swoop down and make the kill — if the price is right).

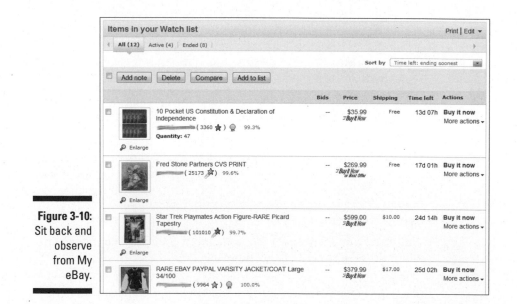

Figure 3-10: Sit back and observe from My eBay.

Also a handy marketing tool, the Watch List page allows you to store listings posted by competitive sellers. That way you can monitor the status of items similar to ones you plan to sell later; seeing whether those items are selling high or low can help you to decide whether it's a good time to sell.

You've probably seen the Add to Watch List link at the top of each item page. If you're watching items (eBay allows you to monitor 200 at a time), you'll see a notation at the top of the page, indicating how many listings you're currently watching.

My number one reason for using the Watch List function is that it allows me to keep my bargain hunting quiet. Everybody — including the competition — knows when you're bidding on an item; nobody knows when you're watching the deals like a hawk. When you're searching for bargains to buy and resell, you may not want to tip off the competition by letting them know you're looking (and kicking off the bidding is a dead giveaway).

Saved searches

A tool that comes in handy for sellers as well as buyers is Saved searches (see Figure 3-11). You can list as many favorite searches as you want; when you want to check one out, simply click the name of the search on the page.

Saved Searches			Edit ▾
		Sort by	Title: A to Z
☐ Delete Add to list			
Name of Search	**Search Criteria**	**Email Settings**	**Actions**
☐ l'occitane immortelle	l'occitane immortelle Category Health & Beauty > Skin Care	Not receiving emails	**Edit search** More actions ▾
☐ La Napoule	La Napoule	Not receiving emails	**Edit search** More actions ▾
☐ lancel		Not receiving emails	**Edit search** More actions ▾
☐ murano lamp		Not receiving emails	**Edit search** More actions ▾
☐ oh deer	oh deer	Not receiving emails (Last sent May-17-08)	**Edit search** More actions ▾
☐ olivetti valentine	olivetti valentine	Not receiving	**Edit search**

Figure 3-11: Some of my favorite searches.

You can view, change, and delete saved searches, or indicate that you'd like to receive e-mail notification when a new item is listed. To add an item to the list, run a search from any search bar on any eBay page and click the Save Search link that appears at the top of the search-results page. The next time you reload your My eBay Saved Searches page, your new favorite will be listed.

Keeping track of saved searches is a valuable tool when you're looking for particular items to resell and want to find them at bargain-basement prices. Be sure to take advantage of asterisks (wildcard characters) and alternate spellings so you can catch items with misspellings in the title. These are your best bets for low prices. (See Chapter 7 for the lowdown on the search engine and how it can help your sales.)

If you choose to receive e-mail when your search locates a new listing, you can request that you receive notification. You're allowed to receive new listing e-mails on any or all of your searches. Just click the drop-down menu and click the Sign Up For Emails link from the drop-down menu next to the saved search. eBay sends its robot to check listings each night, so you'll get notification of a new listing the next morning.

Lists: Saved Sellers

Saved Sellers is where I keep a list of people who sell items similar to what I sell. I can check up on them and see what they're selling, when they're selling it, and for how much. It's a helpful tool that has prevented me from listing an item at the same time the item crops up in one of their auctions.

Saved Sellers is also handy when your competition is selling an item that you plan to sell, but at a deeply discounted price. When that happens, don't offer yours until they sell out of the item, at which time the price will most likely go back up — supply and demand, remember? I have a few quality wholesalers and liquidators listed under my Favorite Sellers, too, and search there for lots I can resell at a profit.

To add a seller to your Saved Sellers list, click the link that says "Save this seller" in the seller's info box (in the upper-right corner of the item page).

Navigation tabs

At the top of all your My eBay pages are four tabs that link to some of the most important parts of your eBay account: Activity, Messages, Account, and Applications.

Activity

Clicking the Activity tab leads to the My eBay information discussed previously. (You'll still see all the links on the left side when you arrive at the page.)

Messages

The Messages tab is where you connect to the eBay e-mail system. This tab is a wonderful tool that gives you your own e-mail hubs for eBay business. Chapter 12 gives you the lowdown on how this feature works.

Account

Mouse over the Account tab to see the drop-down menu shown in Figure 3-12. Clicking the individual links on this tab will bring you to the individual segments of your account. This section is chock-full of important info for you to know. The main Account tab lets you know how much you owe eBay and how much they will charge your credit card that month. This is a quick way to check your last invoice, payments and credits, and your account; all the links are located in one area.

Figure 3-12:
The My eBay Account drop-down menu on my account summary page.

You can also access your PayPal account to see, for example, when deposits were credited to your checking account. (For a complete picture of how to sign up and use PayPal, visit Chapter 13.)

Lots of options are available. I describe the highlights next.

Personal Information

The Personal Information page holds all the links to your personal information at eBay. This is where you can change your e-mail address, user ID, password, and credit-card information; and edit or create your About Me page. You can also change or access any registration or credit card information that you have on file at eBay.

Addresses

On the Addresses page, you can see the address you used to register on eBay and edit (when necessary) your payment address and primary shipping address.

Preferences

An especially nifty aspect of eBay Preferences is that it gives you an opportunity to customize how you run your eBay business. There are sections on your buying, selling, communication, and general preferences. This is an important area for you to check out — because setting some of these tools can make your selling career on eBay go far more smoothly. You can change the following:

- ✔ **Communication Preferences:** Tell eBay whether (and how) you'd like to be notified every time a function occurs in your eBay account. You can customize buying, selling, and other transaction details, notifications, and legal notices issued by eBay.

- ✔ **Site Preferences:** In this area, you take control of how eBay helps you run your business. Here you can customize your checkout procedures, offer shipping discounts, and more. Go to this page and run down the many varied options. These may change from time to time due to eBay policy changes, so it's worth revisiting this area every few months.

  Most importantly, this is the place where you can decide to block certain buyers before they bid or buy from you. By clicking the Buyer Requirements link on these pages, you can block the following:

  - • **Buyers in countries to which I don't ship:** Every eBay seller (until they find out about this option) has had an item won from someone in a country to which they choose not to ship. You may choose not to ship for any number of reasons. Maybe you don't want to ship internationally and accept foreign payments (along with the extra fees from PayPal), or you don't want to risk your packages getting lost in a foreign postal system. When you get a sale like this, however, you basically have to go through with the sale — or risk negative feedback. By indicating that you do not want to accept business from buyers in particular countries, you avoid this problem.

  - • **Buyers with a negative feedback score:** If you don't want to accept customers who have been rapidly building negative feedback, you can remove them from your business here. You have a choice of barring people with a –1, –2, or –3 total feedback score (indicating these people have more negatives than positives).

  - • **Buyers with unpaid-item strikes:** You may prevent those who have had two unpaid-item strikes within the last 30 days. This is a good idea. If they haven't paid for 2 items in the last 30 days, they're likely not to go through with your transaction — thereby costing you time and money.

- **Buyers who may bid on several of my items and not pay for them:** This title is a bit misleading. As often happens in any commerce, some people think shopping is a game. Many hyper-caffeinated (to be kind) eBay joyriders will ferret out a particular seller and buy every item that seller has for sale, with absolutely no intention of paying. They seem to think this is fun.

  Before eBay instituted these blocks, I knew several major sellers who went to bed with several hundred items up for sale — only to wake up to find everything sold. After the initial blush of victory, they realized that everything was bought by the same buyer — often someone with a new account or a low feedback rating. As if that's not bad enough, the poor sellers would check their feedback and find that the buyer left negative feedback for every item bought. eBay is cooperative in helping to clean up a mess like this, but all items then have to be relisted, and the entire repair process is hugely time-consuming. Save yourself some grief and limit your buyers here.

- **Buyers without a PayPal account:** You may choose to bar buyers who don't have a PayPal account, but why? New buyers are the core of eBay, and signing up for a PayPal account is a simple task for those who want to pay you with a credit card.

Seller Dashboard

If you're looking to become a PowerSeller or (even better) a Top-Rated Seller, you should check the Seller Dashboard area with regularity. (Read further on for information on these programs.) Figure 3-13 shows you my Seller Dashboard.

Figure 3-13:
Your all-important Seller Dashboard.

Here's where you can track how your feedback star ratings are going as you sell.

Feedback

Feedback is a crucial area of the eBay experience. Clicking here shows you where you need to leave feedback, as well as your last few feedback comments. This information is also easy to access elsewhere on eBay.

Resolution Center

If you have a buyer who doesn't pay for an item, you need to file an unpaid-item case to get your Final Value fees credited back to your seller account. If payment isn't received, open an unpaid-item case in the Resolution Center. You can do this as early as 4 days — but no later than 32 days — after the listing ended (or *immediately* if the buyer is no longer registered on eBay). If you use this method, you must check back and close the case on your My eBay page.

An easier option is to use eBay's Unpaid Item Assistant (you find this by clicking the Site Preferences link). You set your parameters and eBay will open and close the case for you.

PayPal

Links in the PayPal area allow you to view and update your PayPal account information and profile summary. Clicking these links will take you directly to the PayPal Web site.

Half.com Account

Old-time eBay sellers have been threatened over and over with the possible demise of Half.com (eBay's fixed-price media marketplace), and yet it still hangs on. If you sell or buy on Half.com, you can access your information and transactions from the Half.com Account area.

Seller Account

If you want to check to see how much you owe eBay for your listing and sale, or want to make a payment, the Seller Account area is the place to go.

Subscriptions

When you subscribe to any of the eBay services, such as Selling Manager Pro or Sales Reports Plus, the Subscriptions area is where you can cancel, upgrade, or edit your level(s) of subscription.

The About Me Page

If you're on eBay, you *need* an About Me page. I hate to harp, but eBay is a community, and all eBay members are members of that community. Checking out the About Me pages of people you conduct business with gives you an opportunity to get to know them. Because eBay is a cyberspace market, you have no other way to let prospective bidders know that you're a real person. Don't you shop at some stores because you like the owners or people who work there? The About Me page is your first step toward establishing a professional and trusted identity at eBay.

The About Me page enables you to personalize your business to prospective bidders. (See Figure 3-14 for an example.) Your About Me page also becomes your About the Seller page if you have an eBay store.

Figure 3-14: An excellent example of an About Me page from Beachcombers!

An About Me page benefits you also when you buy. Sellers usually like to know about their bidders to build confidence in their trading partners. If you've put up an About Me page, you're halfway there.

If you don't have an About Me page and you're already on eBay, put this book down and set one up immediately. It doesn't have to be a work of art; just get something up there to tell the rest of the community who you are. You can always go back later and add to or redesign it.

When you plan your About Me page, consider adding the following:

- ✔ Who you are and where you do business.

- ✔ Your hobbies, your interests. This is the place you can personalize your eBay listings with your happy face. If you collect things, here's where to let the world know.

- ✔ Whether you run your eBay business full-time or part-time and whether you have another career. This is more integral information about you; let the world know.

- ✔ The type of merchandise that your business revolves around. Promote it here; tell the reader why your merchandise and service are the best!

- ✔ Tips and information about your products and services.

- ✔ Your most recent feedback and a list of your current auctions.

To create your page, click the Me icon next to any user's name, scroll to the very bottom of the About Me page that appears, find the line that reads "To create your own About Me page, click here," and click. You can also click the About Me page link in the Personal Information of My Account area. Or go to `http://cgi3.ebay.com/ws/eBayISAPI.dll?AboutMeLogin`. Then follow the simple preformatted template for your first page and work from there.

eBay Seller Services

Most eBay users don't know the extent of eBay's seller-specific services. And sometimes sellers are so involved with their auctions that they don't take the time to find out about new helper tools. So I've gone deep into the eBay pond to locate a few excellent tools to help you with your online business. Even if you've used some of these before, it might be time to revisit them because eBay has implemented quite a few changes during the past year.

Bidder-management tools

Did you know that you don't have to accept bids from just anyone? Although many people include notices in their auction descriptions that attempt to qualify bidders ahead of time, this doesn't always prevent "just anyone" from bidding on your auction. Alas, part of the business is keeping an eye on your bidders. With bidder-management tools, you can save yourself a good deal of grief.

Canceling bids

You could have any number of reasons for wanting to cancel someone's bid. Perhaps an international bidder has bid on an auction in which you clearly state you don't ship overseas. Here are a few more legitimate reasons for canceling a bid:

- The bidder contacts you to back out of the bid; choosing to be a nice guy, you let him or her out of the deal.

- Your bidder has received several negative feedback notes and hasn't gone through with other transactions that he or she has won.

- You're unable to verify the bidder's identity through e-mail or the phone.

- You need to cancel the auction (see the following tip).

I don't recommend canceling an auction unless you absolutely have to because normally it's just bad business. People rely on your auctions being up for the stated amount of time. They may be planning to bid at the last minute, or they may just want to watch the action for a while. You may lose potential buyers by ending your listing early. But if you have to . . .

For whatever reason you're canceling someone's bid, you should first e-mail that person and clearly explain why you're doing so. Your bid cancellation appears in the auction's bidding history and becomes part of the auction's official record. For that reason, I recommend that you leave a concise, unemotional, one-line explanation on the cancellation form as to why you've cancelled the bid.

To get to the bid-cancellation form, go to the Site Map link at the bottom of most eBay pages. On the resulting page, under Selling Activities, you will find a Cancel Bids on your listing link. You can also get to the cancellation form directly by typing the following Web address into your browser and then pressing Enter: `offer.ebay.com/ws/eBayISAPI.dll?CancelBidShow`

End your listing early

You may decide to end a listing early for any number of reasons. If anyone has bid on your auction before you end it, you'll be duty-bound to sell to the highest bidder. So before ending an auction early, it's polite to e-mail everyone in your bidder list, explaining why you're canceling bids and closing the auction. If an egregious error in the item's description is forcing you to take this action, let your bidders know whether you're planning to relist the item with the correct information.

Only *after* canceling all bids should you go ahead and close your auction. To end your listing, use the drop-down menu next to the item in your Selling area. Click the End Item link. You can also go directly to `http://cgi3.ebay.com/aw-cgi/eBayISAPI.dll?EndingMyAuction`

Following are some legitimate reasons for closing your auction:

- **You no longer want to sell the item:** Your account may be subject to a "Non-Selling Seller" warning unless you have a really good reason. (See Chapter 4 for more details.)

- **An error occurred in the minimum bid or the reserve amount:** Perhaps your wife said that she really loves that lamp and you'd better get some good money for it, but you started the auction at $1 with no reserve. (Oops.)

- **The listing has a major error in it:** Maybe you misspelled a critical keyword in the title.

- **The item was somehow lost or broken:** Your dog ate it? A meteorite fell on it?

Blocking individual buyers

If you don't want certain buyers bidding on your auctions, you can remove their capability to do so. Setting up a list of bidders that you don't want to do business with is legal on eBay. If someone you've blocked tries to bid on your auction, the bid won't go through. A message will be displayed notifying the person that he or she is not able to bid on the listing and to contact the seller for more information.

You can block as many as one thousand users from bidding on your auctions. However, I recommend that you use this option only when absolutely necessary. Situations — and people — change, and it's best to try to clear up problems with particular bidders.

You can reinstate a bidder at any time by going to the Buyer Blocked Bidder/ Buyer list at `http://pages.ebay.com/services/buyandsell/bidder management.html`

Click the Add an eBay User to My Blocked Bidder/Buyer List link. On the resulting page, you can delete the bidder's user ID from the Blocked list.

Feedback: Your permanent record

Just like your high school permanent record, your eBay feedback follows you forever at eBay. If you change your user ID, it's there. If you change your e-mail address, it's there. When you click the feedback number next to a user's ID, the user's Feedback profile (see Figure 3-15) is displayed. The information shown will tell you a lot about your bidder.

Feedback Profile

marsha_c (7229 ☆) me 📋

Positive Feedback (last 12 months): 100%
[How is Feedback Percentage calculated?]
Member since: Jan-04-97 in United States

This member is a **Top-rated seller**

✓ Consistently receives highest buyers' ratings
✓ Ships items quickly
✓ Has earned a track record of excellent service

Learn more

Recent Feedback Ratings ?
(last 12 months)

	1 month	6 months	12 months
⊕ Positive	29	154	343
◎ Neutral	0	0	0
⊖ Negative	0	0	0

Detailed Seller Ratings (last 12 months) ?

Criteria	Average rating	Number of ratings
Item as described	★★★★★	253
Communication	★★★★★	253
Shipping time	★★★★★	253
Shipping and handling charges	★★★★★	262

The most obvious tip-off to someone's feedback is the star you see next to the user ID. Different colors of stars are awarded as folks reach milestones in their feedback ratings. To decipher the star colors and see what they mean, click the help link and type the words *star rating*.

Your feedback means a great deal to people who visit your auctions. By glancing at your feedback page, they can see

✔ Whether you're an experienced eBay user

✔ Your eBay history

✔ When you started at eBay

✔ How many bid retractions you've had in the past six months

This is valuable information for both the buyer and the seller; it helps the buyer evaluate whether you're the type of person who would make a responsible trading partner. If it's good, it tends to help the seller clinch the sale.

Leaving feedback

Everyone in the eBay community is honor-bound to leave feedback. Sometimes, when you've had a truly dreadful experience, you hate to leave negative or neutral feedback, but if you don't, you're not helping anyone. The point of feedback is not to show what a great person you are but to show future sellers or bidders where the rotten apples lie. So, when leaving feedback, be truthful and unemotional and state just the facts.

Feedback is important to keep eBay going, so you should be sure to leave some for every transaction you take part in. If a week has passed since you've shipped an item, and you haven't heard from the bidder or seen any feedback, drop that bidder an e-mail. Write "Thanks for your purchase. Are you happy with the item?" Also emphasize that you'll be glad to leave feedback after you've heard a reply, and ask for the same in return.

Keep in mind that only buyers can leave positive, negative, or neutral feedback — and sellers can only leave positive.

I suggest that you refrain from leaving feedback on a sale until you're absolutely, positively *sure* that the buyer has received the product and is happy with the deal. Many sellers leave feedback the minute they get their money, but experience can teach them that "it ain't over 'til it's over." A package can get lost or damaged, or the bidder may be unhappy for some reason. If a buyer is unhappy, you want the opportunity to make things right. eBay provides so many different links to leave feedback that I could probably write an entire chapter on it. But I don't want you to fall asleep while reading, so I go through only the most convenient methods:

- ✔ Go to your item page and click the Leave Feedback link, which appears at top left.

- ✔ Click the Leave Feedback link in the drop-down menu next to the completed sale on the Sold page in your My eBay pages.

- ✔ Visit the feedback forum (this link shows up on the bottom of every page) and click the link that shows all pending feedback for the past 90 days.

  When you've fallen behind in leaving feedback, this is a super-fast way to catch up.

Reply to feedback received

You may occasionally get feedback that you feel compelled to respond to. (Did you know that you *could* respond?) If the feedback is neutral or negative, I recommend that you cover yourself by explaining the situation for future bidders to see.

If you receive a negative feedback rating, a well-meaning admission of guilt would work. You could say something like, "Unfortunately, shipping was delayed, and I regret the situation." Prospective bidders will see that you've addressed the problem instead of just letting it go.

To respond to feedback, follow these steps:

1. On the My eBay page, click the Feedback link under Account.

2. On the feedback page, click the Go to Feedback Forum link at the top of the page.

3. On the resulting page, click the Reply to Feedback Received link.

   The Reply to Feedback Received page appears, as shown in Figure 3-16.

Feedback Forum: Reply to Feedback Received

| | Find Feedback |
Enter a User ID or Item Number

An important part of the Feedback Forum is sharing with the community your experience with other members. In addition to leaving feedback, there may be occasions where you want to reply to a comment another member has left in your member profile.

To reply to a comment, click the **Reply** link.

8084 feedback received by marsha_c from buyers and sellers(0 mutually withdrawn)   Page 1 of 324

Comment	From		Date	Item #	Action
⊕ ┆-•¨¨·-┆-•¨ WONDERFUL E-BAYER ¨-┆-¨ "THANK YOU" -┆-•¨¨¨·-┆-	Seller	(456 ☆)	Nov-05-10	150512986114	**Reply**
⊕ Perfect transaction	Buyer	(330 ☆)	Nov-05-10	350405180423	**Reply**
⊕ A pleasure! Thanks for the prompt payment.	Seller	(6392 ☆)	Nov-05-10	160501342659	**Reply**
⊕ worked great	Buyer	(154 ☆)	Nov-04-10	360301455661	**Reply**
⊕ good seller	Buyer	(149 ☆)	Nov-03-10	350405180423	**Reply**
⊕ Great product and fantastic service - couldn't be better!!!	Buyer	(143 ☆)	Nov-02-10	350405180423	**Reply**

Figure 3-16:
Review and respond to your feedback comments.

4. **Scroll to find the feedback comment that you want to respond to and click the Reply link.**

5. **Type your response and then click the Leave Response button.**

The eBay PowerSeller program

I'm sure you've seen the PowerSeller logo on auctions. eBay PowerSellers represent the largest-gross-sales users on eBay. The requirements for becoming a PowerSeller follow:

- You must have gross monthly dollar volume of certain amounts (see Table 3-1). To remain a PowerSeller, you must maintain your level's minimum gross sales for the past three months and keep current with all the other requirements. To advance up the PowerSeller chain, you must reach and maintain the next level of gross sales for an average of three months.

  If you miss your minimum gross sales for three months, eBay gives you a grace period. After that time, if you don't meet the minimum gross figures for your level, you may be moved down to the prior level or be removed from the PowerSeller program.

- You must have at least 100 feedback comments, with 98 percent positive. To calculate your feedback percentage, divide your number of positive feedback comments by your number of total feedback comments (negatives plus positives).

- You must maintain a minimum average detailed seller rating (DSR) of 4.60 or higher for all four DSRs. The DSR rating is based on the star rating you receive when your customer leaves you feedback.

- You must meet a minimum total of $3,000 in sales and 100 transactions with U.S. buyers over the past year.

Table 3-1 shows the benefits and requirement for each PowerSeller tier.

Table 3-1	PowerSeller Benefits and Requirements			
Tier	Monthly GMS ($) or Items Sold	E-Mail / Chat Support	Phone	Manager Support
Bronze*	$1,000 or 100 items	Yes	6:00 a.m.–10:00 p.m.	No
Silver	$3,000 or 300 items	Yes	6:00 a.m.–10:00 p.m.	No
Gold	$10,000 or 1,000 items	Yes	24 hours	Some
Platinum	$25,000 or 2,500 items	Yes	24 hours	Yes
Titanium	$150,000 or 15,000 items	Yes	24 hours	Yes

There's no official indication of it, but I'll bet if you're a Titanium level PowerSeller, John Donahoe (eBay's CEO) will arrange babysitting for you when you're in a jam. (Now, I don't *know* that to be gospel . . . but I'm just sayin' . . . .)

It's a serious matter to comply with eBay policies, but PowerSellers get a little leeway. They also get to know exactly how much "leeway" they can get away with. Table 3-2 shows how much eBay allows the various levels of PowerSellers to get away with per 90-day period.

Table 3-2	Policy Violations by Tier
PowerSeller Tier	Number of Violations in 60 Days
Bronze	4
Silver	5
Gold	5
Platinum	6
Titanium	7

PowerSellers also get a discount off their Final Value fees. If all four of your detailed seller ratings for the past 30 days are 4.6 or higher, you get a 5 percent discount.

Being a PowerSeller means you get an awesome level of customer service, called Priority eSupport. When a PowerSeller dashes off an e-mail to a special customer service department, a reply comes back at the speed of light.

Top-Rated Seller Program

You have to be a PowerSeller before you can become a Top-Rated Seller, but the benefits are well worth the extra effort. As a Top-Rated Seller, you get:

- ✔ Twenty percent discounts on Final Value fees
- ✔ Preferred position in Best Match search results for Fixed Priced listings
- ✔ Top-Rated Seller badge on eBay search results and on your item pages

Maintaining the coveted status is not easy, and your eligibility is examined each month (rather than the three-month PowerSeller period). To see how close you are to becoming a Top-Rated PowerSeller, go to your Seller dashboard. Scroll down to Seller Standing and click the highlighted Performance Standards link.

On the resulting page, you'll see a chart (as shown in Figure 3-17); study where you stand on your DSRs and how close you are to Top-Rated Status.

Performance criteria for: Top-rated ▾			Evaluation Period: Nov 01, 2009 - Oct 31, 2010		
Criteria	**Requirements**		**Your performance**		
	Do not exceed the maximum limits of both percent and count ⓘ				
Low detailed seller ratings*	Max %	Max count	Your %	Your count	
Item as described	0.50%	2	0.00%	0	⊘
Communication	0.50%	2	0.26%	1	⊘
Shipping time	0.50%	2	0.53%	2	⊘
Shipping and handling charges	0.50%	2	0.26%	1	⊘
*Low detailed seller ratings are 1s and 2s.					
Buyer Protection cases	Max %	Max count	Your %	Your count	
Opened cases [See definition]	0.50%	2	0.00%	0 [See cases]	⊘
Closed cases without seller resolution [See definition]	0.30%	2	0.00%	0 [See cases]	⊘
Average detailed seller ratings	Requirements		Your performance		
Item as described	4.60		5.00		⊘
Communication	4.60		4.97		⊘
Shipping time	4.60		4.92		⊘
Shipping and handling charges	4.60		4.98		⊘
Other criteria	Requirements		Your performance		
PowerSeller level	Bronze or above		Bronze		⊘
Transactions (12-month)	100		380		⊘

Figure 3-17: My actual performance versus the Top-Rated Seller performance criteria.

Chapter 4

Safe Selling Equals Profitable Sales

· ·

In This Chapter

▶ Understanding the rules

▶ Watching out for violations

▶ Protecting yourself — and helping make eBay a safe place to trade

· ·

*T*here are a lot of *shoulds* in this world. You *should* do this and you *should* do that. I don't know who's in charge of the *shoulds,* but certain things just make life work better. You may or may not take any of the advice on these pages, but they'll make your eBay business thrive with a minimum of anguish. If you've ever had an auction pulled by eBay, you know what anguish truly feels like.

In the real world, we have to take responsibility for our own actions. If we buy a fifty-two-inch plasma television for $250 from some guy selling them out of the back of a truck, who do we have to blame when we take it home and it doesn't work? You get what you pay for, and you have no consumer protection from the seller of the possibly "hot" TVs. Responsible consumerism is every buyer's job. Lawsuits get filed — and some are won — when people feel they've been ripped off, but my best advice is that if you stay clean in your online business, you'll keep clean.

eBay is a community, and the community was founded on the following five basic values:

▸ We believe people are basically good.

▸ We believe everyone has something to contribute.

▸ We believe that an honest, open environment can bring out the best in people.

▸ We recognize and respect everyone as a unique individual.

▸ We encourage you to treat others the way that you want to be treated.

eBay is committed to these values, and it says so right on its Web site. eBay believes that community members should "honor these values — whether buying, selling, or chatting." So *should* we all.

Is What You Want to Sell Legal?

Although eBay is based in California and therefore must abide by California law, sellers do business all over the United States. Therefore, items sold on eBay must be governed by the laws of every other state as well. As a seller, you're ultimately responsible for the legality of the items you sell — and the way you transact business on eBay. Yes, you can sell thousands of different items on eBay. But do you know what you *aren't* allowed to sell on eBay?

The eBay User Agreement outlines all eBay rules and regulations regarding what you can and can't sell — as well as all aspects of doing business at eBay. If you've never ever read the User Agreement, you really should — at least once. You can find it at the following address: `http://pages.ebay.com/help/policies/user-agreement.html`.

These policies can change from time to time. As an active seller, you should make sure that you're notified of any changes. When eBay makes changes to the User Agreement or Privacy Policy, you'll get a notification of those changes through the eBay Message Center. These e-mails are sent to your registered eBay e-mail address (an important reason to keep this up to date with eBay). To access the correspondence you receive from eBay on the site, follow these steps:

1. **Sign in with your user ID and password.**

   You have to sign in with your password because correspondence is private.

2. **Go to your My eBay page. In the Tabs section on the top of the page, click the Messages tab.**

3. **On the resulting Messages page, click the From eBay link on the left side of the page, as shown in Figure 4-1.**

4. **Click each e-mail individually.**

   The e-mail opens in a reading pane below the Inbox display.

   - After you've opened the e-mail online, it appears dimmed.

   - If you've read the e-mail offline in your e-mail program, it will still appear as unread in your eBay Inbox.

   This arrangement enables you to receive important information that may affect how you run your business.

By now, you should have a firm grasp of the rules and regulations for listing items (if not, check out Chapter 2). But in addition to knowing the rules for listing items, you must consider the items themselves. In this section, I detail the three categories of items to be wary of: prohibited, restricted, and infringing. Some are banned, period. Others fall into a gray area. You're responsible for what you sell, so you'd better know what's legal and what's not.

Figure 4-1:
Your eBay
eMail Inbox:
Messages
from eBay.

Activity	Messages (263)	Account	Applications

Inbox: From eBay (69)

View: All | Unread | Flagged | Others

Inbox
All messages (264)
From members (195)
From eBay (69)
! High priority

Sent

Trash

Folders
My Folder 1
Cashback
Add folder

More options
Save your messages
Find and contact member
Messages Help
Customer Support

Delete | Move to | Mark as

From	Item ends	Subject
eBay	--	Don't forget to redeem your eBay Bucks
eBay	--	eBay Counteroffer Submitted to buyer: NEW eBay For Dummies
eBay	--	You've received an offer for your eBay item, NEW eBay For Dum
eBay	--	eBay Buyer Protection–we've got you covered
eBay	--	You've received an offer for your eBay item, PBS Marsha Collier
eBay	--	You've received an offer for your eBay item, PBS TV Marsha Coll
eBay	--	You've received an offer for your eBay item, NEW eBay For Dum
eBay	--	eBay Counteroffer Submitted to buyer: New ZO Skin Health OSS
eBay	--	You've received an offer for your eBay item, New ZO Skin Health
eBay	--	You've received an offer for your eBay item, Portable PHOTO WIN

Page 1 of 4 — Previous 1 | 2 | 3 | 4 Next

Delete ↓ ↑ Move to

Don't forget to redeem your eBay Bucks
From: eBay
Sent: Oct-21-10 02:30 PM

eBay sent this message to Marsha Collier (marsha_c).
Your registered name is included to show this message originated from eBay.
Learn more.

Use your eBay Bucks Certificate before it expires

If you think it's okay to give away a regulated or banned item as a bonus item with your auction, think again. Even giving away such items for free doesn't save you from potential legal responsibility.

Prohibited and restricted items

Selling violations on eBay come in two different flavors: prohibited and restricted. By either name, they are highly regulated on the site. You want to avoid these violations as they will cause your listing to be removed and place a blemish on your eBay seller record (which can affect your future PowerSeller or Top-Rated Seller status).

A *prohibited item* is banned from sale on eBay. You can't sell a prohibited item on eBay under any circumstances. A *restricted item* is iffy — determining whether you can sell it is tricky. Under certain circumstances, you may be able to list the item for sale.

Take a look at the following list. A little common sense tells you there's good reason for not selling these items, including liability issues for the seller (what if you sold alcohol to a minor? — that's against the law). To fully understand if and when you can list an item, visit the links that I highlight in Table 4-1.

To get the latest information on these types of items, check the following address for updates: http://pages.ebay.com/help/policies/items-ov.html.

**Table 4-1   Prohibited and Restricted Items: Where to
Find the Rules Regulating Them**

Can I Sell This?	Go Here to Find Out*
Adult Only Category	/adult-only.html
Alcohol	/alcohol.html
Animals and wildlife products	/wildlife.html
Art	/selling-art.html
Artifacts, grave-related items & Native American crafts	/artifacts.html
Celebrity material	/celebrity-material.html
Catalytic converters and test pipes	/catalytic-converters.html
Cell phone (wireless) service contracts	/cellphone-services.html
Charity or fundraising listings	/fundraising.html
Clothing, used	/used-clothing.html
Contracts	/contracts.html
Cosmetics, used	/used-cosmetics.html
Counterfeit currency and stamps	/currstamps.html
Credit cards	/credit-cards.html
Currency, selling	/currstamps.html
Drugs and drug paraphernalia	/drugs-drug-paraphernalia.html
Drugs, describing drugs or drug-like substances	/describing-drugs.html
Electronic and surveillance devices	/electronics.html
Embargoed goods and prohibited countries	/embargo.html
Event ticket resale	/event-tickets.html
Firearms, weapons, and knives	/firearms-weapons-knives.html
Gift cards	/gift.html
Food and healthcare items	/food.html
Government documents, IDs, licenses	/government-ids-licenses.html
Government transit and shipping-related items	/government-transit-items.html

Can I Sell This?	*Go Here to Find Out**
Hazardous materials	`/hazardous-materials.html`
Human body parts and remains	`/remains.html`
Imported goods	`/importation.html`
Intellectual property	`/intellectual-property-ov.html`
International trading	`/international-trading.html`
Items encouraging illegal activity	`/encouraging-illegal-activity.html`
Lockpicking devices	`/lockpicking.html`
Lottery tickets and game pieces	`/lottery.html`
Mailing lists and personal information	`/maillists.html`
Manufacturers' coupons	`/manufacturers-coupons.html`
Medical devices	`/medical-devices.html`
Military items	`/military-items.html`
Multi-level marketing, pyramid, and matrix programs	`/mlm.html`
Offensive material	`/offensive.html`
Pesticides	`/pesticides.html`
Plants and seeds	`/plantsandseeds.html`
Police-related items	`/police.html`
Political memorabilia (reproduction)	`/politicalmem.html`
Postage meters	`/postage.html`
Prescription drugs	`/medical-devices.html`
Prohibited services *(wink, wink)*	`/prohibited-services.html`
Real estate	`/real-estate.html`
Recalled items	`/recalled.html`
Slot machines	`/slot-machines.html`
Stocks and other securities	`/stocks.html`
Stolen property and property with removed serial numbers	`/stolen.html`
Transit and shipping-related items	`/government-transit-items.html`
Tobacco	`/tobacco.html`

(continued)

Table 4-1 *(continued)*

Can I Sell This?	Go Here to Find Out*
Travel	`/travel.html`
United States embargoed goods from prohibited countries	`/embargo.html`

* All URLs begin with `http://pages.ebay.com/help/policies`

*Alcohol may be allowed if the value of the item lies in the collectible container (bottle) exceeding the alcohol's retail price. The item should not be currently available at a retail outlet. The auction should state that the container has not been opened, and the seller should be sure that the buyer is over 21. eBay does allow licensed and vetted sellers of wine to sell on the site. For more information, visit `http://pages.ebay.com/help/policies/alcohol.html`.

**Skulls, skeletons, and items that may contain human hair are permissible as long as they're used for educational purposes.

***Old or collectible stock certificates may be sold provided that they're cancelled or are from a company that no longer exists.

****All sellers listing airline tickets, cruises, vacation packages, or lodging must be verified by SquareTrade.

When alcohol becomes collectible

Many people collect rare and antique bottles of liquor or wine. In 1998, I even sold a bottle of Korbel champagne designed by Frank Sinatra on eBay. Korbel bottles have featured artwork by designer Nicole Miller and comedienne Whoopi Goldberg, as well as designs by Tony Bennett and Jane Seymour.

People also collect Jim Beam bottles, Dug's decanters, and miniatures that are even more valuable when they're full. You *can* sell these on eBay as long as you fulfill the following requirements:

✔ The value of the item is in the collectible container, not its contents.

✔ The auction description should state that the container has not been opened, but any incidental contents are not intended for consumption.

✔ The item must not be available at any retail outlet, and the container must have a value that substantially exceeds the current retail price of the alcohol in the container.

✔ Sellers should take steps to ensure that the buyer of these collectibles is of lawful age in the buyer's and seller's jurisdictions (generally 21 years old).

AUCTION ANECDOTE

The Chanel-style purse

I once listed a quilted leather women's purse that had a gold chain strap, which I described as a *Chanel-style purse*. Within two hours, I received an Informational alert from the eBay listing police. I described the item to the best of my ability, but found that it became a potentially infringing item. My use of the brand name *Chanel* caused my auction to violate the regulation against keyword spamming (more on that in the section "Potentially infringing items").

In its informational alert, eBay described my violation:

> "Keyword spamming is the practice of adding words, including brand names, which do not directly describe the item you are selling. The addition of these words may not have been intentional, but including them in this manner diverts members to your listing inappropriately."

Ooops! You can see how my ingenious listing was actually a violation of policy. Think twice before you add brand names to your auction description. Thankfully, the eBay police judge each violation on a case-by-case basis. Because my record was clear, I merely got a reprimand. Had my violation been more deliberate, I might have been suspended.

Note: In addition, in your title, you may not use a brand name along with the words *not* or *like*. As in Chanel-*like* purse or *not* Chanel. This is also considered a violation of the keyword spamming policy.

To see the Chanel USA statement on violations, visit its About Me page. The violations apply to many items that may be listed at eBay: `http://members.ebay.com/aboutme/chanelusa/`.

Potentially infringing items

Potentially infringing items follow a slippery slope. If you list a potentially infringing item, you may be infringing on existing copyrights, trademarks, registrations, or the like, which can bring about what we politely call *legal action*. Get the idea? These items are prohibited for your own protection.

Items that fall under the "potentially infringing" category are generally copyrighted or trademarked items such as software, promotional items, and games. Even using a brand name in your auction as part of a description (known as *keyword spamming*) may get you into trouble.

Keyword spamming manipulates the eBay search engine by including an unrelated item in the listing for a copyrighted or trademarked item, and then diverting bidders to an auction of other merchandise. This is frustrating to the person trying to use the search engine to find a particular item and unfair to members who have properly listed their items.

Keyword spamming can take many forms. Some merely mislead the prospective bidder, whereas others are legal infringements. A few of the most common are

- ✔ Superfluous brand names in the title or item description
- ✔ Using something like "not brand X" in the title or item description
- ✔ Improper trademark usage
- ✔ Lists of keywords
- ✔ Hidden text — white text on a white background or hidden text in HTML code. The white text shows up in the search but is not visible to the naked eye. Sneaky, eh?
- ✔ Drop-down boxes

To get the latest on eBay's keyword spamming policy, go to `http://pages.ebay.com/help/policies/search-manipulation.html`.

Repeating various nontrademarked keywords can get you in trouble as well. eBay permits the use of as many as five synonyms when listing an item for sale. A permissible example of this might be *purse*, *handbag*, *pocketbook*, *satchel*, and *bag*. Adding many nontrademarked keywords would cause the auction to come up in more searches.

The eBay Verified Rights Owners program

eBay can't possibly check every auction for authenticity. But to help protect trademarked items, it formed the Verified Rights Owners (VeRO) program. Trademark and copyright owners expend large amounts of energy to develop and maintain control over the quality of their products. If you buy a "designer" purse from a guy on the street for $20, it's probably counterfeit, so don't go selling it on eBay. eBay works with VeRO program members to educate the community about such items. They work also with verified owners of trademarks and copyrights to remove auctions that infringe on their products. If eBay doesn't close a suspicious or blatantly infringing auction, both you and eBay are liable for the violation.

To become a member of the VeRO program, the owners of copyrights and trademarks must supply eBay with proof of ownership. If you are a legitimate owner, and someone on the site has violated your rights, download the Notice of Infringement form at `http://pics.ebaystatic.com/aw/pics/pdf/us/help/community/notice-infringe2.pdf`.

Note: eBay cooperates with law enforcement. Should you be a violator, they may give your name and street address to a VeRO program member.

To view a list of other VeRO members' About Me pages, go to `http://pages.ebay.com/help/community/vero-aboutme.html`.

Trading Violations

Both buyers and sellers can commit trading violations by attempting to manipulate the outcome of an auction or a sale. Many of the violations aren't necessarily buyer- or seller-exclusive, but apply to both. Regardless of the nature of a violation, such bad behavior harms everyone who's part of the eBay community.

As a valued member of the community, it's partially your responsibility to look out for such violations — so that eBay continues to be a safe venue in which to do business. Should you see a violation, report it immediately to the eBay Security Center (see "eBay's Security Center," later in this chapter). In this section, I detail many common violations so you can be on the lookout for them — and I'll just assume that you won't be committing any yourself.

We need to be watchdogs because we need to protect the other users in our community. Don't feel like a squealer if you make a report. Remember that it takes just one rotten apple to spoil the basket, so if you see a violation, do your duty and report it.

When the competition doesn't play fair

Unfortunately, you may sometimes encounter non-community-minded sellers who interfere with your auctions or sales. This interference can take on several forms, such as sellers who illegally drive up bids or "steal" bidders.

Again, should you fall victim to bad deeds, be sure to report the bad-deed-doer's actions immediately. (Check out "Taking Action: What to Do When Someone Breaks the Rules," later in this chapter.) eBay will take some sort of disciplinary action. Penalties range from formal warnings and temporary suspension to indefinite suspension. eBay reviews each incident on a case-by-case basis before passing judgment.

Shill bidding

Shill bidding is the practice of placing a bid on an auction to artificially inflate the final value. It's the bane of every eBay user (whether buyer or seller) and undermines community trust. Shill bidding may be a violation of the Federal wirefraud statute, which encompasses the practice of entering into interstate commerce to defraud — it's a felony and not something to toy with!

The practice of shill bidding has been a part of auctions from their beginnings. To prevent the suspicion of shill bidding, people in the same family, those who share the same computer, and folks who work or live together should not bid on each other's items.

Should you ever even dream of participating in any sort of auction manipulation, I urge you to think twice. You might think using another e-mail address and username is smart (in a shifty way), but that doesn't work. Every time you log on to your ISP, your connection carries an IP address. So no matter what name or computer you use, your connection will identify you. eBay can use this number to track you through its site.

Shill bidders are fairly easy to recognize, even for the eBay user who isn't privy to things such as IP addresses. By checking a bidder's auction history, you can easily determine a user's bidding pattern. A bidder who constantly bids up items and never wins is suspicious.

Spurious sellers may employ shill bidding to increase the number of bids on an item to make it seem like a "hot" (desirable) item in a hurry. This doesn't mean that all hot auctions are products of shill bidding; it just means that hot auctions are desirable and pull in lots of extra bids (most likely due to the herd mentality). Rogues would like all their auctions to be hot — and may take any road to get there.

Transaction interference

Have you ever received an e-mail from an eBay seller offering you an item that you're currently bidding on for a lower price? This is called *transaction interference,* and it can prevent sellers from gaining the highest bid possible.

Transaction interference occurs also when a troublemaker who "has it in" for a particular seller e-mails bidders participating in the seller's current auctions to warn them away from completing the auction. Tales of woe (and much bitterness) usually accompany such e-mails. If a bidder has a problem with a seller, that bidder can — and should — file a report with eBay and leave negative feedback for that seller. A barrage of negative e-mail is not only a lousy alternative to feedback, but also potentially libelous. Bottom line: It isn't a legally safe thing to practice. If you receive an e-mail like this, ignore its message, but report it to eBay.

Transaction interception

They say the criminal mind is complex; when it comes to transaction interception, it certainly is! *Transaction interception* occurs when an eBay scalawag keeps track of closing auctions and then, when the auction is finished, e-mails the winner as if the scalawag were the seller. The e-mail often looks official and is congratulatory, politely asking for payment. Interceptors typically use a post office box for such mischief. This behavior goes beyond being a trading violation — it's actually stealing.

The best way to protect yourself from such miscreants is to accept payments through a payment service, such as PayPal, by using a Pay Now link. For more about setting up a payment service account, see Chapter 13.

Fee circumvention or avoidance

Basically, *fee circumvention* is the practice of evading paying eBay fees by going around the eBay system. An eBay member can commit fee avoidance in many ways — sometimes without even realizing it. Read this section carefully so you don't fall into this violation by mistake.

You're guilty of fee avoidance if you

- ✔ Use an eBay member's contact information in an attempt to sell, off the eBay site, a listed item.

- ✔ Use an eBay member's contact information to sell, off the eBay site, an item from a closed auction in which the reserve price wasn't met.

- ✔ Close your auction early so you can sell the item to someone who has e-mailed you with an offer to buy the item.

- ✔ Cancel bids to end your auction before it legally closes so you can sell the item to someone who has e-mailed you with an offer of a higher price.

- ✔ Offer duplicates of your item to the unsuccessful bidders in your auction, unless you use the Second Chance option.

Take a look at the discussion on listing policies in Chapter 2 for listing violations that also might fall into this category.

Excessive shipping charges

Although the excessive shipping charges violation falls somewhat in the Fee Avoidance category, it has a rule all to itself. You, as a seller, are required to charge reasonable shipping and handling fees. You may not charge a shipping fee that's disproportionate to the item you're selling. Charging $15 to ship a cell-phone accessory is a good example of unwarranted charges. A cell-phone accessory can most likely be shipped via First Class mail — or at the very most at the one-pound rate.

I know — you're saying that you see sellers violating this rule, but it's a firm policy. Should you want to report another seller's shameless shipping charges, just click the *Report Item* link below the Other Item Info box (below the Seller Info) on every listing page. If sellers are flagrant about breaking this rule, and enough complaints show up in their records, they can be suspended from eBay.

Nonselling seller

Refusing to accept payment from the winning bidder and refusing to complete the transaction is simply wrong. Very, very bad form! You are legally and morally bound to complete any transaction in which you enter.

Bad bidders

Nothing can ruin a seller's day like a difficult bidder, such as someone who asks questions that are clearly answered already in your auction description or someone who asks you to close the auction so that he or she can buy the item offline. Sheesh — you'd think no one read the rules. From the nonpaying bidder to the unwelcome and the shady, you might encounter the buyers (and the gambits) I describe here.

Bid shielding

When two or more eBay members work together to defraud you out of real auction profits, they're guilty of *bid shielding*. Here's how the scam goes down: One member, let's call him Joe, places an early bid on your item, with a *proxy bid* (an automatic bid that increases your bid to outbid any competition, up to the highest amount you specify). Immediately, the accomplice (we'll call her Ann) places a very high proxy bid to drive the bid to the max or beyond. Then, if legitimate bidders bid, they only ratchet up the second bidder's bid — they don't outbid the high bidder's proxy. When the auction is coming to its 12-hour bid freeze, the high bidder (Ann) retracts her bid, thereby granting the winning bid to her buddy (Joe), the original low bidder. The ultimate point of outlawing bid shielding is that it increases the bid to such a high level that normal bidding by authentic bidders is discouraged and they stop watching the listing.

This illegal bidding process is used not only to get bargain-priced merchandise but also to drive bidders away from competitors' auctions by artificially inflating the high bid level.

Unwelcome bidder

In this business, you might think that you couldn't possibly regard anyone as an *unwelcome bidder,* but you just might. Remember how you painstakingly explain your terms in your auction description? That's lost on people who don't take the time to read those descriptions or choose to ignore them. Consider the following points:

- ✔ You state in your description that you ship only within the United States, but you see a bidder with an e-mail address that ends in .jp (Japan), .au (Australia), .uk (United Kingdom), or wherever.

- ✔ A prospective buyer has three Unpaid Item strikes on his or her account in the past 30 days — and decides to bid on (or buy) your item. You probably won't get paid, but you still have the hassle of cleaning up and trying to get fee refunds.

✔ You don't want bidders who have a negative feedback, but someone fitting that description bids on your auction.

✔ You decide to cancel a bid for one of the previous two reasons, but the bidder continues to bid on your auction.

✔ You've blocked a particular bidder who's now using a secondary account to bid on your auctions.

To solve these issues before they occur, you can set your Selling Preferences to prevent bad bidding from ruining your sales. Visit Chapter 3 for instructions on how to block people who could ruin your sales.

Nonpaying buyers

If there's one thing that just ain't tolerated at eBay, it's _unpaid items._ eBay reminds all potential buyers — before they place a bid — that "If you are the winning buyer, you will enter into a legally binding contract to purchase the item from the seller." You'd think that was clear enough, but sadly, many people out there think bidding and buying on eBay is a game. If you see a high bidder on your auction who has very low or negative feedback rating, dropping a line reiterating eBay policy never hurts.

How you, as a seller, communicate with the high bidder is also important. Many times, a well-written, congenial, businesslike e-mail can cajole a basically good person into sending payment. To see some samples that get the job done, drop by Chapter 12.

I've been selling and buying on eBay for more than 11 years. During that time, I've had to file only 20 nonpaying-buyer alerts (see the steps a bit later in this section). I think that nonpaying buyers tend to bid on certain types of items. After you've seen some unpaid items, you'll get an idea of which items to stay away from. My items? A gas-powered scooter, a video game, and some high-priced cosmetics. Serious collector or business items have never been an issue.

To reduce the number of nonpaying buyers, eBay has established that any eBay user who has three nonpaying buyer alerts filed against him or her is suspended indefinitely. An _indefinite suspension_ is a suspension of members' privileges to use the eBay site — it lasts for more than 60 days, with no definite reinstatement date. If users attempt to re-register at eBay and use the system under new IDs, they risk being referred to the United States Attorney General's Office for the Northern District of California for criminal prosecution.

Know that eBay has your back and will send e-mails to buyers who have not paid through PayPal or through eBay's Selling Manager or Selling Manager Pro.

Before filing an unpaid-item dispute, however, give the auction winner a second chance to send payment. If you still don't receive payment, follow these steps to recoup your Final Value fees and be eligible for the Nonpaying Buyer relist credit:

1. **As soon as you have a winner, contact him or her.**

2. **If you don't hear from the winner within three days of the auction's end time, send a payment reminder:**

    a. *Go to the My eBay Views area on the My eBay page. Under Selling, click the Sold link.*

    b. *Click the View Payment Status link next to the pertinent auction.*

    c. *Click the More Actions drop-down menu (see Figure 4-2) and click Contact Buyer to send an e-mail.*

    You may send a reminder between 3 and 30 days after the auction closes.

If you still don't hear from or receive money from your high bidder, it's time to swing into action by filing an alert.

Figure 4-2:
Contacting
a buyer from
your My
eBay Sold
listings.

You must file the alert no earlier than seven days and no later than forty-five days after the auction has ended.

Follow these steps to file an unpaid-item dispute:

1. **In the Sold Views area of the My eBay page, click the Cases⇔ Resolution Center link.**

    Alternately, go to the following address: `http://res.ebay.com/ws/ eBayISAPI.dll?ResolutionCenter`.

2. **Check the Dispute Console to select the transaction that is eligible for filing.**

   eBay sends the buyer an e-mail, and the buyer has the right to respond in the dispute-management process.

Eight days after filing an unpaid-item dispute, you may close the dispute and apply for a Final Value fee credit in the Dispute Console. At this point, eBay offers several options. To close the dispute, you must select one of the following:

- ✔ **We've completed the transaction and we're both satisfied.** You received your payment and you're ready to ship! The buyer will not receive an undeserved Unpaid Item strike.

- ✔ **We've agreed not to complete the transaction.** If you feel sorry for the buyer or believe their tale of woe as to how they cannot possibly buy your item, you can select this option. The buyer won't get a strike on his or her permanent record, and you will receive a Final Value fee credit. (The item is eligible for the standard relist credit.)

- ✔ **I no longer wish to communicate with or wait for the buyer.** You've had it — either no response or no payment. The buyer receives their well-deserved Unpaid Item strike and you get your Final Value fee credit. (This item is eligible for a relist credit.)

You must file for your Final Value fee credit within 60 days of the transaction's close.

Don't forget! When you file for your Final Value fee credit, you also have the option of blocking that buyer from participating in your sales.

If you are the buyer and want to appeal an Unpaid Buyer strike, go to the appeals page at `http://pages.ebay.com/help/buy/appeal unpaid item.html` and click the link to the *Online Unpaid Item Appeal* form. To appeal, a buyer must provide the kinds of proof specified in Table 4-2.

Table 4-2   Acceptable Proof for Nonpaying Buyer Appeal

Proof	*Documentation*
Payment confirmation from PayPal or other payment service	Text of the confirmation e-mail sent from the payment provider
E-mail from the seller indicating payment	Copy of e-mail
Copy of check, money order, or receipt (to be faxed)*	Copies of the front and back of the payment document, which include your eBay ID and item number

* Fax the appeal and documentation to 1-888-379-6251.

Not knowing who's who

eBay members have user IDs so their e-mail addresses remain confidential, not exposed for all (including spammers) to see, in the course of normal business. However, you must supply eBay with your contact information. When you register with eBay, its software immediately checks your primary phone number area code against your ZIP code to verify that the two numbers are from the same city. If you've supplied incompatible codes, the eBay servers will recognize that and ask you to reinput the correct codes.

An eBay member who's involved in a transaction with you can get your phone number by clicking *Advanced* next to the eBay search box and then clicking the Find Contact Information link under the Members area on the left side of the page.

When you arrive at the page, you can then request contact information, as shown in Figure 4-3.

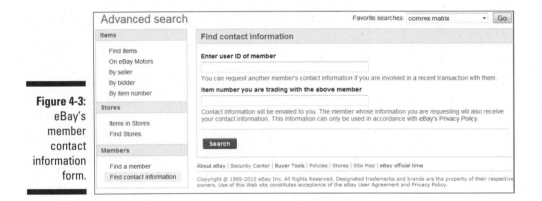

Figure 4-3:
eBay's
member
contact
information
form.

To be on the up-and-up at eBay (and to keep others honest, too), make sure that you

- ✔ **Have your current phone number on file at eBay:** If a buyer can't reach you, you're in violation and you *can* be disciplined.

- ✔ **Have your current e-mail address on file:** If your buyer continually gets e-mail bounced back from your e-mail address, you could get in big trouble.

✔ **Report all underage buyers:** If you suspect that a buyer in one of your transactions is underage (eBay requires that all users be over 18), eBay may close the account. Underage buyers may be using their parents' credit card without permission — or perhaps even a stolen card — for registration.

✔ **Confirm any e-mails purportedly coming from eBay:** Just go to your eBay Messages and check the *From eBay* folder to identify whether an e-mail is really from eBay.

✔ **Verify e-mail purportedly coming from an eBay employee:** If someone e-mails you claiming to work for eBay, be sure to check it out before replying. When eBay employees conduct personal business on the site, company policy requires that they use a personal noncompany e-mail address for their user registration. If you suspect someone is impersonating an eBay employee for harmful purposes, contact the eBay Security Center.

Don't be lured by phishing

Fraudulent e-mail has become a common occurrence. Without warning, a request for confirmation of your personal details arrives — *allegedly* from your bank, Internet service provider, credit card company, PayPal, or even eBay. These e-mails are *phishing* for your personal information and passwords to defraud you of your money or your identity.

These e-mails look just like a legitimate e-mail from the company that holds your data. If you follow the links in the e-mail to "update" your information, you'll be brought to a Web page that duplicates the look of a legitimate Web page. How can you protect yourself from these scammers?

✔ **Never go to the Web site in question from the link in the e-mail.** Open up a new browser and type the URL that you normally use to enter the site. After you log on, you'll know whether there's a problem with any of your information.

✔ **Always look for secure Web site information.** If you're logged on to a secure Web site, the URL will begin with `https://` rather than the standard `http://`. You'll also see a lock symbol in the status bar at the bottom of your browser window.

✔ **Regularly log on to your Internet accounts.** By keeping in regular contact with your providers, you'll know about issues with your accounts before they have a chance to cause a problem.

✔ **Report the e-mail.** If you receive an e-mail supposedly from PayPal, forward the e-mail to `spoof@paypal.com`. Forward an e-mail purportedly from eBay to `spoof@ebay.com`.

Taking Action: What to Do When Someone Breaks the Rules

You need to take a business-like approach to problems at eBay, whatever those problems may be. In previous sections of this chapter, I outline eBay's many rules, as well as the bad deeds and bad seeds you're likely to encounter while doing business on eBay.

As a member of the eBay community, you have the responsibility to know and abide by eBay's rules and regulations. This responsibility includes notifying eBay when someone tries to sell an illegal item (see "Is What You Want to Sell Legal?" earlier in this chapter), an integral part of keeping eBay a safe and lucrative place to do business. In this section, I discuss who to call when someone breaks the rules and what to do when a third party is necessary.

Here are the basic steps you can follow:

- **Contact the buyer:** If you're involved in a transaction, get the buyer's contact information by using the instructions outlined earlier in this chapter. Then call the buyer to see whether you can resolve the situation diplomatically.

- **Seek out eBay security:** Use the Security Center to report any shady actions, policy violations, or possible fraud, such as a community member impersonating an employee or a suspicious auction. Likened to the front desk at your local police station, eBay's Security Center report form gets results. On an item's page, scroll to the bottom and click the Report item link. On most other eBay pages, click the Security Center link, which usually appears at the bottom. Then find the Contact Us⇨Customer Support link at the bottom of the left side Choose a topic area. Alternatively, you can go directly to `http://contact.ebay.com/ws/eBayISAPI.dll?ContactUsNextGen`.

  You'll find an all-purpose security form on this page to help you in your eBay transactions. These forms will be routed to the right department for action.

- **Contact the National Fraud Information Center (NFIC):** If you feel you've become a victim of fraud, be sure to file a report through eBay channels. To really bring down wrath on your nemesis, report the malefactor to the NFIC by calling 1-800-876-7060.

- **Contact local law enforcement:** If you become the target of a check-bouncer, contact local law enforcement in your bidder's hometown.

eBay will supply any information necessary to help law enforcement clear the world of fraud. Provide eBay with the name of the local law enforcement officer, agency, telephone number, and case number or police report number. Also include the offending user's ID and the auction item's number. For a state-by-state list of the possible criminal penalties, visit `www.ckfraud.org/penalties.html#criminal`.

eBay's Security Center

The Security Center is the eBay version of the FBI. By rooting out evildoers, it serves and protects — and puts up with an immense amount of e-mail from users.

If you see an item on eBay that isn't allowed (see "Is What You Want to Sell Legal?"), be sure to make eBay aware of the auction. The Community Watch team will then take over and investigate the item — and, when necessary, end the auction and warn the seller.

When you click the Security Center link — at the bottom of most eBay pages — you see the page shown in Figure 4-4. Click the Report Problem button to get action. You then fill out a step-by-step customer service report. Alternatively, you can get to the Security Center customer service reporting form at `http://contact.ebay.com/ws/eBayISAPI.dll?ContactUsNextGen`.

Figure 4-4: The eBay Security Center.

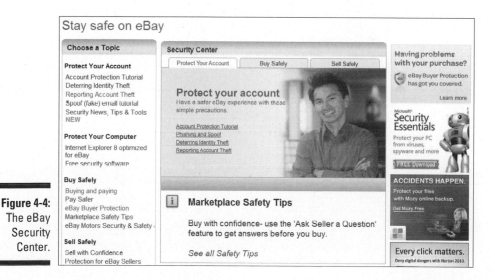

Chapter 5

Expanding Sales with an eBay Store

- -

In This Chapter

▶ Understanding the lure of the online store

▶ Choosing a name

▶ Setting up your eBay Store

▶ Managing your eBay Store

▶ Selling your stuff

▶ Closing your sales

- -

If you're doing well selling your items on eBay auctions, why open a store? Well, have you used the eBay Buy It Now feature in one of your listings? Did it work? In an eBay Store, all items are set at a fixed price and are online until cancelled (or listed at least 30 days), so it's kind of like a giant collection of Buy It Now featured items. Get the idea?

When you open a store, you have just three main rules to remember and apply: location, location, location. If you were going to open a brick-and-mortar store, you could open it in the corner strip mall, a shopping center, or even somewhere downtown. You'd have to decide in what location your store would do best; that goes for an online store as well. You'll find tons of locations where you can open an online store, including online malls (when you can find them) and sites such as Amazon.com, Yahoo!, and, of course, eBay.

You have to pay rent for your online store, but opening and running an online store isn't nearly as expensive as a store in the real world (where you also have to pay electrical bills, maintenance bills, and more). Plus, the ratio of rent to sales makes an online store a much easier financial decision, and your exposure can be huge.

In this chapter, I show you, step by step, how to hang out your virtual shingle and get business booming by opening your own eBay Store.

Online Stores Galore

Amazon.com, Yahoo!, and eBay make up the big three of the online stores. They are the top locations and get the most visitors. These sites garnered an astounding number of *unique* visitors (that counts *all* of one person's visits to the sites just *once* a month) within any given day.

No doubt feeling competition from Yahoo! and Amazon.com, eBay decided to open its doors (in July 2001) to sellers who wanted to open their own stores. Fixed-price stores were a normal progression for eBay in its quest to continue as the world's marketplace. And eBay Stores make sense: It's an approach that benefits all current eBay sellers and opens doors to new shoppers who don't want to deal with auctions.

eBay is an online marketplace that specializes in giving you a place to sell *your* stuff, not *theirs*. It doesn't stock a stick of merchandise, and it isn't in competition with you. In addition to its staggering number of visitors, eBay offers you the most reasonable store rent. You may be able to get an introductory rate for the first few months on any of these services, but the ongoing rates are static. To see what I mean, check out the costs in Tables 5-1 and 5-2.

Table 5-1	Online Starter Store Monthly Costs		
	eBay Basic Store	*Yahoo! Small Business (Starter)**	*Amazon Pro Merchant*
Basic rent	$15.95	$39.95	$39.99
Setup fee	0	$50.00	0
Fixed-price listing fee	$0.20	0	0
Final Value (transaction) fee	See Table 5-2	1.5%	8% to 20%

*Yahoo stores integrate with PayPal.

Table 5-2	eBay Stores Final Transaction Fees			
Final Sale Price	*Electronics**	*Clothing, Shoes and Accessories, Motors, Parts & Accessories*	*Books, DVDs & Movies, Music, Video Games*	*All Other Categories*
Item not sold	No fee	No fee	No fee	No fee
$0.99 to $50.00	8% of the final sale price	12% of the final sale price	15% of the final sale price	12% of the final sale price
$50.01 to $1,000.00	8% of the initial $50.00, plus 5% of the remaining final sale price balance ($50.01 to $1,000.00)	12% of the initial $50.00, plus 9% of the remaining final sale price balance ($50.01 to $1,000.00)	15% of the initial $50.00, plus 5% of the remaining final sale price balance ($50.01 to $1,000.00)	12% of the initial $50.00, plus 6% of the remaining final sale price balance ($50.01 to $1,000.00)
$1,000.01 or more	8% of the initial $50.00, plus 5% of the next $50.01 to $1,000.00, plus 2% of the remaining final sale price balance ($1,000.01 to final sale price)	12% of the initial $50.00, plus 9% of the next $50.01 to $1,000.00, plus 2% of the remaining final sale price balance ($1,000.01 to final sale price)	15% of the initial $50.00, plus 5% of the next $50.01 to $1,000.00, plus 2% of the remaining final sale price balance ($1,000.01 to final sale price)	12% of the initial $50.00, plus 6% of the next $50.01 to $1,000.00, plus 2% of the remaining final sale price balance ($1,000.01 to final sale price)

*This category also includes Pro Audio Equipment, Computers & Networking, Car Electronics, Cameras & Photo, and Video Game Systems.

Even the basic ($15.95) eBay Store gives you a lot of options; here are my favorite highlights:

- ✔ **Selling Manager:** This is the super eBay software that replaces your All Selling page in My eBay. If you have a Premium-level eBay Store, you get Selling Manager Pro for free; the $15.99 a month fee is waived. I use it and love it. Basic stores get basic Selling Manager as part of their package.

- ✔ **Free Picture Pack:** Up to 12 photos and Zoom feature per listing at no extra charge.

- ✔ **Discounted Fixed-Price insertion fee**: Only $.20 per listing (Premium Store only $.05 per listing).

- ✔ **Fifteen custom pages:** You can use custom pages to customize the look of your store, make different landing pages, list store policies, and make the store your own. (I use only a few custom pages and it suits me fine!)

- ✔ **Web address:** Your store has its very own Internet address (URL). This way you can drive buyers directly to your store. Mine is www.stores.ebay.com/Marsha-Colliers-Fabulous-Finds.

- ✔ **Promotion boxes:** By using the promotion boxes, you can highlight featured merchandise at the top of your store pages.

- ✔ **Three hundred store categories:** You can sell (say) sporting goods in one category, women's fashion in another, fine art in one more. . . . You have up to 300 custom categories for your varied merchandise.

- ✔ **Custom store header:** Get your own brand by designing a graphic store header.

- ✔ **Markdown Manager:** Hold a sale in your store! Select items to discount for a period of time and offer discounted pricing! You can run sales on up to 250 listings a day.

- ✔ **Vacation hold:** Ever wish you could make your listings temporarily unavailable or let your customers know you'll be out of town? This great feature allows you to do just that.

- ✔ **Off-eBay E-mail marketing:** Basic eBay Store owners can send up to 5,000 e-mail newsletters per month to those who have selected you as a favorite seller (7,500 per month for a Premium Store). You can find customized e-newsletters and promotional e-mail layouts in your store's marketing area.

- ✔ **Listing feeds:** eBay distributes your listings automatically to buyers, search engines, and comparison-shopping sites via online feeds.

- ✔ **Downloadable promotional flyers:** If you've ever wanted collateral to go with your eBay Store and have wondered about the legalities of using the eBay logo, you're not alone. eBay offers predesigned (perfectly legal to use) downloadable templates for store owners to use. Just print them on your color printer and you're set!

✔ **Search engine keyword management:** You may customize search engine keywords in Manage My Store to improve your store's page rankings in the search engines to which eBay feeds.

✔ **Traffic reports:** Use the eBay Store traffic report to improve your merchandising and listing strategies.

If you want to upgrade to a higher-level store, Table 5-3 shows you your monthly rent.

Table 5-3	eBay Store Monthly Fees		
	Basic Store	*Premium*	*Anchor Store*
Basic rent	$15.95	$49.95	$299.95
Listing fee	$0.20	$0.05	$0.03

I don't think it's going to take a rocket scientist to convince you that having a space in eBay Stores (see Figure 5-1) is better than setting up shop anywhere else. No one I know of gives you more features and improves your chances to grow a business.

To review current prices and rules before opening your store, go to `pages.ebay.com/storefronts/subscriptions.html`.

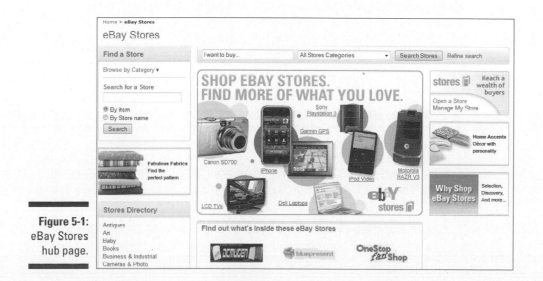

Figure 5-1: eBay Stores hub page.

Mind your underscores and hyphens

If you want to use your eBay user ID for your store name, you can — unless it contains a hyphen (-) or an underscore (_). Remember how eBay recommends that you break up words in your user ID with a dash or an underscore? Uh oh, that's no good for an eBay Store name. I'm in that situation. My user ID is marsha_c; without the underscore, it translates into a user ID that someone else has already taken! Even though it hasn't been used since 1999, someone else has it, which means I can't use it. (marsha_c is probably a crummy name for a store anyway!)

A favorite seller of mine realized that her eBay ID wasn't a good name for a store, either. So she named her store Pretty Girlie Things, which suits her merchandise to a T.

Your eBay Store Name

You've decided to take the plunge and open an eBay Store. Do you have an eBay user ID? Have you thought of a good name for your store? Your store name doesn't have to match your eBay user ID, but both names are more recognizable if they relate to each other. You can use your company name, your business name, or a name that describes your business. I recommend that you use the same name for your eBay Store that you plan to use in all your online businesses. By doing so, you'll begin to create an identity (or as the pros call it, a *brand*) that customers will come to recognize and trust.

Your online eBay Store should not replace your e-commerce–enabled Web site (see Chapter 8) but, rather be an extension of it. When people shop at your eBay Store, you must take the opportunity to make them customers of your Web site through your store's About the Seller page (which is also your About Me page on eBay). Good deal!

Setting Up Shop

It's time to get down to business. Go to the eBay Stores hub from the Sell link on eBay's navigation bar. This takes you to the seller's hub of eBay Stores, as shown in Figure 5-2. If you click all the links you see here, you get the company line about how good an eBay Store can be for your business. Okay, you already *know* how good an eBay Store can be for your business, so skip the propaganda and get right down to business (but don't forget to check for any policy changes that may affect your store's operations).

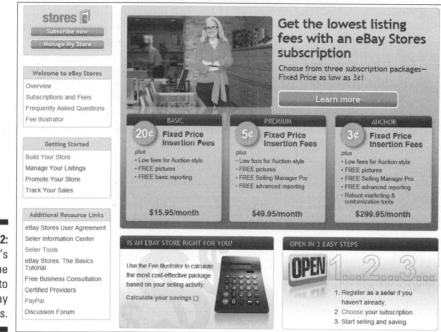

Figure 5-2:
The seller's welcome page to eBay Stores.

Before you click that link to open your store, ask yourself two questions:

- ✔ **Can I make a serious commitment to my eBay Store?** A store *is* a commitment. It won't work for you unless you work for it. You have to have the merchandise to fill it and the discipline to continue listing store and auction items. Your store is a daily, monthly, and yearly obligation. You can close your store temporarily, but eBay will reserve your store name for only 30 days. After that, you have to come up with a new name (and your competition may have taken over your old store name, especially if it's famous).

- ✔ **Will I work for my eBay Store even when I don't feel like it?** You have to be prepared for the times when you're sick or just don't feel like shipping, but orders are waiting to go out. You have to do the work anyway; it's all part of the commitment.

eBay gives you the venue, but it's in your own hands to make your mercantile efforts a success. If you can handle these two responsibilities, read on!

If you're serious and ready to move on, click the Subscribe now link in the upper-left corner of the page (refer to Figure 5-2). You're escorted to a page where you find a reminder that eBay Stores fall under the same User Agreement that you agreed to when you began selling on eBay. Click the Continue button to access the Build Your Store pages similar to the image in Figure 5-3. Because I have an eBay Store, eBay allows me to make changes and redesign my store at any time.

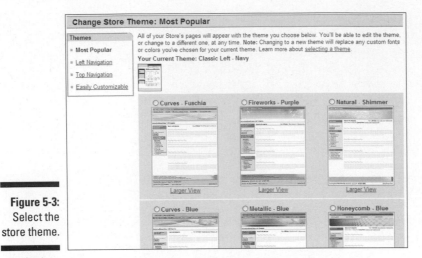

Figure 5-3:
Select the
store theme.

You need to make a few decisions to create a good store. So before building your eBay Store, read the following sections.

Depending on the whims and changes that move through eBay, the order in which you have to make these decisions change, but these are choices that you must make:

1. Choose a color theme.

eBay provides some elegant color and graphics themes (refer to Figure 5-3). You can change the color scheme or layout later, so until you have time to go hog wild and design a custom masterpiece, choose one of the 14 clearly organized layouts, either predesigned or with easily customizable themes. Don't select something overly bright and vibrant; you want something that's easy on the eyes, which is more conducive to a comfortable selling environment.

You have the option of selecting a store theme that doesn't require you to insert a custom logo or banner. I strongly recommend against skipping the logo or banner. You need to establish a unifying brand for your online business.

2. Click Continue.

3. Type your new store's name.

You've decided on a store name, right? Your eBay Store's name can't exceed 35 characters. Before you type it, double-check that you aren't infringing on anyone's copyrights or trademarks.

You also can't use any permutation of eBay trademarks in your store's name.

4. **Type a short description of your store.**

   When I say short, I mean _short._ The paragraph you're reading is 249 characters, and you have only _300_ characters to give a whiz-bang, electric description of your store and merchandise. You can't use HTML coding to doll up the description, and you can't use links. Just the facts please, and a little bit of dazzle.

   The importance of this description is huge. When people search eBay Stores and descriptions, the keyword information you put here is referenced. Also, if the store header contains your description (as in the Classic style themes), search engines such as Google and Yahoo! will look in this description for the keywords to classify and list your store.

   Write your copy ahead of time in Word. Then, still in Word, highlight the text and choose Tools➪Word Count. Word gives you the word count of the highlighted text. Check the character count with spaces, to be sure your text fits.

5. **Select a graphic to jazz up the look of your store.**

   You can use one of eBay's clip art–style banners or create a custom 310-x-90-pixel one of your own. If you use one of eBay's graphics, you must promise (hand over heart) that you won't keep it there for long. (See the text after this set of steps for info on designing your own graphics — or hiring someone to do it.)

6. **Click Continue.**

   Now you should have an idea of what your store will look like. You are about to open an eBay Store, complete with storefront (drum roll, please).

7. **Sign up for the basic store ($15.95 a month) and click the Start My Subscription Now button.**

   Your store is now live on the Internet with nothing up for sale — yet.

8. **Click the supplied link to get in the trenches and customize your store further.**

If you're wondering in which category your store will be listed on the eBay Stores home page, it's all up to you. eBay checks the items as you list them in the standard eBay category format. For example, if you have six books listed in the Books: Fiction and Nonfiction category and five items in the Cameras & Photo category, you'll be in the listings for both of those categories. Your custom store categories (read on) will be used to classify items as they appear in your store.

If you use one of eBay's prefab graphics and just leave it up, people shopping your eBay Store will know that you aren't serious enough about your business to design a simple and basic logo. I've had many years of experience in advertising and marketing, and I must tell you that a custom look will beat out clip art any day. Your store is special — put forth the effort to make it shine.

If you have a graphics program, design a graphic with your store's name. Start with something simple; you can always change it later when you have more time. Save the image as a GIF or a JPG, and upload it to eBay as you would any other image.

A bunch of talented graphic artists make their living selling custom Web graphics on eBay. If you aren't comfortable designing, search eBay for *ebay store banner* or *ebay store design*. Graphic banners on eBay sell for about $5 to $150 — certainly worth the price in the time you'll save.

Don't waste time and money designing a whiz-bang home page for your store. Very few buyers enter your store to begin with; they come once they've viewed or purchased one of your items. At that point, they are already sold on you.

Running Your Store

As part of your store subscription, your My eBay selling area is replaced with eBay's Selling Manager. Selling Manager gives you easy access to customize your store at any time by going to the Manage My Store box (shown in Figure 5-4), on the lower right of your Selling Manager summary page.

Store design

In the Store Design area (see the screen shot of mine in Figure 5-5), you can perform major tasks required for your store.

Figure 5-4:
Here's where you can perform all the necessary tasks for running your store.

Manage My Store	Edit ▼
Manage My Store	
Email Marketing	539 subscribers
Markdown Manager	
Vacation Settings	Off
Display Settings	
Store Marketing	
Traffic Reports	
Store Recommendations	
Quick Store Tuneup	
Feature List	
View My Store:Marsha Collier's Fabulous Finds	

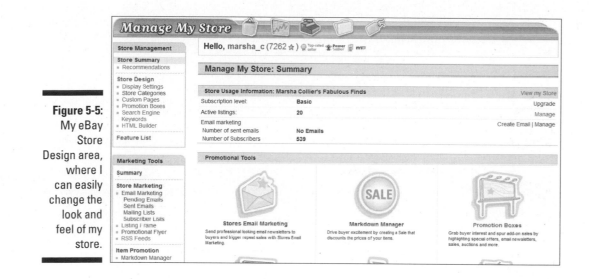

Figure 5-5:
My eBay
Store
Design area,
where I
can easily
change the
look and
feel of my
store.

Here are a just few of the tasks you should consider revisiting:

✔ **Store design:** You can always go back here to change the name of your store or the theme of your pages. You can also change the way your items are displayed: gallery view (as shown in Figure 5-6) or list view. Neither view is inherently better, but I like the gallery view because it shows the thumbnail gallery pictures of my items.

You should also select the order in which your items will sort. Highest Priced First, Lowest Priced First, Items Ending First, or Newly Listed First. I like Items Ending First as my sort, so buyers can get the chance to swoop in on items closing soon.

✔ **Custom pages:** Most successful eBay sellers have (at the very least) a Store Policies page. Figure 5-7 shows you the one for my store. When you set up a policies page, eBay supplies you with a choice of layouts. Just click the Create New Page link to select the template that you want to use. Don't freak out if you don't know HTML, eBay helps you out with an easy-to-use HTML generator, as in the Sell Your Item form.

Following are some important policies to include:

• **Indicate to what locations you'll ship.**

• **Specify the sales tax you plan to collect:** If your state doesn't require you to collect sales tax, leave the area blank. If it does, select your state and indicate the proper sales tax. Most states won't require you to collect sales tax unless the sale is shipped to your home state. Check the links in Chapter 15 to verify your state's sales tax regulations.

- **State your customer service and return policy:** Fill in the information regarding how you handle refunds, exchanges, and so on. Be sure to include whatever additional store information you think is pertinent.

  You can also set up a custom home page for your store, but it's not a popular option. Most sellers feel it's best to let your visitors go right to the listings of what you're selling.

✔ **Custom categories:** Here's where you really make your store your own. You may name up to 300 custom categories that relate to the varied items you sell in your store.

✔ **Promotion boxes:** Set up some promotion boxes and change them every month or so to keep your store's look fresh. Select items for promotion that work well with the particular selling season. You have the option of inserting a filmstrip of your items, as I do on my store home page. When your prospective buyer mouses over one of the photos, it expands. (Take a look at Figure 5-8.)

✔ **Search engine keywords:** Check out this area to see the keywords that eBay forwards to the major Web shopping and search feeds. If you think there are better keywords, be sure to add them.

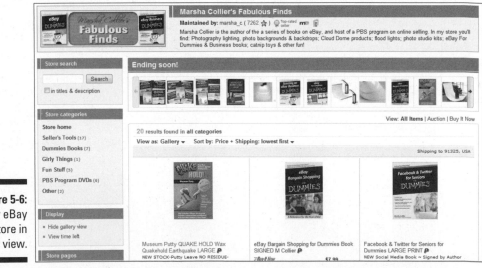

Figure 5-6:
My eBay
Store in
gallery view.

Terms and Conditions Payment and shipment terms may vary on individual items.	Payment methods	**Pay Pal** Money Order/Cashiers Check All credit Card payments are graciously accepted through PayPal only.
	Store ship-to locations	Depending on the item, I will gladly ship Internationally. Because of DVD regions and electrical differences, some of my items may not be appropriate in some countries. United States shipments are sent via Priority Mail unless requested ahead of time. THANK YOU!
	Shipping & Handling	Buyer Pays Shipping and handling.
	Sales tax	8.25% if shipped to CA Resale numbers accepted please email after auction.
	Customer service & return policy	All items are guaranteed to be exactly as stated in the auction description. Any defective merchandise will be cheerfully replaced.
Additional Store Information		I research and personally test out many items to find the most useful and economical items to help eBay sellers. The items that make the grade are the ones I sell in my store!

Figure 5-7:
My eBay Store policies page.

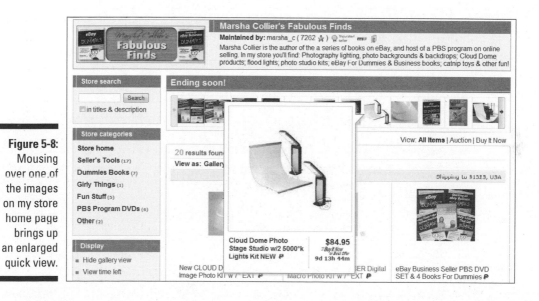

Figure 5-8:
Mousing over one of the images on my store home page brings up an enlarged quick view.

Marketing tools

Under the Marketing tools heading, you can perform many tasks that help bring customers to your store. You have the option of clicking a Summary page, which gives you a quick look at how your store's marketing features are currently set. You have a lot of options in this area. Here are a few of the many offered:

- ✔ **Email marketing:** When you want to design an e-mail campaign to your buyers, you have all the tools here. Create an e-mail newsletter, create one for sending later, manage your subscriber lists — all from one convenient area.

- ✔ **Listing frame:** Select this option once you get an eBay Store. Don't ask questions; just do it. The custom listing header display is one of the best tools you can use to bring people into your store. Since I don't believe in cluttering up my listing pages with a lot of graphics, I use the option to have a store invitation message appear above my description when someone visits to get a look at one of my items. Click the link and select the option to Show Your Custom Listing Header on all your eBay auctions and fixed-price sales. This will encourage shoppers to visit your eBay Store when they browse your eBay listings. When customizing, you can include your store logo as well as a store search box.

Item promotions

eBay has added some excellent ways to promote your store. As an eBay Store owner, you have access to promotional tools that other sellers can't use. One of the most valuable of these is cross-promotions — there's no charge to use it either!

- ✔ **Cross-promotions:** The cross-promotion box appears after a buyer places a bid on or purchases an item from an eBay seller. The beauty of having an eBay Store is that the cross-promotion box appears *twice:* once with your regular listings and again with a different assortment of items (if you want) after someone buys an item. Best of all? You get to select which categories' items are selected from to display with your individual auctions. Figure 5-9 shows a cross-promotion box that appears when someone views one of my auctions.

  You can set up the promotions so that they default to show other items from related store categories. Again, every listing has two sets of options: one for when a user views your listings, and the other for when someone bids or wins your item.

- ✔ **Markdown Manager:** So you say you have to raise some cash to buy new merchandise? Why not run a sale? By clicking here, you can select items to put on sale. After they've been marked down, they'll appear branded as "On Sale."

Create an About the Seller page

If you haven't already created an eBay About Me page, do it now! The About Me page becomes the About the Seller page in your store. This page is a primary tool for promoting sales. (See Chapter 3 regarding About Me pages.) You can put this page together in about ten minutes — max — with eBay's handy and easy-to-use templates!

Logos and branding

As a store owner, you can customize just about everything that you do on eBay. In Logos and Branding, you can add a store banner and a personalized message (if you'd like) on your end-of-auction e-mails and on your eBay checkout invoices. Figure 5-10 shows an invoice customized with my logo and message.

Figure 5-9: A cross-promotion in one of my eBay auctions.

Figure 5-10: Super promotion for your business: Your eBay Store logo can appear on your eBay invoices as well as your e-mails.

Dressing Up Your Listings

eBay has more tempting options that you can use to spruce up your store items. These options work exactly like the ones eBay offers for your fixed-price listings or auctions (see Chapter 10), except you're charged a lower fee than the one for folks who have no eBay Store subscription.

Making a Sale

From the buyer's point of view, shopping at an eBay Store is not much different from winning an auction. eBay Stores feature fixed-price sales; the buyer will get the merchandise as soon as you can ship it (instead of waiting for the auction to run its course). When a buyer makes a purchase from an eBay Store, here's what happens:

1. The buyer clicks the Buy It Now button on the listing page. The Review Payments page appears, where the buyer can review the purchase. This page contains the shipping amount you specified when you listed the item.

2. The buyer provides shipping information (required). When eBay notifies you that a sale has been made, you have all the information you need. You don't have to scurry around looking for the return address on the envelope when the payment arrives.

3. The buyer reviews the transaction and then clicks the Confirm button. The information about the sale is e-mailed to you, and the buyer receives confirmation of the sale.

Your eBay Store will be an essential backup to your auctions. It's a great place to put out-of-season items, accessories for the items you sell actively, and even consignment items between relistings. Considering the price of an eBay Store, you have to make only a few sales per month to pay for it — and when your sales start to build, your efforts will be greatly rewarded!

Part II
Setting Up Shop

The 5th Wave   By Rich Tennant

"Try putting a person in the photo with the product you're trying to sell. We generated a lot of interest in our eBay Listing once Leo started modeling my hats and scarves."

In this part . . .

Your hobby is what you love, and I'm betting you have a houseful of duplicate items — the perfect stuff to start to sell on eBay! Or perhaps you'd like to sell inventory from an existing business or sell for others on consignment. Or maybe you want to start buying wholesale merchandise like the big companies.

As you can see, the options are countless. In this part, I talk about how to find merchandise to sell, the best way to sell it, and how to make the most of your ever-important Web site.

Chapter 6

Finding Merchandise to Up Your Profits

*Y*ou're probably wondering just how you can possibly get enough merchandise to list as many as 20 (maybe 50?) items a day. You're thinking that there aren't possibly enough sources out there to fulfill that kind of volume. Success on eBay isn't easy. Despite the e-mail claims of the huge money that can be made on eBay, it's like everything else: No one has a magic formula. (The only people who really make money from those e-mails are the ones who send them to hopeful new sellers.) Many hours and a good deal of perspiration — along with loads of inspiration — are necessary to make a good living selling online. You *can* do it — if you apply the same amount of effort in acquiring merchandise.

One of my favorite mottoes is "Buy off-season; sell on-season." You can get great bargains on winter merchandise in the heat of summer. January's a great time to stock up on Christmas decorations, and the value of those trendy vintage aluminum trees doubles in November and December. Cashmere sweaters, too! In the winter, you can get great deals on closeout summer sports merchandise. It's all in the timing.

How are you going to acquire the products you need? I've spent hours, days, weeks, okay, even months trying to work out the best ways to stock an eBay business. Ultimately, this depends on you, your personality, and the type of merchandise you plan to sell. I've tried many of the tactics that I discuss in this chapter, as have some eBay sellers that I know, and I pass on the secrets and caveats that each of us discovered along the way.

Dollar Stores

Dollar stores come in all shapes and sizes. They can be filled with junk or treasure, and it takes a practiced eye to separate the wheat from the chaff. Many an item can be found here that makes for great practice for beginning sellers — and often goes for ten times what they paid. Try going in with a teenager, and see whether he or she reacts to any of the items for sale. Sometimes only one in five visits works out, but you'll know when you see the item — and at these prices, you can afford to go deep! Stock at these stores doesn't stay on the shelf for too long; if you pass on an item, it may not be there when you return for it the next day. (Maybe another savvy eBay seller picked up the values.)

99¢ Only stores

The crème de la crème of the dollar-type stores on the West Coast are the 99¢ Only stores. (Okay, $.99 isn't $1.00, but I still think it qualifies as a dollar store!) You can find these stores in California, Nevada, Arizona, and Texas. The highest price in the store is 99¢, and some items can be bought for as little as 29¢.

The bulk of the items sold at 99¢ Only stores are closeouts or special-opportunity buys. When a company changes its labels, for example, it might sell all remaining stock with the old labels to 99¢ Only. I've found some profitable books, Olympics memorabilia, and pop-culture items at this store. And keep in mind that you can go a long way here by being nice. Befriend the store manager, who might alert you when merchandise that matches your specialty comes in. The chain is expanding rapidly, so visit its Web site at www.99only.com to see whether a store is opening near you. Other dollar stores are probably in your area. Pull out the phone book (or bother the 411 operator) and see what you can find.

It's not unusual for dollar store warehouses to sell directly to a retailer (that's you!). If you live in California, Nevada, Arizona, or Texas, you can join their Club99 and buy their merchandise in bulk. It will be delivered at no charge to one of their showrooms. There is a link to Club 99 on the 99only.com home page, or you can go directly to www.99only.com/club99.

If you don't live in one of the states just mentioned, you can purchase merchandise online on their subsidiary Web site at www.bargainw.com and shop for your business. To be able to buy at the site, you must have a business license or a resale number from your state. They also have a minimum order; if it's too high for you, why not split an order with another seller?

Big Lots

Another super selling chain is the Big Lots company, which encompasses the Pic N Save, Mac Frugal's, Big Lots, and Odd Lots stores. They may have items priced at more than a dollar, but they specialize in closeout merchandise. All their merchandise sells for well under what most discounters charge — and at deep discounts to retailers. This is a great place to find toys, household goods — almost anything. Troll their aisles at least once a month to find items that you can resell on eBay. The Big Lots company has stores in 46 states; check its Web site at www.biglots.com for store locations near you.

When you get your state's seller's permit (see Chapter 15), you can take advantage of the Big Lots Wholesale Web site at www.biglotswholesale.com. If you think that Big Lots regular prices are low, you should see their wholesale prices! The minimum order from the Web site is $500, which will get you a lot of merchandise. Before placing an order, be sure to check and see whether the item is selling on eBay. If many eBay sellers are trying to sell the same item now, why not place an order and sell when the other sellers have exhausted their stock? When fewer sellers are selling, the price usually goes up. Supply and demand is the name of the game.

Tuesday Morning

One of my editors is going to kill me for mentioning one of her favorite eBay merchandise sources — but here it is. Tuesday Morning has more than 500 stores scattered over the United States. They sell first-quality designer and brand-name closeout merchandise at deep-deep discounts, 50 percent to 80 percent below retail.

The key here is that the store sells recognizable brand names, the kind of items that eBay shoppers look for. I've seen items at their store from Samsonite, Thomas Kincade, Limoges, Wedgwood, Royal Doulton, Madame Alexander, and even Barbie!

Find your local store at its Web site: www.tuesdaymorning.com. If you sign up for its eTreasures newsletter, you'll get advance notice of when the really good stuff arrives at the store. (Sometimes they have only a dozen of a particular item per store, so you have to be there when the doors open.)

Discount Club Stores

Warehouse stores made their mark by selling items in bulk to large families, clubs, and small businesses. In case you haven't noticed, these stores have recently upscaled and sell just about anything you could want. Their shelves are brimming with current merchandise ripe for the picking.

Sam's Club

In addition to shopping for bargains at the Sam's Club in your neighborhood, you can now visit its wholesale auctions at `auctions.samsclub.com`. What a fantastic place to find merchandise to sell on eBay. The closeouts on the auction site can sell at a fraction of the retail price.

Costco

Believe it or not, one day I was wheeling my cart around Costco (to buy my monthly ration of meat) and right in front of me was a huge display with women jumping and grabbing at the merchandise. I glanced above to read the sign: Fendi Baugette Handbags $199.99. My daughter and I elbowed our way (in a not-too-ladylike fashion, I might add) through the crowd and saw the regularly $450 purses stacked like lunchmeat. In those days, the Baugette was new and sold on eBay for around $350. Needless to say, we bought all that our credit cards could handle.

In the first edition of this book, I talked about a special on the Costco Web site, `www.costco.com`, for a new *Snow White & the Seven Dwarfs* DVD. For $18.49, you could pre-order the *Snow White* DVD and get a second Disney DVD for *free*. When there's an offer like this, you can sell two items on eBay for the price of one. If I had followed my own advice and bought a case of this deal and held some for future sales, I'd be in the money today. It seems that Disney movies are released for a limited time only. That original DVD set sold on eBay for around $40.

When an item is new but has some collectibility, I suggest you buy in bulk, sell some of the item to make up your investment, and save the balance for later. This has paid off for me a good many times with Disney films, Barbies, and Andy Warhol dinnerware.

Garage Sales

What can be better than getting up at 6:00 a.m. to troll the local garage sales? I say nothing — if you're motivated to find lots of good eBay merchandise and prepared for the garage sales. Buy the newspaper or check your local newspaper's classified ads online (just run a Google search for your local newspaper's name), and print maps of the sale locations from MapQuest or Yahoo! You know the neighborhoods, so you can make a route that makes sense from one sale to the next — and figure in bathroom stops and coffee breaks.

Neighbors often take advantage of an advertised sale and put out some stuff of their own. Bring a friend; you can cover more ground faster if two of you are attacking the sales.

A few tips on shopping garage sales:

- ✔ Fancier neighborhoods have better stuff than poor or middle-class ones. I know that sounds unfair, but I know for sure that rich folks' trash is better than mine.

- ✔ Look for sales that say "Early Birds Welcome," and make them the first on your list so you can get them out of the way. It seems like a universal bell goes off somewhere and all garage sales start at 8:00 a.m. *sharp!*

- ✔ The stuff you find at estate sales is often of a higher quality. These sales feature things that have been collected over many, many years.

- ✔ Keep an eye out for "moving to a smaller house" sales. These are usually people who have raised children, accumulated a houseful of stuff (collectibles? old toys? designer vintage clothes?), and want to shed it all so that they can move to a condo in Palm Springs.

  Any toys people are selling while downsizing are usually good ones.

- ✔ I usually put sales that feature "kids' items and toys" on the end of my list, and I go only if I'm not too tired. These sellers are generally young couples (with young children) who are trying to raise money or are moving. More often than not, they're keeping the good stuff and are simply shedding the excess.

Going-Out-of-Business Sales

Going-out-of-business sales can be a bonanza, but be careful and don't be misled. Many states require businesses that are putting on a going-out-of-business sale to purchase a special license that identifies the business as *really* going out of business. Some store ads may read "Going Out for Business" or some similar play on words, so you need to be sure that you're going to the real thing. When a retailer is liquidating its own stock, you're going to get the best buys. A retailer will often run the sale week by week, offering bigger discounts as time goes by. If a company is really going out of business, don't be afraid to make an offer on a quantity of items.

Another benefit of going-out-of-business sales is that many times the stores are selling their fixtures for rock-bottom prices. If you're looking for a mannequin to model your fashions or display pieces for your photographs, run, don't walk, to that sale.

A chain of children's wear went out of business here in Southern California a while back. This chain also carried a smattering of popular dolls. A seller I know made an offer for all remaining dolls and subsequently purchased them at a great price. Throughout the following year, she sold them on eBay for three to four times what she had paid.

Auctions

Two types of auctions where you can pick up bargains are liquidation and estate auctions. (I also discuss charity auctions, where you may be able to find bargains while donating to a good cause.) You'll find perfectly salable and profitable items, but each type of auction has its idiosyncrasies. Before you go to any auction, double-check payment terms and find out if you must bring cash or can pay by credit card. Also, before you bid on anything, find out the *hammer fee,* or *buyer's premium.* These fees are a percentage that auction houses add to the winner's bid; the buyer has the responsibility of paying this fee.

Liquidation auctions

When a company gets into serious financial trouble, its creditors (the people to whom the company owes money) obtain a court order to liquidate the company to pay the bills. The liquidated company then sells its stock, fixtures, and even real estate. Items sell for just cents on the dollar, and you can easily resell many of these items on eBay. A special kind of auctioneer handles these auctions. Look in the phone book under Auctioneers: Liquidators and call local auctioneers' offices to get on mailing lists. This way, you'll always know when something good comes up for sale.

Have you seen this headline before?

"Make Hundred$ of thou$ands in profits by reselling items from Government Foreclosure auctions!" Yes, I've seen this headline too. You send someone money to let you in on the big "secret." Here's the secret: You can find out about many government auctions at these sites:

✔ **www.ustreas.gov/auctions/**: This site gives information on seized Department of the Treasury property auctions held in New Jersey, California, Florida, Texas, Arizona, and other locations. The lists of the lots for sale are posted about a month before the auctions. You can also call the hot line at 703-273-7373 for up-to-date information. They also post the bid results for previous auctions, so you can get an idea about the selling price of various lots.

✔ **www.ustreas.gov/auctions/irs/**: Our buddies at the Internal Revenue Service have their own auction site. Here you can find a wide assortment of real property: patents, livestock, vehicles, planes, boats, business equipment, household goods, and real estate. They sell just about everything. (These guys are serious about collecting their tax money!)

✔ **gsaauctions.gov/gsaauctions/gsaauctions**: This is the official link to the General Services Administration's surplus, seized, and forfeited property auctions. These are electronic bidding online auctions that are held daily. You can even find used crash-test vehicles here (good for selling the undamaged parts on eBay).

✔ **www.usps.com/auctions**: Ever wonder where all the post office's lost packages go? Check this site for auction locations and times. Also search Google for *mail recovery centers*.

✔ **www.govliquidation.com**: This is a private company specializing in government liquidation auctions.

For other sites, run a Google search for *state surplus* (results include tons of links to individual state-seized property auctions), *seized property, tax sales, confiscated property,* and *state auction.* Remember: If you're asked for payment to get the information, then it's not an official site.

Estate auctions

Estate auctions are the higher level of estate garage sales. Here you can find fine art, antiques, ephemera, rare books, and collectibles of all kinds. Aside from the large estate auctions, most auction houses have monthly estate auctions in which they put together groups of merchandise from various small estates. Find out when these auctions are being held and mark them on your calendar.

These auctions are attended mostly by dealers who know the local going prices for the items they bid on. But because they're buying to sell in a retail environment, their high bids will generally be the wholesale price for your area. If a particular item is flooding your market, the high bid may be low. I've seen some incredible bargains at Bonham's estate auctions here in Los Angeles. When you're in a room full of local dealers, they're buying what's hot to resell in your city — not what's going to sell across the country. That entire market will be yours.

Charity silent auctions

I'm sure you've been to your share of silent auctions for charity. A school or an organization will get everyone from major corporations to the local gift shop to donate items. The items are then auctioned off to the highest bidder, usually in a silent format.

You can find many a great item at these auctions. Aside from new merchandise, collectors may feel good about donating some collection overflow to a charity. I purchased the keystone of my *Star Trek* action figure collection at a charity auction: the very rare tri-fold Borg (one of perhaps only 50 in existence). This figure has sold for as high as $1,000 on eBay, and I paid just $60, all while donating to a charity. (Okay, these days it's selling for only about $400 — but heck, it was *still* a deal!)

Goodwill, Salvation Army, and Resale Shops

Participating in a charity such as Goodwill or the Salvation Army is a powerful thing with many benefits. You don't have to worry about having a garage sale to get rid of unwanted stuff (no need to have strangers trodding all over the lawn, crunching the daisy borders while sniffing around at the stuff for sale), and you can pretty much write off many items as a charity tax deduction. And it's simple: You just load the goods into your car and take 'em to the store. It's a win-win-win situation. The extra win is that you can also acquire valuable pieces at bargain-basement prices.

At resale stores, such as those run by Goodwill and the Salvation Army, you'll sometimes uncover treasures; other times you'll find only junk. I recommend befriending the manager, who sees the merchandise as it comes in; he or she will know just what you're looking for (because you said so in a friendly conversation), and will call you before the items hit the floor. This type of relationship can save you from making fruitless trips.

Some stores receive merchandise from a central warehouse, where donations are first sent for minor rehabilitation and cleaning. Other, smaller operations process items in-house, with the store manager supervising. The resale store is a business that runs on a schedule. Ask the manager (whom you've befriended) when the truck regularly comes in. Being there when the truck arrives enables you to view items before the general public sets eyes on them.

A sharp seller I know is always at his local Salvation Army when the trucks come in. One day, as workers unloaded the truck, he saw a plaque-mounted baseball bat. Withholding his excitement, he picked it up and found that it was a signed Ty Cobb bat with a presentation plaque. Although he didn't know exactly what it was, he took a gamble and brought it to the cash register, where he paid $33 minus the senior-citizen discount. He took the bat to his office and made a few phone calls, later discovering that the bat was indeed a rare Louisville Slugger bat that had been presented to *the* Georgia Peach, Ty Cobb. But he'll never sell it because it's his good luck bat, which now hangs above the desk in his warehouse.

Goodwill Industries is definitely gearing up for the twenty-first century. You can shop at its online auctions and get super values on the best of its merchandise. Don't forget to check the going prices on eBay before you buy. Have fun at www.shopgoodwill.com.

Freebies

Freebies come in all shapes and sizes and — best of all — they're free, of course. Freebies are usually samples or promotion pieces that companies give away to introduce a new product, service, or, best of all, media event. Even carefully trimmed ads from magazines can fetch high prices from collectors.

When you go to the cosmetic counter and buy a way-too-expensive item, be sure to ask for tester-sized samples. Name-brand cosmetic and perfume samples of high-priced items sell very well on eBay. Also, look for *gift with purchase* deals. If it's a specialty item, you can usually sell it on its own to someone who'd like to try a sample rather than plunge headlong into a large purchase. Less-special items can be grouped together as lots.

Be sure to put the brand names in the item titles.

Remember the talking Taco Bell Chihuahua giveaway? Those cute little stuffed dogs were all the rage and sold for big money on eBay. It almost seems foolish to remind you of the McDonald's Teenie Beanie Baby giveaways; moms, dads, and dealers were driving in circles through the drive-thru, purchasing as many of the Happy Meals as each store would allow. They'd then drive to the next McDonald's to purchase a different toy. In my house alone, we had frozen hamburgers for three months!

When *Return of the Jedi* was re-released in 1997, the first 100 people to enter each theater got a Special Edition Luke Skywalker figure. These figures are still highly prized by collectors.

In 1995, Paramount network premiered a new show, *Star Trek Voyager.* In selected markets, Paramount sent a promotional microwave popcorn packet as a Sunday newspaper insert. These packets are still selling well (when you can find them), although the value rises and falls according to the current level of popular interest in *Star Trek.*

Before you pass by a freebie, reconsider its possible future resale value.

Salvage: Liquidation Items, Unclaimed Freight, and Returns

The easiest buys of all, *salvage merchandise* is retail merchandise that has been returned, exchanged, or shelf-pulled for some reason. Generally, this merchandise is sold as-is and where-is, and may be in new condition. To buy this merchandise, you must have your resale permit (complete with sales tax number) and be prepared to pay the shipping to your location — unless you're buying the merchandise on eBay.

Available all over the country, the liquidation business has been thriving as a well-kept secret for years. As long as you have space to store salvage merchandise and a way to sell it, you can acquire it for as low as 10 cents on the dollar. When I say you need storage space, I mean *lots* of space. To buy this type of merchandise at bottom-of-the-barrel prices, you must be willing to accept truckloads — think 40- to 53-foot eighteen-wheelers, loaded with approximately twenty-two to twenty-four 4-x-4-x-6-foot (or 7-foot) pallets — of merchandise at a time. Often these truckloads have manifests listing the retail and wholesale price of each item on the truck. If you have access to the more than 10,000 square feet of warehouse that you'll need to unpack and process this amount of merchandise, then you're in business.

Several types of salvage merchandise are available:

✔ **Unclaimed freight:** When a trucking company delivers merchandise, a *manifest* (a document containing the contents of the shipment) accompanies the freight. If, for some reason, a portion of the shipment arrives incomplete, contains the wrong items, or is damaged, the entire shipment may be refused by the merchant. The trucking company is now stuck with as much as a truckload of freight. The original seller may not want to pay the freight charges to return the merchandise to his or her warehouse (or accept blame for an incorrect shipment), and so the freight becomes the trucker's problem. The trucking companies arrive at agreements with liquidators to buy this freight in the various areas that the liquidators serve. This way, truckers are never far from a location where they can dump, er, *drop off* merchandise.

✔ **Returns:** Did you know that after you buy something, decide you don't want it, and return it to the store or mail-order house, it can never be sold as new again (in most states anyway)? Such merchandise is generally sent to a liquidator who agrees in advance to pay a flat percentage for goods. The liquidator must move the merchandise to someone else. All major retailers liquidate returns, and much of this merchandise ends up on eBay or in closeout stores.

If you're handy at repairing electronics or computers, you'd probably do very well with a specialized lot. You may easily be able to revitalize damaged merchandise, often using parts from two unsalable items to come up with one that you can sell in like-new working condition.

✔ **Liquidations:** Similar to the liquidation auctions that I mention in a previous section on auctions, these liquidators buy liquidation merchandise by truckloads and sell it in smaller lots. The merchandise comes from financially stressed or bankrupt companies that need to raise cash quickly.

✔ **Seasonal overstocks:** Remember my motto? Here it is again: "Buy off-season; sell on-season." At the end of the season, a store may find its shelves overloaded with seasonal merchandise (such as swimsuits in August) that it must get rid of to make room for the fall and winter stock. These brand-new items become salvage merchandise because they're seasonal overstocks.

✔ **Shelf-pulls:** Have you ever passed up one item in the store for the one behind it in the display because its box was in better condition? Sometimes the plastic bubble or the package is dented, and you'd rather have a pristine one. That box you just passed up may be destined to become a *shelf-pull*. The item inside may be in perfect condition, but it's cosmetically unsalable in the retail-store environment.

A proportion of liquidation items, unclaimed freight, and returns may not be salable for the reasons that I discuss in the rest of this section. Although you'll acquire many gems that stand to bring you profit, you'll also be left with a varying percentage of useless items. Read on carefully.

Items by the pallet

Some suppliers take the risk and purchase salvaged merchandise by the truckload. They then break up each truckload and sell the merchandise to you a pallet at a time. You'll probably find some local liquidators who offer this service, or you can go online to find one. Here's the rub: finding the right person to buy from.

As in any business, you'll find both good-guy liquidators and bad-guy liquidators. As you know, the world is full of e-mail scammers and multilevel marketers who are in business to take your money. No one trying to sell you merchandise can possibly *guarantee* that you'll make money, so beware of liquidators who offer this kind of promise. I don't care who they are or what they say. Carefully research whomever you choose to buy from. Use an Internet search engine and search for the words *salvage, liquidation,* and *pallet merchandise.*

Some liquidation sellers sell their merchandise in the same condition that it ships in to their location, so what you get is a crapshoot. You may lose money on some items while making back your money on others. Other sellers who charge a bit more will remove less-desirable merchandise from the pallets. Some may even make up deluxe pallets with better-quality merchandise. These loads cost more, but if they're filled with the type of merchandise that you're interested in selling, you'll probably write better descriptions and subsequently do a better job selling them.

Getting a pallet of merchandise shipped to you can cost a bundle, so finding a source for your liquidation merchandise that's close to your base of operations is a good idea. You'll notice that many liquidation sites have several warehouses, which translates to lower shipping costs for the buyer. (They can then also accept merchandise from places close to the various warehouses.) You might see freight on board (FOB) and a city name — which means that when you buy the merchandise, you own it in the city listed. You're responsible for whatever it costs to ship the merchandise to your door. Search around; you may have to go through many sources before you find the right one for you.

When you find a source from which you want to buy merchandise by the pallet, check out a few things before spending your hard-earned cash:

- Does this vendor sell mostly to flea marketers (you might not want that kind of merchandise because you're looking for *quality* at a low price) or closeout stores (more retail-oriented)?

- Did you get a reply within 24 hours after calling or e-mailing?

- Does anyone you speak to appear to care about what you want to sell?

- Are the available lots within your budget?

- Are the lots general or have they been sorted to include only the type of merchandise that you want to sell?

- How long has this liquidator been in business and where does its merchandise come from?

- Does the source guarantee that you *will* make money or state that you *can* make money by buying the right merchandise? **Remember:** No one can guarantee that you'll make money.

> ✔ Does the supplier offer on its Web site references that you can contact to find out some usable information on this seller's items and the percentage of unsalable goods in a box or pallet?
>
> ✔ Is a hard sell involved? Or is it a matter-of-fact deal?

Before you get dazzled by a low, low price on a huge lot and click the Buy It Now button, check the shipping cost. Many so-called wholesalers will lure you in with bargain-basement prices, only to charge you three times the normal shipping costs. Do your homework before you buy!

Job lots

Manufacturers often have to get rid of merchandise, too. Perhaps a particular manufacturer made five million bobbing-head dolls and then sold only four million to retailers. It has to unload this merchandise (known as *job lots*) quickly so it'll have the cash to invest in next season's array of items. Job lots often consist of hundreds or thousands of a single item. You'd best enjoy what you're selling because you'll be looking at the stuff for a while.

Remember supply and demand — don't ever flood the eBay market. Otherwise, your item will become valueless.

Many Web sites specialize in job lots, but you have to visit them often because the deals are constantly changing. One worth checking out is Liquidation.com, shown in Figure 6-1. Visit it at `www.liquidation.com`.

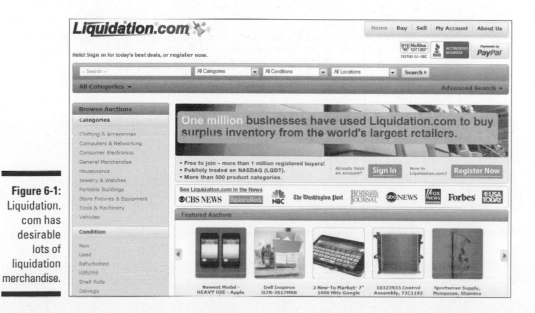

Figure 6-1: Liquidation. com has desirable lots of liquidation merchandise.

Drop-Shipping to Your Customers

Some middlemen, wholesalers, and liquidators specialize in selling to online auctioneers through drop-ship services or warehouses. Some crafty eBay sellers make lots of money selling lists of drop-shipping sources to eBay sellers — I hope not to you. Dealing with a drop-shipper means that you don't ever have to take possession of (or pay for) the merchandise. You pay a monthly fee for accessing the vendor's Web site to select items. You're given a photo of the item and, after you sell the item itself, you give the vendor the address of the buyer. The vendor charges your credit card for the item plus shipping, and ships the item to your customer for you.

This way of doing business costs *you* more and lowers your profits. If you're in business, your goal is to make as much money as you can. Because the drop-shippers are in business, too, they'll mark up the merchandise they sell to you (and the shipping cost) so they can make their profit. Drop-shipping can work as a *supplement* to your basic eBay business.

Be careful when using a drop-shipper. Ask for references. Don't give them your credit card number with carte blanche to keep charging your account month by month if you're not benefiting from their services. See whether a zillion sellers are selling the same merchandise on eBay — and not getting any bites. Check, too, that the price you will pay for the item leaves you room for profit. I've researched some of these items on eBay and noted that many inexperienced sellers only mark up drop-ship goods by a fraction. They seem to be happy making $5 a sale; they don't take into consideration how much the listing fees for unsold items cost them. That's just not smart business on their part; hence they can ruin the market for such items for everyone else.

Also, what happens if the drop-shipper runs out of an item that you've just sold? You can't just say "oops" to your buyer without getting some nasty feedback. It's your online reputation at stake. If you find a solid source and believe in the product, order a quantity and have it shipped to your door. Don't pay for someone else's mark-up for the privilege of shipping to your customers.

True Wholesale Merchandise

Purchasing wholesale merchandise may require that you have your state's resale license, which identifies you as being in the business. Be sure that you have such a license before you try to purchase merchandise directly from another business. Also, when you have a resale number and purchase merchandise from another business — known as a business-to-business

(B2B) transaction — you probably won't be charged tax when you purchase your stock because you'll be paying sales tax when you sell the items. Go to Chapter 15 to find out how to get that magic resale number.

When you have your resale number, you can go anywhere you want to buy merchandise. If you want to buy direct from a manufacturer, you can. Unfortunately, manufacturers often have a monetary minimum for the amount of your order, which may be more than you want to spend (and you'd get more of a particular item than you'd ever want at once). To remedy that, see whether you can find some independent retailers who buy in quantity and who perhaps will let you in on some quantity buys with manufacturers.

To find wholesalers on the Internet, try Google.com. Refine your search to your favorite categories: golf, jewelry, skateboards — get the idea? Then run the following searches (inserting your choice of merchandise as indicated): *Dealer login jewelry; Wholesale login jewelry; Member login jewelry; Distributor login jewelry; Licensed retailers only.*

Sometimes the liquidators that I discuss in the preceding section get cases of perfectly salable goods in their loads. Pallets break up into many cases, and liquidators will often sell these cases individually on eBay. What a great way to acquire goods for your eBay business; I know of several eBay sellers who buy their merchandise this way.

Resale Items on eBay

I'll keep this eBay buying technique short and sweet: Use the magic search engine! But be careful; many a get-rich-quick schemer will use boldface keywords in their auctions to attract your attention. Look only for good-quality merchandise to resell. Remember that the only way to make a living on eBay is to sell quality items to happy customers so that they'll come back and buy from you again. Be sure to search eBay auction titles for the following keywords: *resale, resell, "case of"* (see Figure 6-2), *"case quantity," "lot of," "pallet of"* (see Figure 6-3), *closeout,* and *surplus*. Be sure to use the quotes anywhere that I've included them here because this forces the search engine to find the words in the exact order you write them inside the quotes.

Also be sure you check out the wholesale listings on eBay. After noticing how many sellers were buying from other sellers, eBay enables you to find wholesale items, too. Go to the eBay home page, scroll down the list of categories, and click Everything Else. You'll be brought to the Everything Else category. Just type **wholesale lots** in the search box to find some great deals as shown in Figure 6-4.

Figure 6-2:
Results of a "case of" search on eBay.

Figure 6-3:
Results of a "pallet of" search.

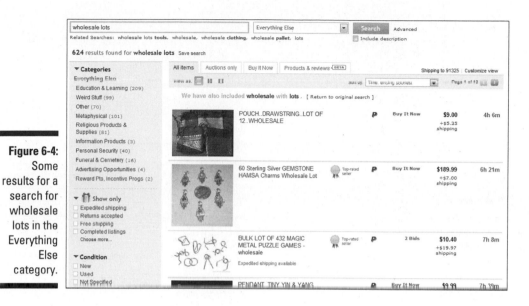

Figure 6-4:
Some
results for a
search for
wholesale
lots in the
Everything
Else
category.

Consignment Selling

Consignment sales are the up-and-coming way for you to help newbies by selling their items on eBay. Lots of sellers do it — and several retail locations base their business on it. You take possession of the item from the owner and sell it on eBay. You're responsible for taking photos and marketing the auction on eBay — for a fee. In addition to the money you earn selling on consignment, you also get excellent experience for future auctions of your own merchandise.

To set up your business for consignment sales, you should follow a few guidelines:

1. Design a consignment agreement (a contract) and send it to the owners of the merchandise before they send you their items. Doing so ensures that all policies are set up in advance and that no questions will arise after the transaction has begun.

2. Have the owners sign and send the agreement to you (the consignor) along with the item.

3. Research the item based on past sales so that you can give the owners an estimated price range of what the item might sell for on eBay.

4. Photograph the item carefully (see Chapter 11 for some hints) and write a thoughtful selling description.

5. Handle all e-mail inquiries as though the item were your own; after all, your fee is generally based on a percentage of the final sale.

What do you charge for all your work? I can't give you a stock answer for that one. Many sellers charge a flat fee for photographing, listing, and shipping that ranges from $5–$10 plus as much as a 30 percent commission on the final auction total (to absorb eBay fees). Other sellers base their fees solely on the final sale amount and charge on a sliding scale, beginning at 50 percent of the total sale, less eBay and payment service fees. You must decide how much you think you can make on an item.

Traditional auction houses handle consignment sales in a similar fashion.

When you've reached the next level of your eBay enterprise and are looking to spend some serious money on your merchandise, check out my book, *eBay Business All-In-One For Dummies.* That's where I delve into the type of wholesale-buying secrets normally reserved for the big-time retailers.

Become an eBay Trading Assistant

After you have 50 feedback messages from buyers under your belt on eBay (and have sold at least 4 items in the past 30 days), you can become a registered eBay Trading Assistant. Check out `http://pages.ebay.com/tahub/` (shown in the figure) to get all the details.

eBay publishes a directory of consignment sellers that you can search by inserting your address. Check out who in your area is a registered Trading Assistant. Read their terms and fees. Consignment sellers charge varied amounts based on their geographic location (some areas can bear higher fees than others).

eBay Trading Assistant Program

Quick Links

Trading Assistant requirements and sign-up

Trading Assistant log-in

Find a Trading Assistant

Learn how to sell

trading assistant on eBay

Trading Assistants are experienced members who sell for others on eBay.

Types of Trading Assistants

Registered eBay Drop-off Location

Similar to a consignment store, this is an eBay Trading Assistant that has a physical store front location with regular business hours. Some may provide a pick-up service or you can drop off your items and they will sell them on eBay. When your items sell, they will pay you the proceeds less

eBay REGISTERED drop off location

Sell for others by becoming a Trading Assistant

Boost your own income by becoming a Trading Assistant and leverage your experience to sell items for other people on eBay.

Through the Trading Assistant Directory, your services are marketed to local eBay members. You can also build your business by downloading flyers, business card templates and the program logo.

Sign up now or click here to learn more about the program and the eBay selling requirements.

Sign-up now!

Find a local Trading Assistant to sell for you

Trading Assistants are experienced eBay sellers in your area who will sell your items for you on eBay for a fee. By hiring a Trading Assistant, you can take advantage of their selling expertise, save time and effort, and still reap the rewards of selling on eBay.

Trading Assistants will do all the work for you, from listing an item and answering customer service inquiries, to collecting payment and shipping the item to the winning buyer.

Find one now!

Chapter 7

Pricing Your Items to Sell

. . . .

In This Chapter

▶ Searching eBay

▶ Finding publications in your area of interest

▶ Using online appraisal services

▶ Authenticating your merchandise

. . . .

*I*f you don't know what your item is worth, you may not get the highest price in any market. If you don't know how to make your item easy to find, it may not be noticed by even the hardiest of collectors. If you don't know the facts or what to say, your well-written title and detailed description (combined with a fabulous picture) may still not be enough to get the highest price for your item.

Knowing your item is a crucial part of successful selling at eBay. This is why I suggest in Chapter 1 that you specialize in a small group of items in the beginning so that you can stay on top of ever-changing trends. An item may be appraised or listed in a book for a high value, but what you care about is the price at which the item will actually sell. Imagine someone uncovering a hoard of your item and, not knowing the value of it, dumping them on eBay with low Buy It Now prices. This frequent scenario drives down the value of the item within a couple of weeks.

The values of collectibles go up and down. *Star Wars* items are a perfect example; values skyrocketed during the release of the latest movie, but now prices have settled to a considerably lower level — and yet there are still buyers. A printed book of value listings is valid only for the *moment* the book is written. If you stay on top of your market in a few specialties, you'll be aware of these market fluctuations. If you're looking for the highest price instead of looking to liquidate excess inventory, I'd hold any special *Star Wars* items until the buzz starts up again.

You no doubt *will* purchase the occasional gem and will want to make the most money possible, so in this chapter I examine the different ways you can find out just how much something is worth. I start with the easiest and most accurate method, and end with the most laborious. I hope you can get your answer the easy way.

The Easy Way: eBay Search

Who woulda thunk it? The best tool for evaluating your items is right under your nose: The eBay search tool is the best and quickest link to finding your pricing information. To see how items like yours have been selling, search the completed auctions. You can search these results also to see in which categories to list your item.

Every type of item has a different type of bidder. This makes sense, right? Would a person searching for collectible dolls have the same shopping habits as a coin collector? Probably not; coins tend to be more expensive than collectible dolls. Although generalities can be dangerous, *profiling* your item's buyer is worthwhile. After you check out the completed auctions for items like yours, you'll be amazed at how the buying patterns of shoppers in different categories become crystal clear. After you arm yourself with this knowledge, you'll know not only how much your items should go for but also the best time to end the auction.

If you're selling a common item, it's also important to check to see how many other sellers are selling the same item — and when their listings close. Nothing can kill your profits like being the second or third item closing with the same piece of merchandise. You have to space your auctions apart from the others, or the law of supply and demand will kick in — and kick you in the wallet.

The way the search system works has changed drastically over the years, so be sure that you know how to use this valuable tool. Almost every eBay page has a small box for searching. Initially you may find it easier to go to the search page, but if you know the search engine *syntax,* or shorthand, you can pinpoint your items with amazing accuracy.

Here are some pointers to help you get the most out of the eBay search engine:

- The search engine isn't case-sensitive, so you don't have to worry about using capitalization in your search.

- To find more needles in the haystack, be sure to select the Search Titles and Descriptions option.

- To find historical pricing (what the item has sold for in the past two weeks), be sure to select the box to search Completed listings.

✔ If you're using common search terms, don't search only auction titles and descriptions; search by category, too. For example, suppose that you're searching for a Winnie the Pooh baby outfit. Type **Pooh outfit** and you'll get a bunch of results. Look to the left of the page, and see the category that more closely matches your search. In Figure 7-1, the matching category is Clothing, Shoes & Accessories. Click the link below it for the Baby & Toddler Clothing subcategory. Now you'll see the search results in the appropriate category — where I guarantee you'll find exactly what you're looking for.

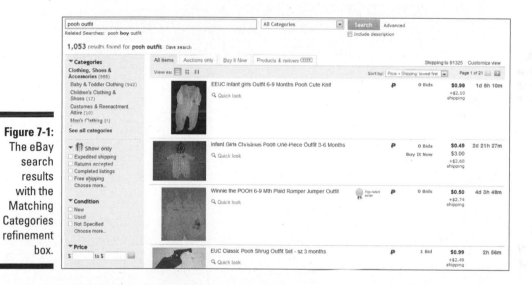

Figure 7-1:
The eBay search results with the Matching Categories refinement box.

✔ Don't use conjunctions *(or, and)* or articles *(a, an, the)* in your search; the search engine might misconstrue these *noise words* as part of your search. Some sellers use the ampersand (&) in place of the word *and,* so if you include *and* in your search, you won't find auctions that use the ampersand. In addition, some sellers (because of the 55-character limit) may not place *the* in their titles; the same goes for *a, or,* and *and*.

Advanced searching methods

If you need to pinpoint a particular item or just want to weed out bogus responses, you can try a variety of advanced search methods, shown in Table 7-1. You can use these shortcuts in any of eBay's search windows.

Table 7-1	Advanced Search Syntax	
Symbol	*Effect*	*Example*
Quotes (",")	Limits search to the exact phrase in the quotes	**"American Staffordshire"** yields auctions relating only to this breed of dog.
Asterisk (*)	Works like a wild card in poker	**196* fashion** displays auctions that relate to 1960s fashion.
Parentheses [()] and comma (,)	Finds items related to either word, or multiple words, between the parentheses	**(shipperke,schipperke)** finds items spelled both ways.
Minus sign –	Excludes words	**watch –digital** gets you a lovely analog watch.
Minus sign (–), parentheses (()), and comma (,)	Excludes more than one word	**Packard –(hewlett,bell)** finds those rare Packard automotive collectibles.

Now that you know how to finesse the search engine, head to the search page and see if you can work some magic.

If you have the item number, you can type or paste it into any of the eBay search boxes to get to that item.

On the search results page, you can choose whether you want to see a mini-gallery of photos, List View, or Fixed price (or Buy It Now) listings in one column and auctions in another. Although this may not ordinarily help when you're doing research, information is key; you might just see a variation of the item in photos that you didn't know about.

Using eBay Advanced Search

By clicking the Advanced Search link just to the right of the Search button at the top of most eBay pages, you can access eBay's advanced search options. With the advanced search, you can narrow your search to check out the competition (who else is selling items like yours). The Advanced Search area has many options; here are a few of the more important:

✔ **Search in categories:** You can narrow your search to one of the 35 top-level categories on eBay. If your product is made for men, women, or children, you may get more efficient results by looking in the category that applies directly to your item. Strangely, when searching for a ladies' watch, I found the following synonyms and abbreviations for *ladies: lady's, ladys, lds,* and *femmes.*

✔ **Completed listings only:** Select this check box to go directly to completed listings for your item research.

✔ **Sort by:** You can find items by auctions that end first (default), newly listed items first, lowest prices first, or highest prices first.

✔ **Location:** If you're selling something big that you can't (or don't want to) ship, you want to deliver it or have the buyer pick it up. This option allows you to check out the competition only in your closest major metropolitan eBay trading area.

✔ **Multiple item listings:** This option lets you search by quantity or lot.

So how can you search completed listings to find bidding and buying patterns on items like yours? Here's a way to dig out all the details you need: Perform a search on the item for which you want information using the search box you see on every eBay page. When the results appear (see Figure 7-2), you'll see how many other sellers are selling the same item you are. That way you can determine whether it's the right time to sell. (If all active auctions for your items have high bids, then okay, it's time to sell — just be sure not to list your auction to end at a time too close to when another one ends.)

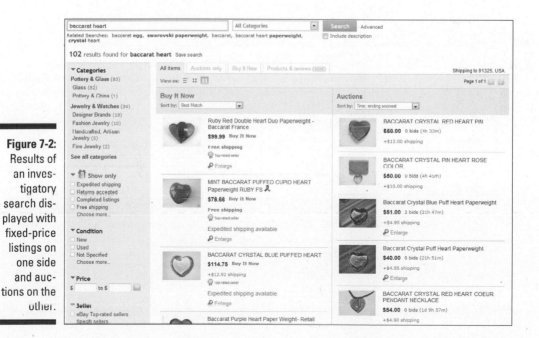

Figure 7-2: Results of an investigatory search displayed with fixed-price listings on one side and auctions on the other.

To dig into the details for historic pricing, you can scroll down (on the left side of any search-results page) to the Search Options area:

1. **Click the Completed Listings check box in the Show Only area of the page.**

   You are presented with the search results of completed listings for the past two weeks.

2. **To sort by price, go to the Sort By drop-down box at the top of the listings and select the Price + Shipping, Highest First option.**

The results of completed auctions of your particular item for the last fourteen days appear, sorted to show highest prices first. Now you're at the heart of the matter (see Figure 7-3). Pull out your calendar and make note of what days your item landed the highest bids. More often than not, you'll find that a pattern appears. Your item may see more action on, say, Sunday or Monday or Thursday or whenever. After you figure out the days that your item gets the highest bids, pull out a copy of the eBay time chart, which appears on the Cheat Sheet at www.dummies.com/cheatsheet/startingebaybiz, or go to www.coolebaytools.com/usa_time_zones.html.

There you can evaluate what time of day your high buyers like to buy.

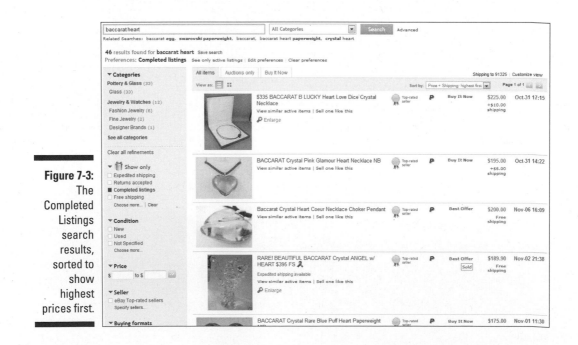

Figure 7-3: The Completed Listings search results, sorted to show highest prices first.

Note that on the results page, items that haven't sold have their prices shown in red; those that have sold are shown in green. This also tells you the high-price breaking point in the current market.

There you have it — the method that will get you the most information that eBay can give you on the sales trends on your item. It's money in the bank. Use it!

If you can't find any listings for your item, you have a few more options. You're not gonna believe I'm saying this, but try searching amazon.com. At least you'll see whether someone else in the world is selling one of your items. None of the cool search features that I previously discuss will work — hey, Amazon ain't eBay.

eBay also has a superior tool for checking your competitor's auctions. After a while, you'll get practiced at identifying the sellers who frequently sell items similar to yours. Aside from keeping them in your Favorite Sellers list on your My eBay page (for more on that, see Chapter 3), here's a way to find out whether one of your competing sellers has an item like yours up for sale.

1. **Go to the Advanced Search area, and click the By Seller link in the Find Items box on the left.**

2. **Enter the seller's user ID in the box provided.**

   a. If you're not sure of the spelling of the seller's ID, select the Show Close and Exact User ID Matches option.

   b. To search completed listings, select the option to Include Completed Listings.

   A drop-down menu appears.

   c. From the drop-down menu, select the time frame in which you want to search.

   You may go back as far as 15 days.

3. **In the next box, type the numbers shown all jumbled up.**

   eBay wants to be sure you're a human being (and not a software site-scraper); only people (so far) can read the jumble.

4. **Click the Search button.**

   You're presented with a list of Seller IDs that closely resemble the one you typed.

5. **When you see the seller you want to check out, click the name.**

Useful Publications

So what if your item isn't for sale on eBay and hasn't been for 15 days? What's the first thing to do? Check out your local newsstand for one of the many publications devoted to collecting. Go over to Yahoo! Local at `local.yahoo.com`. Type your ZIP code to limit the search to your part of the country, and type a search for **newsstand** and **news stand**. You can also search for *Magazines — Dealers* in your area. Let your fingers do the walking: Call the newsstands in your area and ask whether they have publications in your area of interest. If no newsstands are listed in your area, visit your local bookstore.

Here's a list of some popular reference publications:

- ✔ *Toyfare:* Find out who's hot in the action-figure biz in this monthly magazine. Its Web site sells back issues; you can find them at `www.wizarduniverse.com/subscriptions.html`.

- ✔ *Antique Trader:* This magazine has been the bible of the antique collecting industry for more than 40 years. For more articles and subscription information, visit its online home at `www.antiquetrader.com`.

- ✔ *Autograph Magazine:* This magazine (and fabulous Web site) gives the lowdown on the autograph business as well as samples of many autographs for identification. Its Web site, `autographmagazine.com`, also features links to price guides that it publishes.

- ✔ *Collector Editions:* You'll find information on plates, figurines, glass, prints, cottages, ornaments, and dozens of other contemporary decorative collectibles in this monthly magazine.

- ✔ *Doll Reader:* The *Ultimate Authority Doll Reader* has been dishing out the scoop on collectible dolls of all sorts for more than 25 years. It's the place to go to catch the trends on the latest in doll collecting. At `www.dollreader.com`, you'll get an idea of what's in this informative magazine. It even has a newsletter.

- ✔ *Goldmine:* This is *the* magazine for CD and record collecting. The Web site, `www.goldminemag.com`, has many sample articles and information from its issues.

- ✔ *Haute Doll:* Now defunct, *Haute Doll* magazine covered vintage and contemporary dolls and was geared to the adult collector. It covered trends in collecting dolls such as artist dolls, Alex, Barbie, Betsy McCall, Blythe, Brenda Starr, celebrity dolls, Cissette, Cissy, Coco, Coty Girl, Dawn, Elise, Gene, Ginny, Ginger, Jenny, Jill & Jan, Kitty Collier, Little Miss Revlon, Miss Seventeen, Momoko, Somers & Field, Tammy, Tiny Kitty, Tressy, Tyler, Sydney, Vivian, and more! You can purchase back copies by doing a Google search on **Haute Doll**.

✔ *Linn's Stamp News:* I subscribed to this magazine when I was in grade school, and it's still around. Actually it's been around a lot longer, since 1931. (Hey, I'm not that old!) They too have an informative Web site; go to www.linns.com or their superific online magazine at www.linnsonline.com.

✔ *Numismatic News:* Another standard, *Numismatic News*, has been around for more than 50 years. The first issue each month includes a pull-out guide to retail U.S. coin prices. Every three months, it also includes a U.S. paper money price guide. Check out *Numismatic News* on the Web at www.numismaticnews.net.

✔ *Sports Collectors Digest:* Takes sports collectibles to the highest level. Visit its Web site at www.sportscollectorsdigest.com and sign up for a free e-mail newsletter.

✔ *Teddy Bear Review:* Since 1986, this review has offered pages of information on bear collecting. For a free sample issue, go to www.teddybearreview.com.

It seems that every leading magazine has its own Web site. In the next section, I mention some useful Web sites for pricing references.

Online Sources of Information

Because you're all so Internet-savvy (what's better than getting the information you want at a millisecond's notice?), I assume you plan to visit the magazine Web sites that I mention in the preceding section. In this section, I give you a few more fun online sources where you might be able to get even more insight about your items.

Web sites

Many Web sites devoted to different collectible areas list prices at recently completed auctions. These auctions are the best evaluation of an item's value because they're usually directed towards specialists in the specific collectible category. Most of the participants in these auctions *really* know their stuff.

You may have to poke around the following Web sites to find the prices realized at auction — but once you do, you'll have the holy grail of estimated values. Look for links that point to auction archives. Many of these sites will take your item on consignment as well and sell it to their audience:

- Antiques, art, all kinds of rare stuff: www.sothebys.com or www.bonhams.com.

- Art auctions: www.artprice.com charges for its searches by artist, but has an immense database.

- Autographs, movie posters, and comic books: www.autographs.com.

- Art, Comics, Currency and miscellaneous auctions: http://a.uto-graphs.ha.com/. It also has a free online autograph library.

- Collectible advertising glasses: www.pgcaglassclub.com (you have to see this stuff!). It has an online searchable database.

- United States coin price guide: www.pcgs.com/prices/.

- Currency auctions: www.lynknight.com.

- Rare coins: www.bowersandmerena.com.

Online appraisals

I've had a bit of personal experience with online appraisals, which seem quite tempting at first glance. At second glance, though, I realized that unless the person doing the appraisal could actually *see* and *feel* the item, an accurate appraisal couldn't be performed. Also, you have no guarantee that the person at the other end is really an expert in the field that relates to your item.

I had a few items *e-appraised* by a prestigious (and now defunct) online-appraisal company, and the appraisals seemed a bit off. Then I took one, a painting, to Butterfields (now Bonhams) in Los Angeles — and found that the value of the painting was ten times what my e-appraisal read.

The bottom line here is that if it's an item of real value and it's worth appraising, it's worth getting appraised *in person*. Most large cities have auction houses, and many of those auction houses have monthly *consignment clinics* (a way for auction houses to get merchandise for their future auctions). If you bring an item to the auction house, you aren't legally bound to have it sell your item for you, but it may not be a bad idea. All you'll get is a free verbal appraisal; the auction house won't fill out any official paperwork or anything, but at least you'll get an idea of what your item is worth. Real appraisals are expensive, are performed by licensed professionals, and come with a formal appraisal document.

Get eBay pricing history with Terapeak

Terapeak is a new tool for sellers who need to research pricing on eBay. This is a subscription service that allows you to get the lowdown on sales and pricing for your items — as far back as 365 days. You can find this tool at www.terapeak.com/. Because it's a subscription service, you must pay a minimum $9.95 monthly fee, and you can search back as far as 45 days (back 365 days for $24.95 a month). If you sell some fairly pricey items on a routine basis, this tool may be worth looking into.

Authentication Services

Some companies provide the service of *authenticating* (verifying that an item is the real deal) or authenticating and *grading* (determining an item's value based on condition and legitimacy). To have these services performed on your items, you'll have to send the actual items to the service and pay a fee.

Following are a few excellent sites for grading coins:

- ✔ Professional Coin Grading Service (PCGS): www.pcgs.com.
- ✔ American Numismatic Association Certification Service (AMNACS) — sold to Amos Press in 1990: www.anacs.com.
- ✔ Numismatic Guaranty Corporation of America (NGCA): www.ngccoin.com. The site offers lots of information and features a mail-in grading and certification service for your coins.

Stamp collectors (or those who have just inherited a collection from Uncle Steve) can get their stamps "expertized" (authenticated) by the American Philatelic Society. Visit www.stamps.org/services/ser_aboutexpertizing.htm for more information.

For comic books, Comics Guaranty, LLC (CGC), https://www.cgccomics.com/, will seal (enclose in plastic to preserve the quality) and grade your treasured comics.

Sports cards and sports memorabilia have a bunch of authentication services. If you received your autograph or memorabilia directly from the player or team, you can provide personal assurance of its authenticity. Having the item authenticated may or may not get you a higher price at eBay. Try these sites:

- **Professional Sports Authenticator (PSA):** Offers eBay users a discount at http://www.psacard.com/quickopinion/.

- **Beckett Grading Services**. Lots of great information and respected grading at www.beckett.com/grading/.

- **Sportscards Guaranty:** Reviews and grades cards and encapsulates them in tamper-resistant plastic holders. Look at its services at www.sgccard.com/ebay/.

The best way to find a good authenticator in your field is to search the items at eBay and find the most prominent authenticator listed in the descriptions. For example, note that in the coins area, certain grading services' coins get higher bids than those from other services. You can also go to an Internet search engine (Google or Yahoo!) and type the keywords **coin grading** (for coins). You'll come up with a host of choices; use your good sense to see which one suits your needs.

Remember that not all items *need* to be officially authenticated. Official authentication does add value to the item, but if you're an expert on your items, you can comfortably rate them on your own in your auctions. People will know from your description whether you're a specialist (or at least whether you really know your stuff). Your feedback will also work for you by letting prospective bidders or buyers know that your merchandise from past sales has been top-drawer.

Chapter 8

Establishing and Marketing Your Web Site

Success in e-commerce follows a natural progression. There isn't a quick fix. All business expansion will cost you time *and* money. When you're rushing to make the big bucks — listing items so fast you can't count them — you can't possibly learn from your mistakes. Also, expansion costs money, so it only makes sense to *make* some profit before you spend it.

The progression goes like this. One, get started on eBay and get the hang of it (make money). Two, open an eBay Store and stock it (make more money). Keep in mind that no one can master all the intricacies of running an online business in a month or two. That said, here's number three: After you've shown some healthy profit, it's time to expand and invest in your own e-commerce–enabled Web site.

Your eBay Store is important to your business, but it doesn't replace an e-commerce Web site. Yes, eBay is an important site (duh) for your sales and store, but so is your own business Web site. You should establish your own presence on the Web. And although you can — and should — link your site to eBay, don't miss out on the rest of the Internet population.

You don't have a Web site yet? The Web has so many sites with pictures of people's dogs and kids that I just assumed you had your own site, too. The space for a Web site comes *free* from your ISP. One of these sites can be the practice site for your business. Take down pictures of the baby, and post pictures of items you're selling.

You do have a Web site? Have you taken a good look at it lately to see whether it is up to date? Does it link to your eBay auctions or eBay Store?

Most small and medium businesses are increasing their online revenue. In a recent survey of small online businesses, 63 percent of respondents have 5 or fewer employees — does that sound like you?

Well, regardless of whether you have a Web site, this chapter has something for you. I provide a lot of detail about Web sites, from thinking up a name to choosing a host. If you don't have a site, I get you started on launching one. If you already have a site, I give you some pointers about finding the best host. For the serious-minded Web-based entrepreneur (that's you), I also include some ever-important marketing tips.

Free Web Space: Facebook and Blogs

Although I love the word *free,* in real life it seems nothing is *really* free. *Free* generally means something won't cost you too much money — but may cost you a bit more in time. When your site is provided free of charge, there's a tradeoff: You can't have your own direct URL (Universal Resource Locator) or domain name unless you pay an extra fee. Even so, having some kind of site or blog gives you the experience in setting up a site. When you're ready to jump in for real, you can always use your free site as an extension of your main business site.

A free small-business Web site is available from Google Sites. You can find examples of that species at `sites.google.com`. When you get to the Google site, it's just a few clicks to start your own site:

1. **Sign in with your Google Account.**

   If you don't have one, signing up is quick and easy.

2. **Click the Create Site link.**

3. **Select a design template from the Template Gallery.**

You can use the search window to find a template that meets your needs. Figure 8-1 shows a search for store templates.

Be sure you like the template you select; you won't be able to change it later. You'd have to delete your site, give it a new URL, and start over.

Figure 8-1:
Searching
the tem-
plates on
Google
sites for an
e-store
template.

4. **Create and enter a site name and URL.**

5. **Select a theme.**

   The theme determines the site's background and color scheme. (You can change this option at any time.)

6. **Under More Options, select the Everyone in the World Can View This Site option.**

7. **After you are finished selecting your options, enter the provided confirmation code and click Create Site.**

On most of the sites I describe in the following sections, you can add listings of your items to attract buyers. Facebook has its own style of marketing (read further on), but for blogs and sites, you can add widgets and gadgets (of the software variety) or a Really Simple Syndication (RSS) feed that will feature your eBay listings.

Widgets are easy-to-insert snippets of code that carry information to your Web site or blog. Just do a Google search for *eBay widgets*. I did find a site, `www.widgetbox.com`, that has a large selection of eBay widgets.

WidgetBox currently charges a monthly fee of $3.99 (or a discounted fee of $30 a year) to use its widgets. A search on the site netted a selection of more than 1,400 different styles of eBay widgets, as shown in Figure 8-2. If you visit the site, scroll through the selection and read the reviews from other users to decide which widget(s) may be right for you.

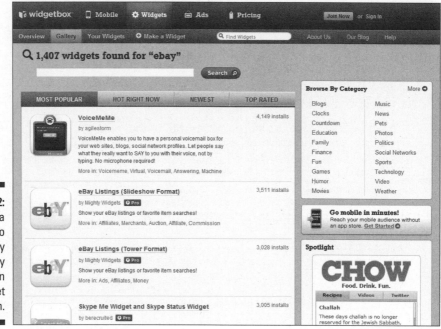

Figure 8-2: Find a widget to display your eBay listings on Widget Box.com.

From your ISP

To access the Internet, you had to sign on with an Internet service provider (ISP), which means you more than likely have your own Web space already. Many ISPs allow you to have more than one e-mail address per account. Each e-mail address is entitled to a certain amount of free Web space. Through the use of *hyperlinks* (small pieces of HTML code that, when clicked, route the clicker from one place to another on the page or on another Web site), you can combine all the free Web space from each e-mail address into one giant Web site.

Many ISPs have their own page-builder (HTML-generating) programs — and offer them free to their users.

Poke around your ISP's home page for a Community or Your Web Space link. For example, after looking around the Comcast ISP's home page, I found and clicked the Member Services link, which led me to a page offering various options. I finally found a Personal Home Page link, which took me to a page that would walk me through setting up my own home page. After agreeing to the Terms of Service, I can simply log on and set up my home page.

Your very own blog

Although we look as Internet blogs as a form of journaling, a blog can serve dual purposes for you. To personalize yourself and your business, putting together a blog that gives content (information, photos, and videos) about the types of products you sell may attract quite a few more viewers.

I'm a big proponent of Blogger (another Google product), a free blogging platform. The difference between Blogger and Sites is that a blog can be far more personal — and if you're a small business, that helps you build your brand as an eBay seller.

By the way, you can have both a Google Site and a Blogger blog, but keep in mind that each site's content needs to be different — and kept up regularly.

Setting up your blog is a similar process to setting up sites, but Blogger has a much more flexible design format. You can make yours look almost any way you want (and you needn't know *any* HTML).

A great example of using Blogger to promote sales is from eBay seller sweet*cherry*pops who sells vintage lingerie on eBay. (Find out more about sweet*cherry*pops in Chapter 18). Her Blogger blog, `sweetcherry vintagelingerie.blogspot.com`, has excellent content for fans of vintage lingerie:

- ✔ Dating Your Vintage Lingerie Garment
- ✔ Vintage Lingerie Labels
- ✔ Vanity Fair Lingerie Source Guide
- ✔ Vintage Lingerie Selling and Buying

Plus she publishes an RSS feed of her eBay listings in a sidebar on the side of her text (see Figure 8-3).

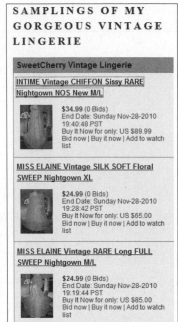

Figure 8-3:
An eBay
RSS feed on
the Sweet
Cherry
Vintage
blog.

The display of the RSS feed is updated based on how often you have set your reader to retrieve data from eBay. Usually new item information crops up every 30 minutes.

Making fans on Facebook

If you're not on Facebook, I hope you will consider joining. Lots of folks are on Facebook for personal and business reasons. And yes, Facebook will allow you to put up a page for your business. It's a good place to send customers to leave comments and reach out to you on a personal basis.

Many small businesses limit their business presence on Facebook to a personal profile. Tidy, I suppose, but they're shutting themselves out from branding and promotion opportunities available on a business page.

Before you can have a business page, you must first have a personal page. Setting up your personal page will familiarize you with how Facebook works — if you don't know already. If you need a little help, I recommend my book *Facebook and Twitter For Seniors For Dummies*. It's a useful, to-the-point book that will get you through the basics, whether you are a senior or not. (But it is in large print.)

Once you've set up your personal page, start another for your business. I have a business page for readers of my books at `www.facebook.com/MarshaCollierFanPage`. On that page, I've installed two important features:

✔ **Welcome page:** When someone new comes to my business page, I want them to feel welcome and not barraged by a bunch of ads. You may see many business pages set up with ads, but the trends in social media are to apply a more personal slant to your business. Figure 8-4 shows my welcome page that was built with an app from hy.ly, which you can find at `www.facebook.com/HylyWelcomeApp`.

✔ **eBay listings:** On my business page, I post my eBay listings with a Facebook app called eBay Items. It pulls your listings directly from eBay and posts them to a separate tab on your Facebook page, as in Figure 8-5. You can find this high-rated app at `apps.facebook.com/ebay items`.

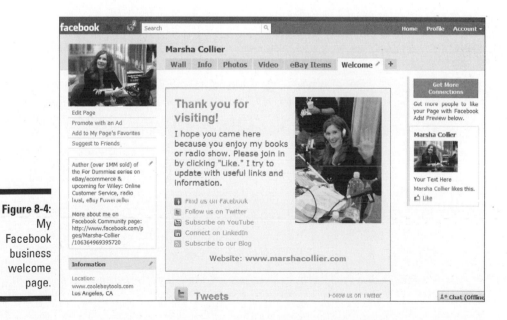

Figure 8-4: My Facebook business welcome page.

Figure 8-5:
My eBay
listings
stealthily
inserted
into my
Facebook
fan page.

Please join me on my Facebook page. I post tips and relevant news about eBay there regularly.

Marketing on Twitter

Lots of people have Twitter accounts and use these accounts to market their eBay sales. There is a trick to this — content. Just as your blog must have content for people to read, so your popularity on Twitter will be based on the content you put there and how engaged with it your visitors are.

A word to the wise: Talk about things that are relevant to you and your business; no one just wants to read a bunch of advertising messages. Your plans on Twitter are to engage and befriend — as well as sell.

Join Twitter and find other eBay sellers through sites like wefollow.com and see whose approach seems to be working. Don't waste your money on any magic marketing programs. Twitter is simple to navigate.

Twitter is one the fastest-growing social media on the Internet. Take a look at my Twitter account twitter.com/MarshaCollier and join me. It's a lot of fun.

Make extra money through the eBay Partner Network

As long as you want to promote your eBay listings elsewhere on the Internet, why not get paid when someone follows your links and buys? In Web-speak, this is called an Affiliate Network — and eBay wants you to join. After you have your Web site or blog set up, go to www.ebaypartnernetwork.com and apply for membership. According to the rules, before you apply, you must fulfill the following requirements:

✔ You own and operate the Web site for which you are applying to promote eBay.

✔ The Web site is functioning, relevant for promoting eBay, and has unique or value-added content or functionality that will drive incremental purchases on eBay.

✔ You are in compliance with the eBay Partner Network Agreement and Code of Conduct.

✔ You have a working phone number and a valid PayPal account or bank account that can receive direct deposits — you will need this payment information during the application process.

eBay offers tools, widgets, and links to carry your affiliate information — even in an RSS feed! Be sure to read all the current legalese before you apply and be sure you agree to all the terms and conditions.

Paying for Your Web Space

If you've been on the Internet for any length of time, daily spam has bombarded you with hosting offers. A *Web-hosting* company houses your Web site code and electronically doles out your pages and images to Web page visitors.

If you take advantage of PayPal's free Pay Now buttons or Shopping Cart, you can turn a basic-level hosted site into a full-on e-commerce store without paying additional fees to your hosting company. The PayPal tools are easy to insert into your pages with a snippet of code provided by PayPal.

Before deciding to spend good money on a Web-hosting company, check it out thoroughly. Go to that company's site to find a list of features they offer. If you still have questions after perusing the Web site, look for a toll-free number to call. You won't find any feedback ratings (as you'd find on eBay), but the following are a few questions to ask — don't hang up until you're satisfied with the answers:

✔ **How long have they been in business?** You don't want a Web host that has been in business only a few months and operates out of somebody's basement. Deal with folks who've been around the Internet for a while and know what they're doing. Is the company's Web site professional-looking? Or does it look like your neighbor's kid designed it? Does the company look like it has enough money to stay in business? You wouldn't want your Web host disappearing mysteriously with your money.

✔ **Who are some of their other clients?** Poke around to see whether you can find links to sites of other clients. Take a look at who else is doing business with them and analyze the sites. Visit several of their client sites. Do the pages and links come up quickly? Do all the images appear in a timely manner? Web sites that load quickly are a good sign.

✔ **What is their downtime-to-uptime ratio?** Does the Web host guarantee *uptime* (the span of time its servers stay operational without going down and denying access to your site)? Expecting a 99-percent-uptime guarantee is not unreasonable; you're open for business — and your Web host needs to keep it that way.

✔ **How much Web space do you get for your money?** Microsoft Network (MSN) Internet access service gives you 30 MB for free; you'd better be getting a whole lot more if you're paying for it!

✔ **What's their data-transfer limit?** *Data transfer* is a measurement of how many bytes are transferred from your site on the server to the Internet. Each hit to your site transfers a certain number of bytes (usually measured in thousands or millions; that is, kilobytes or megabytes) from your host's servers to the viewer's computer.

✔ **Do they offer toll-free technical support?** When something goes wrong with your Web site, you need it fixed immediately. You must be able to reach tech support quickly without hanging around on the phone for hours. Does the Web host have a technical support area on its Web site where you can troubleshoot your own problems (in the middle of the night)?

Whenever you're deciding on any kind of provider for your business, take a moment to call the prospect's tech-support team with a question about the services. Take note of how long you were on hold and how courteous the tech was. Before plunking down your hard-earned money, you should be sure that the provider's customer service claims aren't merely that — just claims.

✔ **What's the policy on shopping carts?** In time, you're probably going to need a shopping cart interface on your site. Does your provider charge extra for that? If so, how much? In the beginning, a convenient and professional-looking way to sell items on your site is to set up a PayPal Shopping Cart or PayPal Pay Now button. When you're running your business full time, however, a shopping cart or a way to accept credit cards is an absolute must.

✔ **What kind of statistics will you get?** Visitors who go to your Web site leave a kind of bread-crumb trail. Your host collects these statistics, so you'll be able to know which are your most and least popular pages. You can know how long people linger on each page, where they come from, and what browsers they're using. How your host supplies these stats to you is important.

✔ **Are there any hidden fees?** Is this host charging exorbitant fees for setup? Charging extra for statistics? Imposing higher charges if your bandwidth suddenly increases?

✔ **How often will the Web host back up your site?** No matter how redundant a host's servers are, a disaster may strike; you need to know that your Web site won't vaporize. *Redundancy* is the safety net for your site. You may be interested in how many power backups a company has for the main system. Perhaps it has generators (more than one is good) and more.

Why learn HTML when Web page editors can do it for you?

If you need some help designing those first pages (I *never* became proficient in HTML and still depend somewhat on software to design my site), try looking for inexpensive HTML Web software. I just checked eBay and searched *Web design* in the Software category. Plenty of inexpensive software is available. The key is to find one that includes a graphical (what-you-see-is-what-you-get, or WYSIWYG) interface that allows you to preview your pages as you design them. Some have predesigned templates.

Then again, the longer you're on the Internet and the more you study, the more you'll learn about HTML. It's often just easier to type out HTML code yourself once you get the hang of it. That's why Patti Louise Ruby and I wrote *eBay Listings That Sell For Dummies*. Only two subjects are covered in the book: HTML and photography for your online business. (Patti covered HTML, and I covered the photography portion.) It also has several HTML templates that you might like to use as your own.

What's in a Web Site Name: Naming Your Baby

What to name the baby, er, Web site? It's almost as much of a dilemma as deciding on your eBay user ID or eBay Store name. If you don't have an existing company name that you want to use, why not use the same name as your eBay Store? (Check out Chapter 5 for details about eBay Stores.) Lock it up now so you can keep your brand forever.

Name your site with a name that identifies what you do, what you sell, or who you are. And be sure you like it because once it's yours and you begin operating under it and establishing a reputation, it'll be with you 20 years from now when you're still selling online! (I know, it should only happen!)

Before you attempt to register a name, you should check to be sure it isn't anyone else's trademark. To search an updated list of registered U.S. trademarks, go to the following site and use the electronic trademark-search system: www.trademarksearchforfree.com.

Registering Your Domain Name (Before Someone Else Takes It)

Talk about your junk e-mail. I get daily e-mails advising me to *Lose 40 pounds in 40 days, Accept credit cards now,* and of course *REGISTER MY NAME NOW!* The last scam seems to be geared to obtaining my e-mail address for other junk mail lists rather than trying to help me register my Web site. Choosing a *registrar* (the company that handles the registering of your site name) is as important as choosing the right Web host. You must remember that the Internet is still a little like the Wild West, and that the cyber equivalent of the James Gang might be waiting to relieve you of your hard-earned cash. One of the ways to protect yourself is to understand how the registry works (knowledge *is* power), so read on.

In October 1998, U.S. government officials decided to expand the domain-registration business by breaking up the Network Solutions site (previously the only place that you could register your Web site). This opened up the Web to all kinds of people selling domain names.

Domain parking

Suppose you've come up with a brilliant name for your site and you get really big and famous. Then someone else uses your Web site's name but registers it as a .net — while yours is a .com. To avoid this situation, when you're ready to register your site, make sure you register *both* domains (.com and .net) and park them with your registrar. For example, www.ebay.net and ebay org are registered to (guess who?) ebay.com. You can check the owner of any domain name at any of the Web-hosting or registrar sites.

Before you decide on a registrar for your domain name, take a minute to see whether the registrar is accredited by the Internet Corporation for Assigned Names and Numbers (ICANN) — the international governing body for domain names) or is reselling for an official ICANN-accredited registrar. (You'll have to ask who they register with.) The Accredited Registrar Directory is updated constantly, so check the following URL for the most recent list: www.internic.com/regist.html.

You'll usually get a substantial discount from the more expensive registrars when you register your domain name for multiple years — a good idea if you plan on staying in business. Also, if you register your name through your hosting service, you might be able to cut the price in half! The only drawback is that your prepaid registration might go out the window if you choose to change hosting companies.

Making your personal information private

ICANN requires every registrar to maintain a publicly accessible WHOIS database that displays all contact information for all domain names registered. Interested parties (or fraudsters) can find out the name, street address, e-mail address, and phone number of the owner of the site by running a *whois* search on the domain name. You can run a whois search by going to www.whois.net and typing the domain name in question.

This information can be useful to spammers who spoof your e-mail address as their return address to cloak their identity, identity thieves, stalkers, and just about anyone up to no good. To see the difference between private and public registrations, run a *whois* search on my Web site, www.coolebaytools.com, and on www.yahoo.com.

Registrars such as Network Solutions offer private registration for an additional $9 a year. Check to see whether your registrar offers this service and how much they charge.

If you're registering a new domain name but already have a site set up with your ISP, you need a feature called *URL forwarding*. This feature directs any hits to your new domain name from your existing long URL address. Some registrars offer this service, but watch out for hidden surprises, such as a free offer of the service, which means they will probably smack a big fat banner at the bottom of your home page. Your registrar should also have some available tech support. Trying to troubleshoot domain name system (DNS) issues is a job for those who know what they're doing! Remember, sometimes you get what you pay for.

Marketing Your Web Site (More Visitors = More Business)

After you set up your Web site, it's time to let the world know about it. Having spent many years in the advertising business, I can spot businesses that *want* to fail. They open their doors and expect the world to beat a path to them and make them rich. This doesn't happen — ever.

You must take an active approach to letting the world in on the goodies you have for sale. This means spending a good deal of time promoting your site by running banner ads and getting your URL into a search engine. There are no shortcuts.

About a trillion people out there want to take your money for advertising your Web site. As with all transactions regarding your Web site, knowing who you're dealing with is absolutely vital. If you want to run your banner on someone else's site, don't spend money; ask to do an exchange. The more advertising you can get for free, the better. If you decide that you want to pay for advertising, I recommend that you wait until *after* you've made a profit selling merchandise from your site.

A simple link to your Web site from your eBay About Me page will draw people to your site initially. You'll be pleasantly surprised.

Getting your URL into a search engine

For people to find your site (and what you're selling), they must be able to locate you. A popular way that people do this is by using a search engine to hunt up things they're interested in. So you should submit your site to search engines. Go to the search engines that interest you and look for a link or a help area that will enable you to submit your site. Be sure to follow any specific instructions on the site; some may limit the number of keywords and the characters allowed in your description.

To submit your URL to search engines, you need to do a little work. (Nothing is easy, is it?) Write down 25 to 50 words or phrases that describe your Web site; these are your *keywords*. Now, using as many of the words you came up with, write a description of your site. With the remaining words, create a list of keywords, separating each word or short phrase by a comma. You can use these keywords to add metatags to the header in your HTML document for your home page. *Metatags* are identifiers used by search engine *spiders,* robots that troll the Internet looking for new sites to classify on search engines. Metatags look like this:

```
<META NAME = "insert your keywords here separated by
        commas" CONTENT = "short description of your
        site">
```

If you have a problem coming up with metatags, check out the free metatag generator at www.metataggenerator.org.

Google

Google crawls the Internet regularly with its spider, Googlebot, looking for new sites to index on Google Search. If Googlebot has missed your site, go to the following site and let Google know that your site is ready for listing: www.google.com/addurl.html. Google doesn't guarantee that your site will be listed, but the process takes less than a minute. What could it hurt?

Yahoo!

Yahoo! is one of the more difficult sites to list with, although you *can* get a free listing if you fill out all the forms correctly and wait six to eight weeks. Instructions for the free listing are at http://search.yahoo.com/info/submit.html.

You'll hear a lot about *search engine optimization (SEO)* when getting your Web site set up. This basically means that you want to use the right keywords in your metatags to get the spiders to see your site.

Paid search advertising

Paid search advertising helps you get visitors to your site. When you go to a search engine, you'll see several searches on the right side of the page (Google) or on the top of the search results (Yahoo!); these are the paid listings that match your search. Each time you click one of these links, the site owners pay a fee for directing a new visitor to their site.

The two major players in the field are Google Adwords (adwords.com) and Yahoo! (smallbusiness.yahoo.com/marketing/).

In my book, *eBay Business All-In-One for Dummies,* I go into far more detail on how to take advantage of these services.

Part III

Business Is Business — Time to Get Serious

The 5th Wave   By Rich Tennant

"Come on Walt — we need a shot of the product to bring in more bids."

In this part . . .

Let's delve into the dollars and sense of your eBay business. In this part, I discuss automating your business by using online and offline tools, sprucing up your listings, setting up your home photo studio, and handling shipping (the bane of most businesses). I also give you the lowdown on two other important aspects of your business: working with customers and collecting payments.

Chapter 9

Software Built for Online Auctions

*N*ow that eBay has become a world marketplace, a single-page auction or item listing is becoming an increasingly valuable piece of real estate. Millions of potential buyers view your sale — and the more auctions and fixed-price items you can list, the better your chance to make a good living. Time is money: You need to post your auctions quickly and accurately.

Auction posting, recordkeeping, inventory cataloging, photo managing, and statistic gathering are all tasks that you can automate. It's worth a try; after all, the more your business grows, the more confusing things can become. Automated tools can help you keep it all straight. But remember that the more tools you use, the more expense you may be adding to your business. Always keep your bottom line in mind when evaluating whether to use fee-based software and services.

In this chapter, I discuss how to automate different tasks, software you can use to automate them, and Web sites that offer services to make your daily chores considerably more bearable. After you read this chapter, you'll be well equipped to decide whether to automate your business.

Considering Tasks for Automation

You'll have to perform certain office tasks, no matter how few or how many auctions you're running. Depending on your personal business style, you may want to automate any or all of the following tasks. You may choose to use a single program, a manual method, or some features from one program and some from others. For those who aren't ready for the automated plunge, I offer alternatives. Where appropriate, I insert references guiding you to where in this book or on the Web you can find more information about the automated services I discuss.

Setting up images for automatic FTP upload

You have several ways to store the images in your auctions. If you're using an auction-management service or software (such as Auctiva.com or Vendio, both of which I discuss later in this chapter), an *uploader* is usually included as a part of the software. Many online services merely fetch the photos from your hard drive without the need for additional File Transfer Protocol (FTP) image-uploading software.

With this format, you merely click the Browse button to access the Open File window, and then find the location of the images on your hard drive. When you've located the images that you want to upload (one per line), click the Upload button and the images will be on their way to the service's servers.

If you choose to keep images on your own Web site (which makes the images available for your Web site, too), you'll have to use some sort of FTP software. You probably aren't using close to the total space that your hosting service allots for your Web site, which leaves plenty of room to store a separate folder of eBay images.

The Mozilla Firefox Internet browser uses a free FTP add-on called FireFTP. Go to `https://addons.mozilla.org/en-US/firefox/addon/684/` and download the app. After you install it, go to the Tools drop-down menu at the top of the Firefox window and click FireFTP. It's a straightforward FTP software program that should be part of your auction arsenal, even if you use a service or other software. You can download a free version of Firefox at `www.mozilla.com/en-US/firefox`.

Sorting auction e-mail

A vital function of any auction software or system is to give you a way to customize and send e-mails to your winners. Many sellers use the default letters in these programs, which tend to be a bit — no, incredibly — impersonal and uncaring. (To see some examples of customer-friendly e-mails and tips on drafting your own, head to Chapter 12.) You must decide whether you want the program to receive e-mail as well.

Most computer-resident auction-management programs have their own built-in e-mail software as part of the program. When you download your winner information from eBay, the program automatically generates invoices and congratulatory e-mails.

How you handle your auction-related e-mail is a personal choice. Although
I currently use eBay's Selling Manager Pro to send auction-related e-mails,
I receive auction e-mail through Outlook, using a separate folder titled
Auctions that contains subfolders for eBay Buy and eBay Sell.

Automating end-of-auction e-mail

you want to set up e-mails to be sent automatically after an auction ends,
must use a software application to do so. (I use Selling Manager Pro.)
software should download your final auction results, generate the e-mail,
et you preview the e-mail before sending it out. Many online sites that
ss later in this chapter (see the section "Online auction-management
send out winner confirmation e-mails automatically when an auction
be sure that you set your preferences to Preview the e-mail before
if you want to use this option.

g inventory

werSellers depend on the old clipboard or notebook method —
ms as they sell them. If that works for you, great. Others prefer
spreadsheet to keep track of inventory.

on-management packages that I detail later in this chapter
Auction-management software") handle inventory for you.
m from inventory automatically when you launch an auc-
ice of handling inventory directly on your hard drive or
ry online with a service that's accessible from any com-
re.

n my desktop through QuickBooks. When I buy mer-
t the bill to QuickBooks, it puts the merchandise into
When I input my sale, it deducts the items sold from
rint a status report whenever I want to see how
have to order.

Generating HTML

Fancy auctions are nice, but fancy doesn't make the item sell any better.
Competitive pricing and low shipping rates work in your favor — especially
with eBay's Compare Items feature in Search. Also, a clean listing with only

BAMA THEATRE

BAMA ART HOUSE
FILM SERIES
SUMMER 2014

June 10
A Night in Old Mexico
June 17
Only Lovers Left Alive*
June 24
Joe
July 1
Alan Partridge
July 8
Under the Skin*
July 15
Fading Gigolo

bamatheatre.org

*Sponsored by
Left Hand Soap Company

Screenings:
Tuesdays at 7:30 p.m.
Admission:
Discount Punchcard Tickets: $50
General:
$7 gen, $6 sr & stu and
$5 AC members

as many photos as necessary goes a long way to sell your product. Some software and services offer a large selection of templates to gussy up your auctions. But you must think of your customers; many of them are still logging on with dial-up connections, which are notoriously slow. The use of simple HTML doesn't slow the loading of your page, but the addition of miscellaneous images (decorative backgrounds and animations) definitely makes viewing your auction a chore for those dialing up. And forget the background music — that *really* slows things down!

Don't fret; you can make do by repeatedly incorporating two or three simple HTML templates, cutting and pasting new text as necessary. Most auction-management programs offer you several choices of templates. I recommend that you stick with a couple that are similar; that gives a standardized look to your listings, the way major companies give a standardized look to their advertising and identity. Your customers will get used to the look of your auctions and feel comfortable each time they open one.

One-click relisting and selling similar items

Using auction software or an auction service speeds up the process of posting or relisting items. After you input your inventory into the software, posting or relisting your auctions is a mouse click away. All the auction-management software packages that I detail later in this chapter include this feature.

Inserting your hosted pictures into your description

An important line of HTML code that everyone seems to forget is the one that inserts a picture into your auction description. On the Sell Your Item page, click the tab to view in HTML mode, and insert the following line below where you'd like your image to appear in your description:

Be sure to substitute your own server and image name. If you want to put one picture on top of another, just type <P> between the lines of code — repeat the HTML line with a different image name for each image that you want to display.

```
<img src="http://www.
    yourserver.com/imagename.
    jpg" />
```

TIP

If you buy your items in bulk, you might want to take advantage of eBay's free relisting tool. By clicking the Sell a Similar Item link (shown in Figure 9-1) on any ended listing, you can relist your items automatically. Sell a Similar Item starts the listing as new, so if your item doesn't sell, you can avail yourself of the Relist feature. This way, if the item sells the second time, your listing (insertion) fees for the first listing will be credited.

Paid with PayPal on Oct 18, 2010. | Leave feedback

- Print shipping label
- View order details
- View PayPal transaction
- View purchased item
- Contact buyer
- Sell a similar item
- Relist
- Unmark as shipped
- Unmark as payment received

Listing info

High bidder ID: jmc061789 (3) 0%
Duration: 7 days
Start time: Oct 18, 2010 19:41:11 PDT
Start price: $99.00

NEW Apple iPod Touch 3rd Generation 8 GB MC086LL/A
★★★★★ 309 product reviews

Item condition: New
Ended: Oct 18, 2010 20:10:41 PDT
Bid history: 1 bid

Sold For: **US $179.00**
Add to list

Shipping: **FREE shipping** Expedited Shipping |
See all details
Delivery: Estimated within 3-5 business days

Top-rated seller
marsha_c (7262 ★) me
100% Positive feedback
✔ Consistently receives highest buyers' ratings
✔ Ships items quickly
✔ Has earned a track record of excellent service
Save this seller
See other items
Visit store: Marsha Collier's Fabulous Finds

Other item info
Item number: 350405501565

Figure 9-1: When a listing is over, the Sell a Similar Item link appears at the top of the page.

Although eBay says that Sell a Similar Item is for relisting items, it also works when you're listing a duplicate of an item that has sold successfully. The only difference is that you aren't credited for the unsold item's listing fee.

Scheduling your listings for bulk upload

If you want to schedule the unattended launch of your auctions without incurring eBay's 10-cent fee, you must use an online management service (check out the "Online auction-management sites" section, later in this chapter). If you can be at your computer to send your auctions to eBay singly or in bulk, you can use the Turbo Lister application, which eBay offers at no charge. (For details, see the "Turbo Lister" section, later in the chapter.)

Researching your statistics

There are so many questions when you're selling on eBay. What is the best time to end my auction? What day should I start my listing? Is it better to run a five-day or a seven-day auction? Now an online service can help you separate the rumors from the facts.

Lots of eBay "experts" out there will give you hard-and-fast rules to guarantee success with your listings. It's a lot of bunk. Every category and every type of item may draw shoppers at different times of the day and different days of the week. The best experts are those who are selling every day on eBay, day in and day out. They are usually PowerSellers and do their own research for their listings. They don't have the time to spout off and give you secrets. I'm a regular seller on eBay (a PowerSeller. too), and I've noticed distinct variations in my sales through a fantastic online service called Sellebrity Analytics. It's really one of a kind.

Sellebrity tracks your listings automatically. The site gives you loads of information about your visitors without violating anyone's privacy. Here are some of the key features:

- ✔ Track visitors with emphasis on geography and click patterns
- ✔ The date and time the visitor arrived at your auction, and what city, state, and country your visitor is from
- ✔ Use real-time SPY to watch your sales occur in Real Time
- ✔ Widgets for your Web site or blog

You get all this information and a free one-page eBay item lister. Sellebrity offers a 30-day free trial at `http://marsha.sellebrity.com/`. After that, services start at $4.99 a month.

To end an old wives' tale about what days and times your listings get the highest hits, Figure 9-2 shows you some charts from my Sellebrity account, showing how many visits my listings got each day. Verrry interesting.

Figure 9-2: Seems like my fixed-price sales go all over the lot with no pattern to sales.

Automating other tasks

That's not all! You can automate a few more tasks. Having so many options is like being in a candy store: You may want it all, but that might not be good for you. For example, if you use online postage, you may not want to print your labels because that would be doubling your work. Take a serious look at the options you're offered and see whether they fit into your particular work style.

Checking out

When someone wins or buys an item, eBay's checkout integrates directly with PayPal — and will also indicate your other preferred forms of payment. If you're closing less than 100 auctions a day, that's all you need. eBay and PayPal will also send an e-mail to you and the buyer so you can arrange for payment.

Some online auction-management services offer your own private checkout area, which will cost you a percentage of your sale, so you must decide whether your business warrants this option. A personalized winner's notification e-mail can easily contain a link to your PayPal payment area, making a checkout service unnecessary.

Printing shipping labels

Printing shipping labels without printing postage can be the beginning of a laborious two-step process. Two companies, Endicia.com and Stamps.com, print your labels and postage all in one step. (Endicia's software even sends the tracking numbers directly to eBay). Check out Chapter 17 for information on how this works.

Some sites print your winners' address labels without postage. That works well if you don't mind carrying your packages to the post office for postage. (Why would you do that? A burning need to stand in line, I guess!)

Tracking buyer information

Keeping track of your winners isn't rocket science. You can do it in an Excel spreadsheet by downloading the information from PayPal. If you choose to have an online management service do this for you, be sure that you can download the information to *your* computer (in case you and the online service part ways some day).

Generating customized reports

Sales reports, ledgers, and tax information are all important reports that you should have in your business. Online services and software supply different flavors of these reports.

PayPal allows you to download your sales data in a format that's compatible with QuickBooks, a highly respected and popular bookkeeping program. You can also choose to download your data to an Excel spreadsheet. PayPal reports are chock-full of intensely detailed information about your sales and deposits. Putting this information in a standard accounting software program on a regular basis makes your year-end calculations easier to bear. (In Chapter 16, I detail what else you might need for this task.)

Submitting feedback

If you're running a lot of auctions, leaving feedback can be a chore. One solution is to automate the submission of feedback through an online service or software. But timing the automation of this task can be tricky.

Don't leave feedback for an eBay transaction until *after* you've heard from the buyer that the purchase is satisfactory. Leaving positive feedback immediately after you've received payment from the buyer is too soon. After you receive an e-mail assuring you that the customer is satisfied, leaving feedback manually by going to the feedback forum (or the item page) can be just as easy as — if not easier than — bulk-loading your feedback. The Selling Manager Pro program on eBay has a setting that will post positive feedback for a buyer automatically.

Managing Your Business with Online Resources and Software

If you searched the Internet for auction-management services and software, you'd come up with a bunch. For simplicity's sake, I've chosen to examine just a few of these services in this chapter. After speaking to many sellers, I've found online services that offer uptime reliability (uptime is key here; you don't want the server that holds your photos going down or mislaunching your auctions) and software that's continually updated to match the ongoing changes in eBay.

Using a site or software to run your auctions takes practice, so I suggest that you try any that appeal to you and that offer free preview trials. Along with the descriptions of these different applications, I include a link so you can check them out further. Table 9-1 compares the costs of many auction-management and online services.

Table 9-1	Cost Comparisons for Auction-Management Services and Software
Site Services or Software	**Entry-Level Cost**
AAASeller.com	$9.95/month
Auction Wizard 2000 (`auctionwizard2000.com`)	$100.00 year
Auctiva	$2.95 /month
eBay Blackthorne Basic	$9.99/month
eBay Blackthorne Pro	$24.99/month
eBay's Selling Manager	Free
eBay's Selling Manager Pro	$15.99/month; free to Premium Store owners
InkFrog.com	$9.95/month
Vendio	$10.00 month + Final Value fee (FVF)

Some software and services work on a monthly fee, whereas others work on a one-time–purchase fee. For a one-time–purchase software application to truly benefit you, it *must* have the reputation for updating its software each time eBay makes a change in its system. The programs I discuss in this chapter have been upgraded continually to date.

Most services have a free trial period. Be sure that you don't spend a bunch of your precious time inputting your entire inventory, only to discover you don't like the way the service works. Instead, input a few items to give the service a whirl.

Online auction-management sites

Auction-management Web sites handle almost everything, from inventory management to label printing. Some sellers prefer online (or hosted) management sites because you can access your information from any computer. You might use every feature a site offers, or you might choose a bit from column A and a bit from column B and perform the more personalized tasks manually. Read on to determine what service might best suit your needs.

Although quite a few excellent online services for automating sales are available, I have room here to show you only a few. Remember that the whole time you're using an online service, your information resides on a server out there in cyberspace; if you're a control freak, it may be a bit much to bear. Many services are similar in format, so in the following sections I point out some of the highlights of a few representative systems.

When selecting a service, look for a logo or text indicating that the service is an eBay Certified Developer, Preferred Solution Provider, or API licensee. These people have first access to eBay's system changes and can implement them immediately. Note that these logos do not guarantee the quality of their service — only that they subscribe to eBay for the logo and use of the API.

Auctiva

If you are new on eBay and you'd like to try a little automation to get you started, Auctiva is your entry-level choice. Auctiva has been serving eBay sellers since my first edition of *eBay For Dummies* in 1999. They offer some very good free tools that you can try to get an idea of whether you want to use their service. Now, I always say you get what you pay for, but with Auctiva you get a bit more than that; you get free image hosting and scrolling galleries.

Auctiva offers online item-listing software and image hosting for eBay sellers. The easy-to-use site guides you through the process: creating auction listings, posting them on eBay, communicating with buyers, collecting payments, organizing shipments, keeping records of sales, marketing your listings, and much more.

Their basic plan, at $2.95, gives you 15 listings a month from their site. It features 500MB Image Hosting, a Scrolling Gallery on your eBay listings, and an efficient, one-page listing form with design templates.

Here are some of the site's features:

- **A one-page listing tool:** You can create your professional-looking listings with a complete one-page listing tool — and if you like variety, you can choose from 1,500 template options.

- **Image hosting:** Auctiva enables you to upload hundreds of images at a time, and you can keep your account organized by managing your images within Auctiva's online folder structure.

- **Auctiva Scrolling Gallery:** You may have notice that at the bottom of many listings you see on eBay, there is a scrolling gallery showing other items for sale by the seller. This is an excellent tool for selling even more merchandise.

✔ **Profiles:** After you generate your profile information, your Auctiva profile is set to appear automatically in all your listings by default.

For these features and more, visit the Auctiva Web site at www.auctiva.com.

Vendio

Vendio was founded in 1999 by a couple of eBay sellers looking for a new way to organize their listings. In 2010, they were acquired by Chinese e-commerce giant Alibaba. Their market is small-to-medium-size merchants, for whom they offer an integrated solution to manage their sales. They integrate with Amazon.com, eBay, Google, Shopzilla, and more to give sellers a wider market for their sales. Each year, more than 80,000 merchants use Vendio's award-winning multichannel platform and applications to sell nearly $2 billion in merchandise.

Vendio offers users a free Vendio store. The Vendio platform lets you manage items, orders, buyer communications, and your very own store all through one integrated Platform. Some of the features of a Vendio store:

✔ More than 50 professionally designed store templates

✔ One hundred percent customizable templates (HTML, XML, CSS)

✔ Template code that you can edit in the browser

✔ What-you-see-is-what-you-get (WYSIWYG) drag-and-drop design editor

✔ Pre-built SEO features (for editing metadata, titles, keywords, and descriptions)

✔ Selling items on Facebook

✔ Stores that are compatible with the iPhone

✔ Acceptance of Google Checkout, Authorize.net, and Payflo Pro

✔ Acceptance of offline payments (checks, money orders)

Aside from the free store, Vendio's eBay integration is deep, and its offerings are kind of like a Chinese restaurant menu: You can use (and pay for) only what you need:

✔ **Buyer appreciation:** This automates the process of personalized customer communication. Vendio will send your customers a thank-you e-mail the first time they bid or buy. Best of all? This service is free.

✔ **Counters:** This free service from Vendio will let you see the number of visitors to your item, as well the total number of bids. Er, by the way, this is also free.

✔ **Image hosting:** Store your images for use in your Vendio store or Vendio Marketplace listings on their site.

✔ **Research:** Study what's going on in the market. See what's selling. This service keeps you up with what the competition is doing. Feature analysis and more is available for $20 a month.

✔ **Free Gallery Pro:** You can get a great free service from Vendio: its Gallery Pro. This service gives you a small bit of text that you add to your listings that displays a scrolling gallery of your items for sale when someone views one of your listings.

To use Vendio's eBay integration, you pay $10 a month, plus a FVF when your items sell, as shown in Table 9-2.

Table 9-2	Vendio Final Fees
Monthly Sales Revenue	*Successful Listing Fee*
Your first $1,000	1.95% of sales
$1,000.01 to $2,500	1.75% of sales
$2,500.01 to $5,000	1.5% of sales
$5,000.01 to $25,000	1.2% of sales
$25,000.01 and above	1% of sales

Auction-management software

Many sellers prefer to run their auction businesses from their own hard drives. I happen to like being able to refer to my old auctions on my backups. Luckily, some valuable auction software programs are available to perform all the same tasks you get from the online services.

To those who would rather have the software at home, there are some solid choices other than the ones I examine in the next section. There are always new programs available — but the ones I mention here are time-tested.

You can accomplish almost all the same tasks on your own computer as you can with online services — except online auction checkout. You can always use eBay's checkout as your final stop or include a link in your end-of-auction e-mails. And if you want, you can set up a checkout page on your own Web site that gathers your auction information.

eBay's Selling Manager

eBay replaced the All Selling tab of your My eBay page with Selling Manager, which displays a summary of your current transactions. Many sellers (even some PowerSellers) rely on Selling Manager to handle their eBay management chores.

From Selling Manager, you can

✔ **View listing status:** You can see which sales activities you've completed and what you still have to do.

✔ **Send custom e-mail and post feedback:** Customize your e-mail templates and set up stored feedback comments to help you run through the post-sales process quickly.

✔ **Relist in bulk:** Relist multiple sold and unsold listings at once.

✔ **Maintain sales records:** See individual sales records for every transaction, including a history of the transaction status.

✔ **Print invoices and shipping labels:** Print labels and invoices directly from sales records.

✔ **Download sales history:** Export your sales records to keep files on your computer.

✔ **Keep track of nonpaying bidder (NPB) and FVF:** File nonpaying bidder alerts and Final Value fee requests.

There is no fee for using Selling Manager. It also offers a Pro version that incorporates inventory management and more for $15.99 a month (free to Premium Store subscribers). Many sellers (myself included) love the Pro version. The figure shows a Pro summary page.

Most of the software packages will perform the following operations:

- Maintain inventory
- Prepare and list auctions
- Manage e-mail
- Automate feedback
- Provide HTML templates
- Track income and expenses

Auction Wizard 2000

Way back in 1999, Standing Wave Software developed a product that would handle large inventories and meet the needs of the growing eBay population. Enter Auction Wizard. In 2000, the company introduced a more robust version, Auction Wizard 2000, to meet the challenges presented by changes on eBay.

This software is a *tour de force* of auction-management programs whose pieces are integrated into one program. Aside from the processes just described, you can also

- Keep track of consignment sales by consignees, including all fees.
- Import your images; and crop, rotate, or resize them before uploading.
- Upload your pictures with built-in FTP software while you're working on your auctions, eliminating the need for another piece of auction-business software.

The program interface is straightforward. I always plunge into new programs without reading the instructions, and I was able to use this program right off the bat. I'm still not an expert, but that's probably because Auction Wizard 2000 has so many features that I haven't had the time to study them all.

To begin using the software, simply download your current eBay auctions directly into the program. When your auctions close, send customized e-mails (the program fills in the auction information) and manage all your end-of-auction business. Some sellers launch their auctions using Turbo Lister (see the "Turbo Lister" section at the end of this chapter), and then retrieve them and handle the end-of-auction management with Auction Wizard 2000. For a free trial, go to the Auction Wizard site at www.auction wizard2000.com.

Blackthorne Basic and Pro

Of the two versions of Blackthorne Basic and Pro, the professional version is what you're going to need for your eBay business (but it's also the toughest to learn). Because the software is owned by eBay, it's the first to have updates for eBay's latest changes.

eBay's Blackthorne Basic is a solid listing program, offering a variety of templates. Blackthorne puts your standard shipping information and auction messages into your auctions automatically so you don't have to retype them every time. You can customize your e-mail correspondence, and Blackthorne will generate the appropriate e-mail messages after retrieving your completed auction information from the site. The program is available as a monthly subscription fee charged to your regular eBay bill.

The Pro version (which supports multiple user IDs) takes things up a notch, handling your auction listings as well as automating bulk listing and end-of-auction business. For example, the Pro version will

✔ Spell check your auction listings

✔ Schedule your auction launches for a later posting (see the following tip)

✔ Keep track of your inventory

✔ Launch items directly from stock at hand

✔ Automate bulk-feedback postings

✔ Print shipping labels

✔ Create sales reports

One of the finer points of the Pro edition is that you can schedule your auction listings for a particular time — *and* space out your auctions (within a group of items to be listed) by a set number of minutes. (You can also do this in eBay's free Turbo Lister.) This is valuable because so many bidders bid during the last few minutes of an auction, when the highest bids take place.

To check out the latest changes and upgrades, and to compare *all* of eBay's selling program versions, visit pages.ebay.com/selling_manager/comparison.html.

Turbo Lister

I like Turbo Lister because it's simple and easy to use. It has a built-in WYSIWYG HTML editor and makes my listings easy to prepare offline. When I'm ready, I just click a button and they're all listed at once. I can also stagger listings and schedule them for a later date for a fee.

Using Turbo Lister is as simple and straightforward as posting a listing using the Sell Your Item page on the eBay site. One of the benefits of Turbo Lister is that it allows you to prepare auctions while offline — and group them for launching all at once to eBay. You can also keep listings in the program for relisting in the future.

Using the program is a two-step process. First, you download the application from eBay at pages.ebay.com/turbo_lister/download.html. Next, you install Turbo Lister on your computer. What could be simpler?

Chapter 10

Dollars and Sense: Budgeting and Marketing Your Sales

. . . .

In This Chapter

▶ Marketing your listings by choosing the right category

▶ Using promotional options to your advantage

▶ Paying eBay: The lowdown on basic fees

. . . .

*Y*our entire online business is just that: a business. In every business, decisions are made regarding how much money is spent for each division of the company. Because you're the head of your company, you must make these decisions. Even if you're selling on eBay on a part-time basis, you still have to address budget concerns. When you list an item for sale on eBay, you must consider what the item will sell for, in what category to list it, and whether to add any eBay listing options. You also need to figure out whether you can afford to give free shipping or charge an average figure to cover shipping to any part of the country.

Establish a minimum percentage that you assign as your profit so that you can determine how much to spend on your advertising (marketing) budget. If your item has considerable competition from similar items in its category, you may want to add some of the options eBay offers to make folks notice it and want to buy it. The cost of these options (or advertising) needs to fit into your established budget for the particular item.

In this chapter, I give you a preview of the various options eBay offers its users, highlighting the cost of these options along the way and the pros and cons of each. I also detail the basic eBay fees. When you've finished reading this chapter, you should be well on your way to establishing a working budget and have a handle on marketing your items.

Listing Your Items

With tens of thousands of categories, finding the right place for your item can be daunting. (For more about eBay categories, see Chapter 2.) You have to apply some marketing techniques when deciding where to place your auctions to best advantage. You should always also be thinking about your budget; for example, you can list an item in two separate categories, but you have to pay double for that. Does your budget allow for it? Will the added expense really bring in more customers? Figure 10-1 shows you how eBay lists the categories where your searched items appear. It helps you hone your choice of popular category to a finer edge.

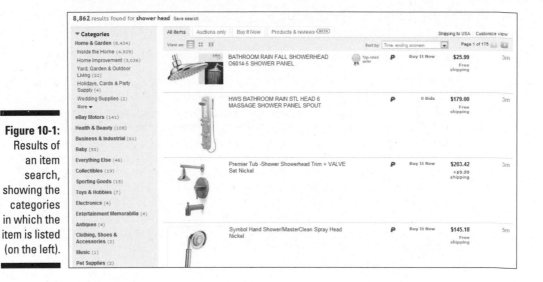

Figure 10-1:
Results of
an item
search,
showing the
categories
in which the
item is listed
(on the left).

To find where other sellers have listed items that are similar to yours, perform a completed item search for your item. In the Search box, type your item keywords. When you get the results, click the option on the left side of the page to Show Only: Completed Listings. When you get the results, indicate that you want them sorted by highest prices first by using the drop-down menu.

After you have your results, click the completed listings with the highest bids. At the top of the auction page, you'll see the listed category. You may find that your item is listed successfully in more than one category.

Check the active listings; are lots of people selling your item? If you see that you're one of 40 or 50 selling the item, you need to get creative as to where to list your item. Evaluate the item and its potential buyers. In what categories would someone shopping for your item search?

Over my eBay career, I have sold several things in "iffy" categories. My catnip cigars come to mind. I was selling these adorable seven-inch cigars filled with organic catnip and was being blown away by the zillions of listings in the *Cat Toys* category. So I got a little creative. It is a cigar, and one of eBay's popular categories is Tobacciana, so I listed it there. If someone is a cigar buff, they may be browsing that category. And perhaps they just may happen to own a cat they'd like to share a cigar with! I'm just stretching the category rules a tad. I normally would list the cigars solely in my store, but at other times (like holidays), I listed them for auction.

Suppose that you've found two perfect categories in which to list your item. eBay allows you to list an item in two categories when using the Search Categories tool, as shown in Figure 10-2, but does that mean it's the best marketing decision for your listing? That depends. When you list an item in two categories, you must pay two listing fees. Depending on the time, the season, the availability of your item, and how much you paid for it, you probably don't have the money to budget for paying double listing fees (and double any options you use). In addition, most eBay buyers (busy people that they are) use the search engine because they can find what they're looking for quickly. If they search for your item using the search engine rather than by browsing the categories, listing the item in two categories is a needless expense; list in one and let the search engine find it.

Figure 10-2:
You can list
an item
in two
categories.

Select a category	? Help

Find a matching category

Enter a UPC, ISBN, or keywords that describe your item.

ebay book   [Search]

For example: Levis 501 women's jeans

| Search categories | Browse categories | Recently used categories |

Buyers will see your listing in the category that you select.

Books
- Nonfiction
- Other
- Fiction & Literature
- Textbooks, Education

Gift Cards & Coupons
- Coupons

Everything Else
- Education & Learning > Adult & Career Education > Business > Entrepreneurship

You can change your category midauction, starting it in one category and ending it in another, as long as your listing has no bids. And at the end of an auction in which your item doesn't sell, you can use the relisting feature to run the auction again in another category.

eBay's Optional Listing Features

When you're listing an item for sale, you'll no doubt be presented with eBay's recommendations to improve your listing. This usually consists of recommending that you add one of the options that (according to eBay's research) will improve your final selling price. Sounds pretty good, doesn't it? But getting carried away with these options is easy — and can lead to spending all your profits before you earn them.

In classes taught on eBay selling, many instructors quote auction success rates for the various features, but in the real life of your business, success varies from listing to listing and category to category. If you take the boldface option and then your listing appears in a category full of boldface titles, the bold just doesn't have the punch you expected to get (and paid for). Your item would stand out more without the bold option.

You need to weigh the pros and cons in terms of how these options affect your eBay business. Will spending a little extra money enhance your item enough to justify the cost? Will you be able to make the money back in profits? You must have a good understanding of what the options are, and when and how you can use them to their fullest advantage.

For every item you put up for sale, you have to pay a minimum of two fees: an insertion fee for listing the item *and* a Final Value fee. (I discuss these two fees in the "eBay's Cut of the Action" section, later in this chapter.) Accepting credit card payments through PayPal means you must also pay a fee to them as well. Estimate your expenses from these basics before you consider spending money for advertising. When I get a new product, I put together a chart to calculate my fees *before* I list the item. I run it through once or twice with my expected sales figures to get an idea of the costs for listing the item.

I use a Web-based calculator to help me wade through the numerous options and fees that eBay charges for. Visit www.rolbe.com/ebay.htm for an easy-to-use calculator. Figure 10-3 shows you how it works estimating costs for a sample listing. The Web site also sells a great spreadsheet program that can help you figure out not only eBay fees but business markups as well.

Fees are different for sellers who have an eBay Store and those who do not.

Figure 10-3: Calculating your fees before you list your item can save you from making a serious pricing mistake.

Subtitle

You may use 55 characters for your item's title. Title search is the de facto, number-one way people search on eBay. From the statistics I've seen of my own items, 90 percent of searches were made for title only, versus title and description. But how can you make your item stand out when it shows up with hundreds of other items that look the same? Use the subtitle option! This can be a great marketing tool when you offer something special or have a little more information to give those who are searching or browsing.

When your item has something special about it or could use some extra punch, the subtitle option allows you more space to catch the eye of the prospective buyer. Take a look at my example in Figure 10-4.

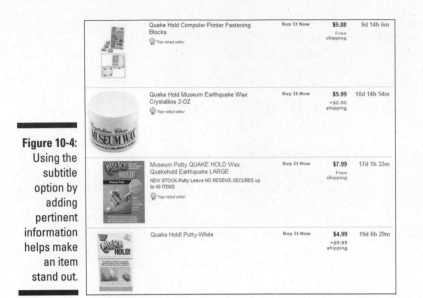

Figure 10-4:
Using the subtitle option by adding pertinent information helps make an item stand out.

Listing Designer

eBay comes up with options to fill the needs (or wants, in this case) of users. Sellers enjoy putting colorful graphics around their descriptions. It will also help you design your description, placing pictures in different places on the page. But if you have a good description (creatively done with HTML color and emphasis) plus a good picture (inserted with the HTML code I gave you), your item will draw bids just the same as if you spent $0.10 extra (per listing) for the Listing Designer option.

If you want your descriptions surrounded by graphics, make sure the graphics aren't too intensive; keep the number of them and their file size down. Otherwise the pages will load too slowly for dial-up users. Also, take a look at *eBay Listings That Sell For Dummies,* a book I wrote with eBay guru Patti Louise Ruby. It's a comprehensive book that covers eBay photography and HTML for listings. After you've set up your own templates from the easy samples in the book, you'll never have to lay out another penny for more. In Chapter 9, I show you how you can buy reasonably priced templates from savvy eBay graphics experts.

You can use a graphics template to "brand" your listings on eBay, giving them a uniform look. If you want to use a template, decide on one and make it your trademark.

eBay's special combo deals

Any restaurant that serves up a menu of tempting treats will usually offer combo deals. Surprise — so does eBay. They can be a great way to save money while combining options:

Value Pack: I use the Value Pack all the time. It's only $0.65 and combines some of eBay's best features at a bargain-basement price:

✔ Gallery Plus: When a prospective shopper mouses over your image in a search, eBay displays a larger picture, up to 400 x 400 pixels (regularly $0.35).

✔ Subtitle: Give your item some extra selling power with the extra information you put in your subtitle (regularly $0.50).

✔ Listing Designer: This can be a little iffy. Choose from one of the many colorful graphics eBay has to offer if one appeals to you. But you may have your own template, or you may just not want to use one of the kitschy graphics. That's okay, too. You don't *have* to use Listing Designer to get this deal; just leave the Listing Designer box empty when you get to that part on the Sell Your Item form (regularly $0.10).

So you actually get $0.95 worth of options for $0.65. Even if you don't use the Listing Designer, you're saving money.

Boldface option

The boldface option is probably the most-used option in the eBay stable. An auction title in boldface type stands out in a crowd, unless . . . you got it, unless it's in a category loaded with boldface auction titles. If the $2 that eBay charges for this benefit is in your auction budget, odds are it will get you a good deal more views than if you *don't* use it.

To recap your title option costs, see the "Insertion (listing) fees" section later in this chapter.

View counter

Counters have become a popular free option in the online world. Placed on your listing in the Sell Your Item form, the numeric *view counter* ticks up by one each time someone loads your page from eBay. This can add up to numbers that impress bidders (convincing them they're viewing a hot deal) or impress other sellers to run out and sell the identical item at eBay.

A counter is a terrific tool for marketing your auctions — sometimes. If you have an auction with no bids and a counter that reads a high number, newbie bidders may be dissuaded from taking a flyer and bidding on your auction. They'll think along these lines: "Gee, if that many people looked at this listing and didn't bid, something must be wrong with the item." They'll tend to doubt their own instincts as to what is and isn't a good deal. In a situation such as this, however, what might be going on is that savvy bidders are just watching your auction, waiting to bid at the last minute.

Also offered by eBay is a *hidden counter* that shields the numbers from the eyes of casual lookie-loos. The figures are available only to you, after you sign on to eBay and click the item in your My eBay page. The number of page views appears at the top of the page.

Professional counters can be more sophisticated and can give you valuable marketing data about your items. Smart counters offer a breakdown of visitors hour by hour. Others can let you know where your customers have come from and what keywords they used to find your item. The specialized type of counter that I use is Sellebrity Analytics from Sellebrity.com (see Figure 10-5 — more information on how to get it is in Chapter 9). eBay offers you a free counter, but it's not a very smart one. By the way, readers of this book can get a 30-day free trial Sellebrity Analytics by going to `analytics.sellebrity.com`.

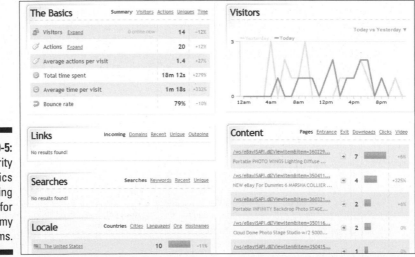

Figure 10-5: A Sellebrity Analytics marketing counter for one of my items.

Buy It Now

The Buy It Now feature, shown in Figure 10-6, has many significant benefits. If you have a target price for the item you're listing in an auction, make that your Buy It Now price. You can also use this option during frenzied holiday shopping times or with very hot items. Try posting a slightly higher than normal price and perhaps you'll get a bite, er, sale.

REMEMBER

Keep in mind, when deciding on your Buy It Now price, that eBay requires the price be at least 10 percent more than your opening bid.

Figure 10-6:
The Buy It Now feature.

The Buy It Now feature disappears when someone bids on the item or, if you've placed a reserve on the auction, when a bidder meets your reserve price.

Buy It Now adds costs to your listing on a graduated scale that's based on your selling price, as shown in Table 10-1. If your item will sell for a low price, remember my golden rule: Before paying for a feature, ask yourself whether it's in your listing budget.

Table 10-1	Buy It Now Fees
Buy It Now Price	*Auction Fee*
$0.01 to $9.99	$0.05
$10.00 to $24.99	$0.10
$25.00 to $49.99	$0.20
$50.00 or more	$0.25

eBay's Cut of the Action

Becoming complacent and blithely ignoring your eBay costs as you list items for sale is easy to do. As sellers, we easily can fall into the habit of listing and relisting without reevaluating the profitability of our final sales. As a person in business for yourself, you must always take into account outgoing costs as well as incoming profits. The cost of your initial listing is just the beginning of your advertising budget for that item; you have to factor in the cost of all the options and features you use as well. Then, when the item sells, you pay eBay an additional Final Value fee. (For fees regarding your eBay Store, check out Chapter 5.) In this section, I review the costs for listing an auction and for a fixed-price listing on eBay.

The fees I detail here aren't the end of your fees. If you use a credit card payment service such as PayPal, that service also charges you a fee. In Chapter 13, I examine the costs of the most popular credit card payment services.

Insertion (listing) fees

Your *insertion fee* is based on the highest dollar amount of two things: your minimum opening bid or the dollar amount of your reserve price. If you start your auction at $0.99 and have no reserve, the listing fee is free (for the first 100 items per month) if you don't have an eBay Store. (By the way, if you start your listing at $1.00, your fee is $0.50 — why add fees for a start price of just a penny more?) But if you start your auction at $0.99 and set an undisclosed reserve price of $50.00, your auction costs $2.00 to post. When you place a reserve on your item, you're charged an insertion fee based on the amount of the reserve — plus the reserve price charge.

Fixed-price listing fees are pretty clear-cut. If your Buy It Now price is $0.99 or higher, you pay eBay $0.50 per listing.

For a summary of eBay insertion fees, see Table 10-2. (The fees for eBay Motors are in Chapter 2.)

Table 10-2	eBay Auction Listing Fees	
Opening Bid or Reserve Price	*Insertion Fee*	*Basic Store Subscriber Insertion Fee*
$0.01 to $0.99	Free*	$0.10
$1.00 to $9.99	$0.25	$0.25
$10.00 to $24.99	$0.50	$0.50

Opening Bid or Reserve Price	Insertion Fee	Basic Store Subscriber Insertion Fee
$25.00 to $49.99	$0.75	$0.75
$50.00 to $199.99	$1.00	$1.00
$200.00 or more	$2.00	$2.00

* If you do not have an eBay Store, you may list up to 100 auction listings in a month for free as long as your starting price is between $0.01 and $0.99, and you have no reserve price. If you exceed 100 listings with this starting price per month, you will be charged a $0.10 fee per listing.

If your item doesn't sell, don't think you can get your insertion fees back. They are nonrefundable. You do have the option of relisting your unsuccessful item without being charged a second listing fee, but *only* if your item sells with the second listing. If it doesn't sell the second time, the charge for the second listing will stand. Writing a better title, starting with a lower opening bid, or adding a snappier description will help in selling the item. Maybe you should think about changing the category as well.

I recap the cost of the valuable eBay listing options in Table 10-3. Note that eBay will no doubt come up with other tasty add-ons for your listings.

Table 10-3	Listing Option Fees	
Option	**Fee: Auction or Fixed Price 3, 5, 7, 10 days**	**Fee: Fixed Price 30 days**
Subtitle	$0.50	$1.50
Bold	$2.00	$4.00
Listing Designer	$0.10	$0.30
Gallery Plus	$0.35	$1.00
Scheduled listing	$0.10	$0.10
List in two categories	Double fees	Double fees
Additional pictures	$0.15	$0.15
Picture Pack 1–6 pictures	$0.75	$0.75
Picture Pack 7–12 pictures	$1.00	$1.00

eBay Final Value fees

eBay's version of the Hollywood back-end deal is the Final Value fee. Big stars get a bonus when their movies do well at the box office; eBay gets a cut when your auction sells. After your auction or fixed-price listing ends, eBay charges the Final Value fee to your account in a matter of minutes.

Final Value fees on auctions are pretty easy to figure out. If your item doesn't sell (duh), there's no Final Value fee. If it sells, you pay eBay 9 percent of the selling price to a maximum of $50.00.

Even a rocket scientist would have trouble figuring out exactly how much eBay receives at the end of fixed-price listings. Its Final Value fees are based on the category you listed your item in, as well as how much the item sold for. To help you calculate Final Value fees, see Table 10-4.

Table 10-4	Fixed-Price Final Value Fees by Category			
If Your Item Sells for	**Electronics***	**Clothing, Shoes & Accessories; Motors, Parts & Accessories**	**Books, DVDs & Movies, Music, Video Games**	**All Other Categories**
Item not sold	No fee	No fee	No fee	No fee
$0.99 – $50.00	**8%** of the final sale price	**12%** of the final sale price	**15%** of the final sale price	**12%** of the final sale price
$50.01 – $1,000.00	**8%** of the initial $50.00, plus **5%** of the remaining final sale price balance ($50.01 to $1,000.00)	**12%** of the initial $50.00, plus **9%** of the remaining final sale price balance ($50.01 to $1,000.00)	**15%** of the initial $50.00, plus **5%** of the remaining final sale price balance ($50.01 to $1,000.00)	**12%** of the initial $50.00, plus **6%** of the remaining final sale price balance ($50.01 to $1,000.00)
$1000.01 or more	**8%** of the initial $50.00, plus **5%** of the next $50.01 to $1,000.00, plus **2%** of the remaining final sale price balance ($1,000.01 to final sale price)	**12%** of the initial $50.00, plus **9%** of the next $50.01 to $1,000.00, plus **2%** of the remaining final sale price balance ($1,000.01 to final sale price)	**15%** of the initial $50.00, plus **5%** of the next $50.01 to $1,000.00, plus **2%** of the remaining final sale price balance ($1,000.01 to final sale price)	**12%** of the initial $50.00, plus **6%** of the next $50.01 to $1,000.00, plus **2%** of the remaining final sale price balance ($1,000.01 to final sale price)

The Final Value fees for eBay Store subscribers are different when it comes to auctions. The fees are based on the final selling price. Table 10-5 lists the store subscriber's auction final fees for you.

Table 10-5	Auction Final Value Fees by Category for eBay Store Subscribers
Selling Price	**Final Value Fees**
Item not sold	No fee
$0.01 to $50.00	8.75% of the final selling price
$50.01 to $1,000.00	8.75% of the initial $50.00, plus 4% of the remaining final selling price ($50.01 to $1,000.00)
Equal to or over $1,000.01	8.75% of the initial $50.00, plus 4% of the next $50.01 to $1,000.00, plus 2% of the remaining final selling price ($1,000.01 to final price)

To avoid brain-drain, use an eBay fee calculator to check your fees before you set prices. See Chapter 9 for software that will do this for you.

Chapter 11

Setting Up Listings That Sell

· ·

In This Chapter

▶ Writing a great description

▶ Setting up a photo studio

▶ Shooting great pics

▶ Scanning your items

▶ Kicking it up a notch with imaging software

▶ Hosting your pics

▶ Finding HTML templates

· ·

Rule #1: A good photograph and a concisely written description should be the goal for all your auctions. My years of advertising and marketing experience have proven this to me repeatedly in almost every type of media. If you're trying to fetch the highest possible price for an item, keep your listings simple and professional: no dancing clowns (unless you're selling clowns), no overdone graphics, and no difficult-to-read typefaces. Less is more.

In this chapter, you find out how to write eye-catching descriptions and improve the visual elements of your listings. Once you have some solid recommendations, you can make your own decisions regarding what you want to do and how to best accomplish your goals.

Writing Winning Text

When you write descriptions for your listings, be sure that you describe your items clearly and completely. Mention everything about the article; if the item is used or damaged, be sure to describe the flaws. When you're honest up front, you'll have a happy buyer. Remember to include your terms of sale and specify the types of payment and credit cards you accept. Be sure to include appropriate shipping charges, too. Following is a checklist of some of the things to mention:

> ✔ Size, style, color (garment measurements in inches are also valuable because sizes aren't universal across brands)
>
> ✔ Condition (new, new with tags, used, gently used, well-worn)
>
> ✔ Manufacturer's name
>
> ✔ Year of manufacture (if vintage, it's always good to mention an era at least)
>
> ✔ Fabric or material
>
> ✔ Any damage to the item
>
> ✔ Special features
>
> ✔ That you've stored it in a clean, dry place (if you have)

After you list all the facts, get excited and add a little showmanship in your description. Think *infomercial!* Think *Shopping Channel!* Whoopee! These people know how to make things sound so good that you feel that you *must* have whatever item they're selling. You can do the same, if you just get those creative juices flowing. In Chapter 12, I give you some more pointers on how to write the best descriptions possible.

Outfitting Your eBay Photo Studio

Taking pictures? No problem! You have a digital camera, and you know how to use it. Just snap away and upload that picture, right? Sorry, but no. There's a good way and a bad way to take photos for eBay and, believe it or not, the professional way isn't necessarily the most expensive way.

I recommend that you set up a mini–photo studio for taking your eBay pictures. That way you won't have to clean off your kitchen counter every time you want to take pictures.

If you must use the kitchen counter or a desktop, be sure to use a solid color, inexpensive photo stage, which you can find — where else? — on eBay.

Beware of following instructions in books about digital photography. In most cases, their instructions are valid for pictures that you want to print. Online images are a horse of a different color (oooh, did I really say that?). Be sure you follow instructions that are written for Web images, such as in the steps in my *eBay Listings That Sell For Dummies*.

You need several basic things in your photo studio; the extras you should have are based on the type of merchandise you're selling. An eBay *generalist,* someone who will sell almost anything online — like me! — should have quite a few extras for taking quality photos.

What you find in this section might be more than you thought you'd need to take good pictures. But quality photographs will sell your merchandise, so you need to take this technical part of your business seriously. Of course, if you sell only one type of item, you won't need such a varied selection, but you should have the basic photo setup. Go into it slowly, spending only as much as is prudent at the time. Also check my Web site (`www.coolebay tools.com`) for more ideas.

For the best images of your item, be sure to zoom in on it. No one needs to see the background — they want to see the merchandise up close and personal. Also, when it comes to background, be sure it's all one solid (and preferably neutral) color.

Digital camera

Digital cameras are mysterious things. You may read about *megapixels* (a million pixels) and think that more is supposed to be better, but that doesn't apply to eBay applications or to Web images. Megapixels measure the image resolution that the camera is capable of recording. For online use, all you really need from a camera is 800 x 600 pixels (or at most 1024 x 600) because the majority of computer screens are incapable of taking advantage of more pixels. If you use a higher-resolution picture, all you'll do is produce a pixel-bloated picture that can take a looooong time to load online.

You don't need a million pixels, but you do need the following:

- **Quality lens:** I'm sure anyone who has worn glasses can tell the difference between good lenses and cheap ones. Really cheap cameras have really cheap plastic lenses, and the quality of the resulting picture is accordingly lousy. Your camera will be your workhorse, so be sure to buy a well-known brand from a manufacturer known for making quality products.

- **Removable media:** Taking the camera to your computer and using cables and extra software to download pictures to your hard drive is old-fashioned and annoying. Removable media eliminate this annoyance. The most popular are Secure Digital (wafer-thin), Compact Flash cards (the card comes in a plastic shell), and Sony Memory Sticks; all are no larger than a matchbook. Just remove one of these cards from your camera and insert it into your computer, if your computer has a port for it — or you can get an adapter that connects to your computer through a USB port (adapters often show up on eBay for a few dollars).

- **Tripod and tripod mount:** Have you ever had a camera hanging around your neck while you're trying to repackage some eBay merchandise that you've just photographed, and the camera is banging into everything? Or perhaps you've set down the camera for a minute (in a safe place) and then can't find it? Avoid all this by using a tripod to hold your camera. Tripods also help you avoid blurry pictures from shaking hands — and when you're shooting in macro mode, shaking comes with the territory. To use a tripod, your camera needs to have a tripod mount, which is the little screw hole that you see on the bottom of most cameras. In the following section, I give you some tips on finding the right tripod.

✔ **Macro setting capability:** If you're ever going to photograph coins, jewelry, or small detailed items, you must have a macro setting on your camera (usually symbolized by a little flower icon). This setting enables you to get in really close to items while keeping them in focus.

✔ **White balance setting:** Without getting into a long-winded discussion of measuring Kelvin and color rendering (I did this in another book), just know that good cameras have a sensor that ensures that colors are represented faithfully. It can be an automatic function of the camera, or you can select presets based on the type of light you are using: daylight, tungsten bulb, fluorescent bulb, and so on.

✔ **High optical zoom:** When you're shopping for a digital camera, you'll see optical zoom and digital zoom. Optical zoom enlarges the pictures through traditional quality lenses. The digital version pseudo-enlarges your images with a software interface within the camera. If you've ever enlarged a low-resolution photo and found that it got grainy and out of focus, you have an idea of what happens with digital zoom. The quality just isn't there.

✔ **Autofocus:** This option just makes life easier when you want to take pictures.

The bottom line here is to buy a brand-name camera. I use only a few. One is an older model Sony Cybershot DSC-H1; it's too bulky to carry around, but easy to find in a messy office. It has a 12x optical zoom with image stabilization to overcome shaky hands — available on eBay for under $100. My second is a new, very portable Canon SD 3500 IS, which I use at a low-resolution Web setting. It's got a 5x optical zoom (plus image stabilization) and can be found on eBay for under $300. Although one uses an SD card and the other a Sony Memory Stick, my notebook has ports for either of those media.

I bet you could find a camera that fits your needs right now on eBay for less than $100. Remember that many users of digital cameras tend to buy the newest camera available and sell their older, lower-megapixel cameras on eBay for a pittance. Don't forget that many brick-and-mortar camera stores also sell used equipment.

Other studio equipment

Certain endeavors seem to be open pits that you throw money into. I promise that your eBay photo studio will not be one of these pits — now or later.

Tripod

A *tripod* is an extendable aluminum stand with three legs (get it? tripod?) that holds your camera steady for shooting pictures. Look for one that has a quick release; that way, if you want to take the camera off the tripod for a close-up, you don't have to unscrew the camera from the base and then screw it back on for the next picture.

The tripod can be a tabletop version or one with extendable legs. The legs should extend to your desired height, should lock in place with clamp-type locks, and should have a crank-style geared center column so you can raise or lower your camera as needed for different shots. Most tripods also have a panning head for shooting from different angles. You can purchase a tripod from a camera store — or on eBay — for as low as $25.

Power supplies

If you've ever used digital cameras, you know that they can blast through batteries faster than sugar through a five-year-old. A reliable power supply is a must. You can accomplish this in a couple of ways:

- **Rechargeable batteries:** Many specialists on eBay sell rechargeable batteries and chargers. Pick up quality Ni-MH (nickel-metal hydride) batteries; unlike the older Ni-Cad (nickel-cadmium) batteries, batteries of this newer type have no memory effect. That means you don't have to totally use them up before you put them back in the recharger. If you want to try a budding technology that's now coming to the fore, try lithium-ion rechargables; they have all the benefits of Ni-MH and don't lose their charge quickly when being stored.

- **Lithium-ion batteries:** This new kind of battery has no memory effect and only a slow loss of charge when not in use. Lithium batteries are the longest-lasting and lightest batteries available — but they're also expensive.

- **CR-V3 lithium-ion batteries:** Some smart guy figured out a way to put the equivalent of two batteries into one unit; considerably cutting the price: One CR-V3 takes the place of two standard AA batteries, and can average 650 photos before you have to change it. The CR-V3 is available also in a rechargeable form, which extends its life even farther (and reduces your battery budget significantly). Some cameras can use them; some cannot. Check out yours before making the purchase.

If your eBay photo studio includes a camera on a tripod (and it should), you can use a good, old-fashioned AC adapter (you know, the one that plugs into the wall). As long as you pay your electric bill, you're going to have power to your camera.

Lighting

Trying to take good pictures of your merchandise can be frustrating. If you don't have enough light and use the camera's flash, the image might be washed out. If you take the item outside, the sun might cast a shadow.

In the early (stone-age) days of eBay, I used my camera's flash and had my daughter shine a flashlight on the item as I took pictures from different angles — all the while hoping that the color wasn't wiped out. Also, the autofocus feature on many digital cameras doesn't work well in low light.

After consulting specialists in the photo business to solve the problem of effective lighting for a digital camera, I put together an inexpensive studio-lighting set for online auction photography. It's easy to assemble your own kit, once you've figured out everything you need for your types of items. And yes, some helpful hints are coming right up.

To eliminate shadows, it's best to have at least two lights, one for either side of the item.

Professional studio lights bulbs aren't necessary. Although they do the trick, professional lights are very expensive and short-lived.

Cloud Dome

If you're going to attempt to photograph jewelry, collectible coins, or other metallic items, you'll quickly become frustrated at the quality of your pictures. (Touching up the pictures in PhotoShop is a time-wasting option.) Metallic objects pick up random color from any kind of light (other than true color) that you shine on them when you're trying to capture them in a picture. Gold jewelry will photograph with a silver tone; silver will look goldish!

After much experimentation, I learned the secret of getting crisp, clear, close-up pictures: Use a Cloud Dome. It stabilizes your camera (just as if you were using a tripod) and filters out all unwanted color tones, resulting in image colors that actually look like those of your item.

The Cloud Dome is a large plastic bowl on which you mount your camera. You take pictures through a hole in the top of the dome. The translucent white plastic diffuses the light so your item is lit evenly from all sides, eliminating glare and bad shadows. Check out the manufacturer's Web site at www.clouddome.com to see some amazing before-and-after pictures.

The Cloud Dome also manages to get the best images from gems. You can actually capture the light in the facets! Pearls, too, will show their luster. Several eBay members (including yours truly) sell the Cloud Dome; I highly recommend it because it works!

Cube Tent

Cube Tent is an ingenious product that replaces the traditional (and expensive) photographer's tent. Professional product photography requires pictures with no glare, no harsh shadows, and no burnout of item details. The Cube Tents are made of translucent white fabric that diffuses the light and provides a perfect lighting condition for many objects. There are plenty of these for sale on eBay, and most sellers include wrinkle-free backgrounds. The Cubes are also combined in kits along with floodlights, as in my own photo studio.

Props

To take good photos, you need some props. Although you may think it strange that a line item in your accounting program will read "Props," they do qualify as a business expense. (Okay, you can put it under "Photography Expenses" if you like; *props* just sounds so Hollywood!)

How often have you seen some clothing on eBay from a quality manufacturer, but you just couldn't bring yourself to bid more than $10 because it looked like it had been dragged behind a car and then hung on a hanger over the bathroom door to be photographed? Could you see how the fabric would hang on a body? Of course not. Take a look at Figure 11-1; that dress looks simply fantastic, darling!

Figure 11-1: Midge the Mannequin, modeling one of my eBay successes.

Diane Von Furstenberg BRAND NEW with tags!

100% Silk Jersey dress
Fits Size 6 or 8

This lovely silk number is THE sexiest dress! It's by hot designer Diane Von Furstenberg (who is featured in the new issue of Vogue). It's a fabulous silk jersey spaghetti strap dress, with a sexy cowl neckline. The original price of the dress is $220, and it can be yours for the highest bid. Draping beautifully on the body, it's got a sexy below the knee length and a very flattering cut.

Bid with confidence and bid whatever you feel this great dress is worth to you as it is selling with NO RESERVE! Winning bidder to pay shipping & handling of $5.25, and must submit payment within a week of winning the auction. Credit cards are accepted through Billpoint and PayPal.

GOOD LUCK, HAPPY BIDDING!

Click below to...
View my other auctions - Win more than one and $AVE on shipping!

Mannequin

I hate to even say it, but if you're selling clothing, you'll get higher prices for your apparel if you photograph your items on a mannequin. If you don't want to dive right in and buy a mannequin, at least get a body form to wear the outfit. Just search eBay for *mannequin* to find hundreds of mannequin forms selling for less than $20. I've seen the high-quality kind (like the ones in store windows) show up on eBay for a low as $75. If you sell children's clothing, get a child-size mannequin form as well. The same goes for men's clothes. If worst comes to worst, find a friend to model the clothes. There's just no excuse for hanger-displayed merchandise in your auctions.

I got my mannequin (Midge) at a department-store liquidation sale here in Los Angeles. I paid $25 for her. She's showing her age and her face paint is a little creepy, so I often crop her head out of the photos. She has a great body and everything she wears sells at a healthy profit. Many stores upgrade their mannequins every few years. If you know people who work at a retail store, ask when they plan to sell their old mannequins; you may be able to pick one up at a reasonable price.

Steamer

Clothing is usually desperately wrinkled when it comes out of a shipping box. It may also get crumpled lying around, waiting for you to photograph it and sell it on eBay. If the clothing isn't new, but is clean, run it through your dryer with Dryel (the home dry-cleaning product) to take out any musty smells and loosen the wrinkles. There's nothing like old, musty-smelling clothes to sour a potentially happy customer.

The clothes you want to sell may be wrinkled, but ironing is a bear (and may damage the fabric), so do what the retail professionals do: Use steamers to take the wrinkles out of freshly unpacked clothing. Get the type of steamer you can use while the article of clothing is hanging up, so you can just run the steamer up and down and get the wrinkles out. The gold standard of steamers is the Jiffy Steamer. It holds a large bottle of water (distilled only), rolls on the floor, and steams from a hose wand. Some models sell on eBay for under $100. Until you're ready to make an investment that big, at least get a small handheld version that removes wrinkles; search eBay for (*garment, clothes steamer*) to find some deals.

Display stands, risers, and more

Argh. I just browsed the Jewelry category and saw some horrendous pictures. Many sellers use photos supplied from the manufacturer, and those are beautiful, but the majority of sellers either didn't zoom in on the piece or the colors were off. Jewelry does not photograph well on most people's hairy hands (that's why hand models make the big bucks). It looks a lot better when you display it on a stand or a jewelry display, or flat on a velvet pad. If you're selling a necklace, why not display it on a necklace stand? I bought my display stands from a manufacturer, but had to wait several months to receive them. These days the manufacturers and sellers have moved to eBay with ready-made goods. Just search for *ring stand, necklace display,* and the like.

Risers can be almost anything you use to prop up your item to make it more attractive in a picture. Put riser pieces that aren't attractive *under* the cloth that you use as a background. (You can also find risers on eBay.)

You wouldn't believe what the back of some professional photo setups look like. Photographers and photo stylists think resourcefully when it comes to making the merchandise look good — from the front of the picture, anyway! Throughout my years of working with professional photographers, I've seen the most creative things used to prop up items for photography:

- ✔ **Small bottles of sand:** Use small bottles (prescription bottles work well) filled with very heavy sand to prop up small boxes and other items in a picture. (A photographer I once worked with used little bottles of mercury, which is a heavy liquid metal but is also a poison, so I don't recommend using it.)

- ✔ **Beeswax, putty, and clay:** To set up photos for catalogs, I've seen photographers prop up fine jewelry and collectible porcelain with beeswax (the kind you can get from the orthodontist works great) or clay. Beeswax is good because it's also a neutral color and doesn't usually show up in the photo. However, you must dispose of beeswax often because it gets filthy when it picks up dirt from your hands and fuzz from fabric.

- ✔ **Museum Putty and Quake Hold:** These two products are invaluable when you want to hold a small object at an unnatural angle for a photograph. (They're like beeswax and clay, but far cleaner.) Neutral-colored Museum Putty works very well — but be careful not to use the clear version, because it often leaves a residue and is difficult to get off the item. I discovered these products after losing everything breakable in my home in the Northridge earthquake. Museums use these clay-like puttys to secure and keep breakables in one place — even during an earthquake!

- ✔ **un-du and Goo Gone:** un-du is a clear liquid that will get sticky residue off almost anything. If your item has sticker residue on it, it's bound to show up in the picture. Squirt on a little un-du and use its scraper to remove the goo and bring back the shine. Goo Gone is another product useful for cleaning items. The product comes in several forms, including a sticker lifter. Some sellers use lighter fluid when they can't find un-du. The problems of working with lighter fluid are obvious (or should be — how's your fire insurance?); I don't recommend it.

✔ **Clamps and duct tape:** These multipurpose items are used in many photo shoots — in some of the strangest places. Your mannequin may be a few sizes too small for the dress you want to photograph. How do you fix that? Don't pad the mannequin; simply fold over the dress in the back and clamp the excess material with a metal clamp (even a heavy-duty plastic hair clamp), or use a small piece of duct tape in the back (off-camera, of course) to hold the fabric taut.

Keep a collection of risers and propping materials in your photo area so they're always close at hand.

Backgrounds for your images

Backgrounds come in many shapes and sizes. You can use paper, fabric, or one of the portable photo stages for smallish items.

In professional photo-talk, *seamless* is a large roll of three-foot (and wider) paper that comes in various colors and is suspended and draped behind the model and over the floor. (Ever wonder why you never see the floor and wall come together in professional photos?) Photographers also drape the seamless over tabletop shots for an *infinity* look. Some people use fabrics such as muslin instead of seamless.

I keep several backgrounds on hand. (If you use velvet, be sure to clean it with sticky tape before you use it in a picture — lint appears huge in pictures.) I recommend using neutral fabrics, papers, or plastics, such as white, light gray (18%), natural, dark blue, and black, so that the color of the fabric doesn't clash with or distract from your items.

The Cloud Dome people have also invented a cool photo stage. I like it because it's portable (easy to store), nonbreakable, simple to clean, and inexpensive. It's sold on eBay and is pictured in Figure 11-2.

Figure 11-2: Cloud Dome's photo stage (seltzer bottle not included).

Taking Good Pictures

If you have a small photo studio setup (see the preceding section) with a quality camera, a tripod, props, and lights, you're well on your way to taking some quality shots for your auctions. A few things to remember:

✔ **Zoom in on your item:** Don't leave a bunch of extraneous distracting background in your pictures. Crop any extra background in your photo-editing program (see the "Image-Editing Software" section, a bit later in this chapter) before you upload the images to eBay or your image-hosting site.

✔ **Watch out for distracting backgrounds:** If you don't have a studio tabletop, or if the item is something that won't fit on a table, try to make the background of the photo as simple as possible. If you're shooting the picture outside, shoot away from chairs, tables, hoses — you get the idea. If you're shooting in your home, move the laundry basket out of the picture.

One of my favorite eBay pictures featured a piece of fine silver taken by the husband of the lady selling the piece on eBay. Silver and reflective items are hard to photograph because they pick up everything in the room in their reflection. (This is when you need the Cube Tent). In her description, the lady explained that the man reflected in the silver coffeepot was her husband and not part of the final deal. She handled it with humor so that even this little faux pas added pizzazz to the listing!

✔ **Be sure the items are clean:** Cellophane on boxes can get nasty-looking, clothing can get linty, and all merchandise can get dirt smudges. Not only will your items photograph better if they're clean, they'll sell better too.

Clean plastic or cellophane with WD-40 (no kidding); it will take off any sticker residue and icky smudges. Of course, un-du or Goo Gone StickerLifter are the best adhesive removers for paper, cardboard, clothing, and such — plus they come with a handy plastic scraper. I also keep a kneaded rubber art eraser around to clean off small dirt smudges on paper items. Any cleaning solution helps your items (even a little Method or 409), but use these chemicals with care — check to make sure they don't react with the stuff your item is made of. Accidentally destroying your items while cleaning them is, well, counterproductive.

✔ **Check the camera's focus:** Just because a camera has an autofocus feature doesn't mean that it makes pictures come out crisp and clear automatically. Low light, high moisture, and other things can contribute to a blurred image. Double-check the picture before you use it.

Using a Scanner

Scanners have come a long way in the past few years. This once-expensive item can now be purchased new for a little more than a hundred dollars. If you sell books, autographs, stamps, or documents, a scanner may be all you need to shoot your images for eBay.

When shopping for a scanner, don't pay too much attention to the resolution. As with digital cameras, images for the Internet (JPEGs) needn't have any higher resolution than 96 ppi (pixels per inch). Almost any scanner can get that resolution these days. Quality makes a difference in the manufacture of the scanner, so stick with brand names.

You should use a *flatbed* scanner, on which you lay out your items and scan away. I replaced my old scanner with an HP all-in-one product that combines a scanner, fax machine, copier, and printer in one handy little unit that saves me lots of space in my office. I've seen HP flatbed units, new in the box, sell on eBay (and even at Office Depot) for as low as $100.

There's many an eBay store that sells new and refurbished items — cameras, scanners, and even computers for the lowest prices I've ever seen. Search eBay Stores for the item name (new or refurbished). A few tips on scanning images for eBay:

- ✔ If you're taking traditionally processed photographs and scanning them on a scanner, have them printed on glossy paper because they'll scan much better than those with a matte finish.

- ✔ You can scan 3-D items, such as a doll, on your flatbed scanner and get some respectable-looking images. To eliminate harsh shadows, lay a black or white t-shirt over the doll or her box so that it completely covers the glass. That way you'll have a clean background and you'll get good light reflection from the scanner's light.

- ✔ If you want to scan an item that's too big for your scanner's glass, simply scan the item in pieces, and then reassemble it to a single image in your photo-editing program (see the following section).

- ✔ Scanner settings are often complex. There's no need to scan your online image at any higher resolution than 100dpi (but at least 90). Be sure to set the scanner for 24-bit color; although some scanners will just let you select between Normal and Best, use whichever setting is closest to 24-bit.

- ✔ Boxed items are a natural for a flatbed scanner. Just set them on top of the glass and scan away. You can crop the shadowed background with your photo-editing software (see the following section).

Editing Your Images with Software

Lose the idea that the software that comes with your scanner is good enough. It may be just fine for some simple uses, but the kind of control you need is only available in *real* image-editing software, not in a mere e-mail picture generator.

Because I have a graphics background, I've always been happy using Photoshop, but it's a large and expensive program. It's also overkill for eBay images. Most of the time I use Fast Photos by Pixby Software (although, alas, it won't work with Windows 7 or a Mac); it's a small-but-professional program at a fraction of the price of Photoshop, offering just the tools that eBay sellers need for Web images — no more and no less. It's also one of the easiest-to-learn programs on the market because it works intuitively. You can go to the manufacturer's Web site `http://www.pixby.com/marshacollier` and download a twenty-one-day free trial for my readers.

If you've taken quality photographs to begin with, they won't need major editing. But for minor alterations, your computer's operating system has a few tools you can use. For the Mac OSX Leopard, you can use the native program, Preview. For Windows Vista, you can touch up photos in the Preview mode, and in Windows 7, the Media Center.

And don't forget that you'll be working with images not only for eBay items but also for your Web site. (Check out Chapter 8 for more about putting together a Web site.)

Finding a Home for Your Images

You need a safe place to store your pictures for eBay. If your images don't appear when someone clicks your auction, or if your images take too long to load, a user might click off your auction and go to the next one. If you have more than one possible place to host your images, test each with a few pictures; you want one that's reliable.

On eBay's Create Your Listing form, you can upload up to 11 images for the top of your listing. You can upload images directly from your computer, or host them on a server. If you're hosting your own pictures, you can insert additional images into your description — not only storing the photos for future use, but also showing off your item's details.

When you store your own photos on a service or your ISP's storage area, you may have to use an FTP (File Transfer Protocol) program to upload the pictures. In the old days, this meant buying a program or getting shareware (free, noncommercial software). Now, if you use the free Firefox browser (I keep Firefox on my computer, right along with Microsoft's Internet Explorer, and often switch back and forth), you get a built-in FireFTP program. Firefox is stable and updated frequently, so there's no reason to fear installing it on your system. Just go to `https://addons.mozilla.org/en-US/firefox/addon/684/` for your free download and more information.

When you use auction-management software to build your listings, you most likely won't need an FTP program to upload your images. Generally the complete management programs integrate an FTP program as part of the package — and may include storage space for your images on their server. Check out Chapter 9 for more about auction-management software packages.

You should always put your eBay images in a separate directory — *not* in an active part of your e-commerce Web site (if you have one). You may think that your business Web site ought to be a good place to store your images, but it isn't. If you want to keep track of your site statistics, such as the number of hits, hosting your own images may ruin the data. A call for one of your eBay images counts as a hit on your site, and if people are looking at your images rather than dropping by to buy, you'll never get accurate Web-site stats.

Free ISP space

Most ISPs (Internet service providers) give you at least 5 MB of storage space for your personal home page. Although this space isn't appropriate for your final business site (too small), it's a perfect place to host your pictures. Everyone has an ISP, and most all ISPs give you space. You may have to use an FTP program to upload to your Web space, or your ISP may supply its own uploader. Go to the home pages for your ISP (the member area), and check out what it offers. Visit Chapter 8 for more information on ISP space.

Auction-management sites

If you're using one of the auction-management Web sites that I discuss in Chapter 9, you're covered for most of your back-office (clerical) tasks. These Web sites supply enough Web space to hold all your eBay images. They also have a convenient one-click upload from your hard drive.

If you find that you truly have no place to host your images, take a look at some of the less-expensive auction-management sites. As of this writing, you can get image hosting *and* other auction utilities for around $10 a month at the following: AAASeller.com, Auctiva.com, Inkfrog.com, and SellerSourceBook.com.

eBay's Photo Uploader

To get those snappy images that appear at the top of the listing page, you're going to have to use eBay's Photo Uploader. You can upload images directly from your computer, or you can indicate the Web address where your image is stored and it will show up in the space. To clearly illustrate your listing, I recommend you add other photos within your description — and the way to do that is to use Web-hosted pictures.

You can use eBay's photo uploader to host your top-of-listing photos for eBay. I recommend that the image you upload be around 1024 pixels on the long side (no smaller than 1000 pixels). Then eBay reformats your photo to fit in the layout at the top of the page and then compresses the file for quick viewing. This process can destroy the quality of your carefully photographed images if you haven't saved them in a compatible size. You're running a business, so be businesslike and use the method that presents your photos in their best light.

I upload images from my computer for the top of listing images, and should I want more images in my description, I use images hosted on my Web site.

When you get to the Create Your Listing page, you'll get to the point where it's time to upload the photo(s) that you want to appear at the top of the page. Let's examine the options first. Note in Figure 11-3 that there is a link to *Add or Remove Options*.

Figure 11-3:
Click to
select your
options for
uploading
photos.

Bring your item to life with pictures   Add or remove options | Get help

All pictures are free.

Add pictures

Click to add
pictures!

When you click this link, a box with your options will appear. Each item has its own check box. If you click the box, a check mark will appear, indicating that you've chosen this option. Your choices are:

- ✔ **Show option for copying picture files to eBay from a Web server.** If you already have the images on an existing Web page, this option allows you to upload your pictures from a Web site instead of from your hard drive. When you click to add pictures, you will be asked for the URL (Web address) of pictures to copy from your site's Web Server.

- ✔ **Host pictures on your server instead of eBay servers.** If you have your images stored with an image-hosting service, or if you keep your merchandise photos in a directory or your Web site, this is the option to use. The difference between the previous option in this list and this one is that eBay will link to your Web server instead of copying the image to the item page. If you decide to use your own photos at the top of the listing, eBay recommends that each one have a total file size of under 75 KB and measure at least 600 pixels on its longest side.

- ✔ **Enable watermarking with my eBay user ID.** Enabling this feature will watermark your photos with your eBay ID.

- ✔ **Enable watermarking with the eBay camera icon.** Rather than watermarking with your user ID, this option puts a small camera icon in the corner of the image.

When you've got the options set, click the square to add pictures and a window will open, as shown in Figure 11-4.

Figure 11-4:
The basic uploading page for pictures.

This is the basic version — here's where you can upload eBay-ready images as they appear on your computer. Click the Browse button to find pictures stored on your hard drive or media card.

To upload your pictures, after clicking Add Pictures on the Create Your Listing page, you get a new Standard Uploader window as in Figure 11-5. If you want to rotate or crop the picture, click the Standard Uploader link (on the far right in Figure 11-5) to access this more advanced tool.

Figure 11-5:
The
Standard
Uploader
window is
ready to
upload your
images.

Follow these steps to upload your pictures to eBay:

1. **Click Browse.**

   A browsing window appears.

2. **Locate the directory that holds your eBay images on your computer.**

3. **Click the image (or multiple images) in the browsing window.**

   The image name (or names) appear in the Filename box.

4. **Click the Open box.**

   The selected image appears in the picture frame on the eBay uploader

5. **To rotate the image, click the circular arrow (at the upper-left of the main image box).**

6. **To crop the image to remove unnecessary background:**

   a. **Click the crop box in the right corner of the larger image.**

      Two squares appear at opposite corners of your main image.

   b. **Click the frame on the outside of your image,** and move the bar until the offensive area is cropped out. You can do this from all sides of the picture.

7. **After you're happy with the results, click Save.**

   The image appears on the Create Your Listing page.

Unless you have an eBay Store, eBay charges for any photos you upload after the first one. Each additional picture costs you 15¢, so inserting photos into your description will save you precious cents and increase your bottom line.

Inserting images in your description

Assuming you have your images hosted on a hosting service or your Web site's server, you can place pictures anywhere within the description. You can display them at the top, at the bottom, one after the other, or side by side. Let me fill you in on a little HTML trickery to accomplish this.

To use any HTML in your description, you must select the HTML tab above the description box to insert the code. You can still design your ad in eBay's Standard mode, but you'll have to switch to the HTML tab to insert the photos. Putting HTML coding in the Standard box will not pull in your image (if you try it, all you get is a bit of gobbledy-gook text).

To get one picture centered on the page, here's the code I use:

```
<center><img src=http://ISP.com/mmyUsername/myImage.jpg></center>
```

This little bit of HTML code translates into a centered image, from your Web address and the file location and name, (Please substitute your own image-hosting site, user name, and the filename for your image).

HTML and You

My small grasp of HTML gets me only so far. I usually use a shareware program to produce code for my Web site or eBay listings. Luckily, you don't have to know a lot of code to produce glorious eBay listings.

The Create Your Listing form has an excellent, basic HTML generator that has a toolbar similar to the one in a word processor. As you can see in Figure 11-6, you can use the toolbar to change the size, font, or color of the text. You can also insert code by switching from the Standard design view to the HTML view of the description area to include your own hosted images in the listing description.

For a quick and easy HTML fix, go to my Web site at www.coolebaytools.com. Then go to the Tools area and click Cool Free Ad Tool. You'll get a quick HTML generator; feel free to use it as often as you like. There's no charge. You can select border colors and include an image in your description area. Nothing fancy, mind you, just nice clean HTML. You type your information as indicated and then select colors, as shown in Figure 11-7.

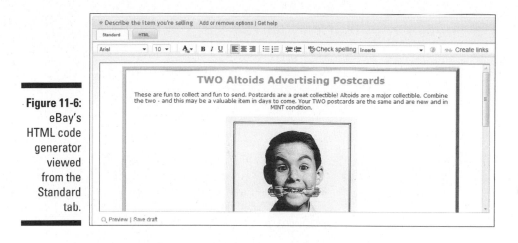

Figure 11-6: eBay's HTML code generator viewed from the Standard tab.

Figure 11-7: The Cool Free Ad Tool page.

When you're finished, click the View Ad button. On the next page, you'll see HTML code for your auction description that you can cut and paste into the auction-description area of the Create Your Listing page. It's pretty painless.

Chapter 12

Providing Excellent Customer Service

. . . .

In This Chapter

▶ Making a good first impression

▶ Reaching out to customers

▶ Writing the perfect e-mail

▶ Sending out-of-office replies and adding your signature

. . . .

*e*Bay is supposed to be buckets of fun! But if you're making money, you're in business. When you're in business, you must always deal with a few boring and very un-fun details.

First and foremost, you must remember that your customers are number one. Businesses become successful by providing fantastic customer service and selling quality merchandise. The image that you project through your e-mails and listings identifies you to the bidders as a good guy or a bad guy. No kidding. Your e-mails should be polite and professional. You shouldn't make prospective customers feel like you're hustling them, sneaking in hidden fees, or being pushy with overbearing rules.

You don't have to have the most beautiful listings on eBay to succeed. You need products that people want, and you need to take the time to build good customer relations. By doing so, you can begin working your way to Top Seller status (and receiving the fee discounts that fatten your bottom line). In this chapter, I cover some ways to let your customers know that they're number one in your book: from writing effective auction descriptions to sending cordial e-mails.

Meeting Your Customers

eBay is a person-to-person marketplace. Although many sellers are businesses (like you), the perception is that sellers on eBay are individuals earning a living (versus big business). The homespun personal approach goes a long way to being successful when selling on eBay. One of the reasons many buyers come to eBay is that they want to support individuals who have the gumption to start their own small enterprise on the site.

After you've written a brilliant title for your auction *(not IN ALL CAPITAL LETTERS, please),* prospective buyers click your listing and scroll down to your description. Do they have to dodge through pointless verbiage, losing interest in your item along the way? Or do you get right down to business and state the facts about what you're selling?

Here are a few things to remember when writing your auction description (see Chapter 11 for more tips for your listings):

- ✔ **Write a factual description.** Do you carefully describe the item, stating every fact you know about it? Are you clear in your description and careful not to use any jargon? Finally, does it answer almost any question a potential buyer might ask? If not, do some revising.

- ✔ **Include some friendly banter.** You want to make the customer feel comfortable shopping with you. Don't be afraid to let your personality shine through!

- ✔ **Update your About Me page.** The small *me* icon that appears next to eBay usernames is an invitation to click. When prospective customers click the icon, they see a page that's all about you and your business. Let people know who they're dealing with. When deciding between two people selling the same item and when all else is equal, buyers will more than likely do business with the seller who makes them feel secure. (Visit Chapter 3 for info on how to set up your About Me page.)

- ✔ **Limit the number of terms of sale.** Some sellers include a list of rules that's longer than the item's description. Nothing will turn off a prospective buyer more than paragraph after paragraph of rules and regulations. If you really *must* put in a litany of rules, make it short and use the following bit of HTML to make the size of the text smaller: `<font size=-1>insert your rules here</font>`.

- ✔ **Choose a reasonable typeface size.** Many users are still looking at eBay on an 800 x 600 display. If you design your listings at 1024 x 768, your typefaces may be way too large for the average user. Forcing a user to scroll and scroll to find the details only leads to frustrated customers.

Telling your story

Being honest and forthright encourages customers to consider your offerings on eBay. Also, if you go the extra mile and give some bonus information, the customer will feel more at ease.

An excellent example comes from an eBay Motors seller who throws in a few special touches to draw in the customer.

When you shop eBay Motors, a prospective buyer has the option of ordering a vehicle history report from the car's listing page. This costs the buyer $7.99 just to view the report. This seller orders a CarFax report himself and puts a link to a PDF version of it right into his auction descriptions. Saving the prospective buyer the cost of the report doesn't seem like much, but it's one of those simple touches that set a customer at ease.

He also posts his business philosophy at the end of his auctions. Here's part of it:

"My dealership is entirely focused on the sales of vehicles via the eBay format. I make all purchasing and sales decisions and am 100% responsible for the content of my auctions, including all text and photography. I personally answer every email and conduct all business regarding the sale of this vehicle.

I buy and list approximately 5–10 units per month; I look at hundreds of vehicles each week that do not make the cut . . .

This is my living. *I do this full time. I do not have a "car lot." eBay has been my dealership for years and all operations are focused towards bringing you the best vehicle possible at the best price you will find. I am committed to this format and take your vehicle purchase very seriously. You are dealing with a secure seller."*

Wow, don't you just want to buy a car from this guy?

✔ **Quote a flat shipping amount and expedite shipping.** Make use of eBay's shipping calculator to give your customers a fair shake at the shipping costs. But if many other sellers offer the same item, flat rates stand out in a search, and the lowest rate may help you reel in an undecided buyer. Also, eBay gives you a lot of leeway when quoting expedited shipping (First Class Mail, Priority) and your listing will stand out when people feel they won't have to wait weeks to get their item.

It's just plain bad taste to overcharge on shipping (and a violation of eBay's rules — you can be suspended for it). eBay buyers expect that you'll add something for handling costs, but overdoing it can make you look like you're trying to squeeze every penny out of your bidder . . . not a good feeling when you're on the other end!

✔ **Keep photos a practical size.** Some users still connect with a slower connection, and if they have to wait for your large pictures to load, they may go elsewhere. If your listing doesn't fully open within a few seconds, the person will simply back out and go on to another listing.

Reaching out through social media

One up-to-the-minute way to meet your customers is through a savvy use of online social networking. After you've joined these sites, put a link to your social media accounts on your e-mails, promotional pieces, and thank-you notes. As social media usage grows, you may find your customers looking you up on these sites.

Your customers become part of the conversation and your community. This can benefit your business because you can crowd source (poll) your online connections to help you select new merchandise to sell and promote.

Knowing your customer is important to cementing an ongoing relationship. On Facebook, you can even send a "Happy Birthday" discount to your customers. Take a spin through Chapter 8 to get a feel for what Facebook and Twitter can offer as you get your online business up and running.

Communicating with Your Customers

Perhaps English class wasn't your favorite, but when it comes to being a professional, incorporating good grammar, proper spelling, and punctuation in your communications portray you as a pro. Before writing this book, even I hooked up with some grammar and punctuation sites to brush up on my writing skills. (Okay, I also have brilliant editors covering up my transgressions, and they didn't even ask me to write that.)

Throughout the rest of this section, I provide some examples of effective seller e-mails. Don't forget your good manners when writing, but don't be too formal — remain personable and polite.

The initial inquiry

The first written communication you may have with a prospective buyer is an inquiry e-mail. Buyers can ask you a question about your item by clicking the *Ask a Question* link on the listing page, which can generate an automatic e-mail addressed to you through eBay's e-mail system. Often these questions are brief.

At least 50 percent of the inquiries that I send to sellers don't get a response — guaranteeing that I *won't* be buying that product. Often, when I do get a response, it's a terse, brusquely written note. Many people choose not to use punctuation or capitalization in their e-mails. How professional looking is that? Not very. Sellers who take the time to write a short, considerate reply that includes a greeting and a thank-you for writing will get my money.

Helping your buyers buy safely

When selling items of high value, you can attract new customers by bonding your eBay sales. *Surety bonding* has been used for about 5,000 years to guarantee business transactions between buyers and sellers who don't know each other. It may be new to you and me, but lots of people know about it, and when prospective buyers look at your listing and see that the transaction is covered up to $25,000, they may be more likely to bid higher or pay more. BuySAFE is a service that bonds select sellers through various insurance companies. Shoppers like seeing a warranty; when they see a BuySAFE seal on your listings, they know they'll get just what they want.

BuySAFE will bond your transactions on eBay or on your own Web site. To be eligible for the BuySAFE seal, you must pass a rigorous check, which proves to BuySAFE that you're a solid seller. After you get your seal and bond your transactions, you are charged 1 percent of your final selling price for the bonding. You don't have to bond all your listings. After you've been approved, you can bond just the ones you think will need the boost. I've found that the seal easily boosts the bids on my listings by 1 percent, so it works for me. For more details and an introductory offer for readers of this book, check out the BuySAFE site at www. buysafe.com/coolebaytools.

To respond, the safest way is to go to your My eBay Messages page. (This way, you won't get sucked into responding to a spammer who's impersonating an eBay e-mail just to confirm that your e-mail address is live). That said, respond quickly, clearly, and politely — and (should you feel like it) give a little sales pitch. You can remind the soon-to-be buyer that you can package several items in one box to save on shipping costs. And why not use this opportunity to point out other listings you have that may also interest the writer? That's good customer service as well as good marketing.

Your note can be brief and straightforward. For example, I wrote the following note in response to a question regarding the condition of the Christmas tree in one of my auctions:

Hello,

Yes, the aluminum Christmas tree in my auction is in excellent condition. The 58 branches are full and lush and will look great for the holidays. Please write again if you have any more questions or concerns.

Don't forget to check my other auctions for a color wheel and a revolving tree stand. They would look great with this tree, and I can combine your wins so you can save on shipping.

Thank you for writing,

Marsha
www.coolebaytools.com

Isn't that nice? The note addresses the question in a respectful and personable manner. Writing a note like this doesn't take long. You should be doing it.

Also, putting your Web site or eBay store URL in your signature is a great way to get new customers to view your personal Web site or blog.

If you subscribe to eBay's Selling Manager Pro, you can customize and set your stock e-mails to your buyers.

The winner's notification letter

Have you ever received a bulk-generated, boilerplate winner's confirmation letter? The seller hasn't bothered to fill in half the blanks, and you're almost insulted just by reading it? Receiving a note like this after you've requested that the seller combine purchases (and the letter pays no attention to your request) is especially annoying. E-mails can cross, but a personal approach goes a long way with customers.

I'm not saying you shouldn't automate your eBay business. I'm merely suggesting — strongly recommending — that you take the time to personalize even your canned e-mail responses. I admit that since I have my account set up to send out invoices automatically when someone purchases something, I do send out an automated e-mail. The following letter is just to let the customer know that there's a real person behind the automation:

Good news! You won eBay item #120089481873 Cloud Dome Photo Stage Studio.

Thank you for winning my eBay item. Buyers tend to go unrecognized on eBay a little too often, so I want you to know that your purchase is very much appreciated. If I can be of any assistance to you, please let me know. While this first e-mail is being generated automatically, I do welcome one-on-one contact with you. Just send a reply to this mail and I'll answer your inquiries directly.

I am serious about my business and look forward to the opportunity to serve you. I'd also like to invite you to check out my other items available on eBay.

marsha_c

Marsha Collier
Author, "eBay For Dummies" and "Starting an eBay Business For Dummies";
Host of the PBS program "Making Your Fortune Online"
www.coolebaytools.com

Leaving feedback for buyers

Keep in mind that you can only leave a positive feedback for your buyers; but you may type any comments about the transaction that you want. After you leave feedback, you can't rephrase or change an erroneous evaluation of another user. I *know* that it's easier to leave feedback after payment is received, but waiting to see how the transaction evolves afterward is prudent — especially if the package gets lost in the mail, which can turn even a previously kind and sweet buyer into an insane screaming nutcase. Same thing if the item is damaged. You should evaluate a buyer based on more than whether the person pays for an item. (Buyers are supposed to do that — it's a contract, remember?) When leaving feedback for buyers, consider the following:

✔ Did they return your communications quickly?

✔ Did they pay in a timely manner?

✔ If a problem occurred with the item or in shipping, did they handle it in a decent manner or did they try to make your life a living hell?

Remember that sellers are judged on communication, shipping time, the quality of packaging, and friendliness.

If you aren't selling many items at a time, I suggest a more personal approach. Here's the tried-and-true winner's notice that I have sent out:

Congratulations!

Yours was the winning bid on eBay item #122342911 for the Emilio Pucci book. You got a great deal! I am looking forward to a pleasant transaction and positive feedback for both of us.

If you pay through PayPal, I'll send your order right away.

Thank you for buying my item. I am delighted to be dealing with you and know you will enjoy your purchase.

Marsha_c

Marsha Collier
www.coolebaytools.com

The payment reminder

Writing a payment reminder can get sticky. You don't want to aggravate the buyer, but time is wasting, and you could spend this time reposting your item. When writing a payment reminder, you need to be firm but pleasant. Real things can happen in people's lives. Family members get sick, and people just plain forget. Perhaps your payment fell between the seats of the car on the way to the post office. (I've had occasion to use that one when I forget to send a payment — it's less embarrassing to refer to something that actually happens now and then — so feel free to use it yourself.)

When you honestly forget to send a payment, nothing is more humiliating than someone debasing you through e-mail. So remember that people do make mistakes, and check the winner's feedback before you send the letter. If you can garner from the feedback that this winner has a habit of not following through on bids, you can definitely be a bit firmer in your wording. Always set a clear deadline for receiving payment, as shown in the following letter:

Hello,

You won an auction of mine on eBay last week for the Emilio Pucci book. Your payment was due yesterday and it still has not arrived. Perhaps sending payment has slipped your mind considering your busy schedule. I know it can easily happen.

Please e-mail back within 48 hours and let me know whether you want to go through with our transaction. I'd like to put the item back up for sale if you don't want it.

Thank you for your bid,

Marsha Collier

How firm you choose to get with a nonpaying bidder is up to you. I've dealt with a few nonpaying bidders on eBay, but I've left only two negative feedbacks. Some people who tend to overbid are indeed violating the contract to buy, but legitimate reasons might explain why someone hasn't followed through on an auction. You must decide which method to take and how far you want to stretch your karma (what goes around comes around). Assess each case individually, and don't be hasty in leaving negative feedback until you know the whole story.

The payment received and shipping notice

I know that you probably aren't going to send out a payment-received letter for every transaction, but it would surely be nice if you did. Staying in constant communication with your buyers will make them feel more secure with you and with buying on eBay. You want them to come back, don't you?

When you receive payment and have shipped the item, sending a short note helps to instill loyalty in your customer. I always send out the automatic e-mail from UPS or FedEx announcing the shipment tracking number. You can additionally have PayPal send out an e-mail by inserting the tracking number into the PayPal payment record. Because PayPal e-mails aren't very personalized, I follow up with my own, more personal note:

Subject: SHIPPED: eBay item: eBay Listings That Sell For Dummies

Hi (insert buyer's name)!

Thank you for buying my eBay Listings That Sell For Dummies and paying so promptly! I'm looking forward to a smooth transaction — and positive feedback for both of us.

If you paid through PayPal, please check your PayPal account because I have posted your package's delivery confirmation number in our transaction record. Please note that if you purchased shipping insurance, you will not see the insurance reflected on the package. I insure my packages with a private insurance policy from U-Pic. (More information is on my Web site.)

If there is any question when the package arrives, PLEASE e-mail me immediately. Your satisfaction is my goal, and I'm sure any problem can be easily taken care of. Please let me know when the package arrives so that we can exchange some very positive feedback!

Marsha Collier
www.coolebaytools.com

Good customer service will get you many repeat customers and lots of positive feedback. Good communication will head off problems before they start. If your customers have received communications from you during the entire transaction, they'll be more likely to discuss a glitch with you rather than make a knee-jerk reaction and leave negative feedback.

Using eBay's E-mail System

Thanks to the many innovations on the site to protect user privacy, you can now use eBay's Messages for your eBay business correspondence.

You may notice that when you get an e-mail through eBay Messages from another eBay member, that the return e-mail address looks a little bizarre, like this: `marsha_erdb3225pb@members.ebay.com`. eBay assigns each member a special e-mail address that routes its way through the eBay system.

If you decide to answer an e-mail that comes through eBay through your smartphone or from your computer, you can just reply as you normally would. Your e-mail will route through the e-mail messages at eBay and go directly to the sender's personal e-mail box. A copy will also appear in the person's Messages inbox. I know it may sound confusing, but it works.

Because I don't think you need a lesson on how to send e-mail, let me show you a couple of tricks that you can do with eBay Messages.

Sending an out-of-office reply

If you plan to be out of town or incommunicado for a few days, you can set up an automatic response to prospective buyers who try to contact you. Any e-mail that is sent to you through eBay will be replied to with the message you set up in this area.

Here's how to set it up:

1. **Go to your My eBay page and click the Messages tab**

2. **Click the Change settings link, which is to the right of the tabs on the Messages page.**

3. **In the Out of office email response area, select the Turn On Out of Office Reply option.**

   A window opens, as shown in Figure 12-1.

4. **Indicate the dates you will be unavailable, so eBay will know when to send out the messages.**

   You can type the dates or use the drop-down calendars.

5. **In the text box, type your personal response.**

   This response will be sent to your buyers while you are away.

6. **Once you're satisfied, click the Apply button at the bottom of the page.**

Figure 12-1:
Setting up
your eBay
out-of-office
automatic
response.

After you've set up your out-of-office reply, you'll see an alert at the top of your inbox. When you've returned from your time off, go to the same area and turn off the reply.

Adding an e-mail signature

Have you noticed how e-mails look more professional with a nicely set up signature? You can add a personalized touch to your outgoing eBay e-mails by adding a signature. You can even add your eBay store logo (if you have one).

To add an e-mail signature to your e-mails sent from eBay, do the following:

1. **Go to your My eBay page and click the Messages tab.**

2. **Click the Change settings link, which is to the right of the tabs on the Messages page.**

3. **In the Email Signature area, select the Show Signature option.**

4. **In the window that appears, type the signature as you'd like it to appear.**

 5. **If you have an eBay store and want the logo to appear, select the Add My Store Logo option.**

 6. **Click the Apply button.**

   Now all your e-mails from this time forward will have your new signature.

Note that you can change your signature and logo at any time by returning to the Change Setting page.

Chapter 13

Collecting Your Money

*T*he hours spent selecting your items, photographing them, touching up the pictures, and writing brilliant auction copy all come down to one thing: getting paid. At first thought, you might be happy to take any form of negotiable paper, bonds, and stocks. As you become more experienced and collect for more auctions, however, you'll decide which payment methods you prefer and which are more heartache than they're worth.

Receiving and processing payments through multiple processors will take time and patience. The more payment methods that you accept, the more methods you have to keep track of.

If you will be selling on eBay, you'd do best to sign up with PayPal at the same time. Most buyers on eBay want to pay for their purchases through PayPal because of their Buyer Protection. You may use other payment methods, but every seller should offer PayPal as a payment option. eBay Seller Protection is available for transactions paid by approved payment providers.

Aside from using the approved providers in the next section, you may have your own merchant credit card (more about that in a later section) or accept payment upon pickup. In-person payment methods can include checks, money orders, cash, PayPal, or credit card. Be clear about which of these payment methods you'll accept if you indicate you'll allow the pickup of merchandise.

Most sellers do not accept checks or money orders for in-person pickup. Since there is a clearing time for checks and money orders, the seller has fewer options for resolving any problems that might crop up.

Approved eBay Payment Providers

Person-to-person payment systems, such as eBay's PayPal, allow buyers to authorize payments from their credit cards or checking accounts directly to the seller. These services make money by charging percentages and fees for each transaction. It all happens electronically through an automated clearinghouse — no fuss, no muss. The payment service releases to the seller only the buyer's shipping information; all personal credit card information is kept private. This speeds up the time it takes the buyer to get merchandise because sellers are free to ship as soon as the service lets them know that the buyer has made payment and the payment has been processed.

From the seller's point of view, person-to-person payment service transaction fees are lower than the 2.5 to 3.5 percent (per transaction) that traditional credit card companies charge for merchant accounts. (Get the details in the "Your very own merchant account" section, coming up.) Even traditional retailers may switch their online business to these services to save money. In this section, I discuss the top payment services and how each works.

Before you decide which credit card payment service to use, get out your calculator and check the company Web sites for current rates. Calculate your own estimates; don't rely on a site's advertised samples. I've found that the charts on the Web tend to leave out certain minor fees. I've also found that comparison charts quoting the competition's prices tend to include optional fees. Watch out for the fine print and do your own math.

When you pay the fee to your payment service, realize that the total amount of your transaction — including shipping fees, handling charges, and any sales tax that you charge — incurs a fee. The payment service charges a percentage based on the total dollar amount that's run through its system.

eBay's approved payment providers are

- **ProPay:** Visit www.propay.com to check out its eAuction for eBay PowerSellers services. ProPay requires an annual $5 signup fee and have low transaction fees based on your PowerSeller ranking on eBay:

Bronze PowerSeller	3.1% and $0.30 USD
Silver PowerSeller	2.7% and $0.30 USD
Gold PowerSeller	2.4% and $0.30 USD
Platinum PowerSeller	2.4% and $0.30 USD

- **Moneybookers:** Popular with international sellers, this payment service is based in the U.K., and payments are figured in Euros.

- **Paymate:** Based in Australia, Paymate enables international payments. As of the date of this writing, it does not publish its transaction fees.

Selling with PayPal

PayPal (see Figure 13-1) allows buyers to safely click and pay with a credit card, instant transfer, or e-check directly from eBay (or thousands of other online stores) after they've won an auction or made a purchase. PayPal conveniently integrates into all eBay transactions and has a streamlined checkout on other sites. If your auction uses the Buy It Now feature or is a fixed-price listing, you can require buyers to pay for their purchases immediately with PayPal payments.

When you go to PayPal.com for the first time, you will land on the consumer landing page (as shown in Figure 13-1). Once you've signed up for a business account, you will land on the business hub, shown in Figure 13-2.

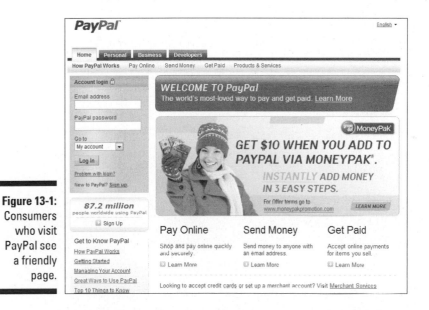

Figure 13-1:
Consumers who visit PayPal see a friendly page.

To accept credit card payments, you must have a Premier or Business account. Buyers may join when they win their first auction and want to pay with PayPal, or they can go to www.PayPal.com and sign up. The story is slightly different for the seller. You need to set up your PayPal account *before* you choose to accept it in your auctions or sales.

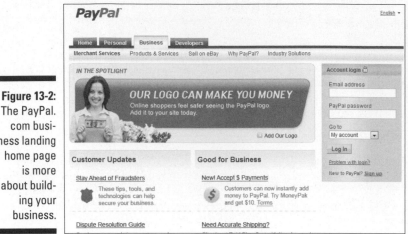

Figure 13-2:
The PayPal.
com busi-
ness landing
home page
is more
about build-
ing your
business.

Here are more than a few particulars about PayPal accounts:

✔ Auction payments are deposited into your PayPal account. Choose one of several ways to get your money:

• Have the money transferred directly into your registered checking account.

• Receive payment by check (PayPal charges $1.50 for the check).

• Keep the money in your PayPal account for making payments to other sellers.

• Withdraw the cash from an ATM with a PayPal debit card. If you enroll in PayPal Preferred Rewards, you'll get back 1 percent of the money spent on purchases.

✔ PayPal assesses your account $20 for any chargeback. The fee is waived if you've fulfilled the requirements in the PayPal Seller Protection policy (see the next bullet). To specify whether you want to accept a credit card payment from a buyer without a confirmed address, log on, go to your account, and then click the Profile tab. Next, scroll down Selling Preferences and click Payment Receiving Preferences. If you accept payment from a nonconfirmed address, that transaction will not be covered by the PayPal Seller Protection policy.

✔ The PayPal Seller Protection policy protects you for the full amount of the eligible payment, unauthorized card use, and non-shipments. To qualify for this protection, you must do the following:

• **Be a verified member of PayPal with a Premier or Business account:** Allow PayPal to confirm with your bank that your checking account and address are your own.

- **Ship only to a confirmed address:** PayPal confirms that the buyer's ship-to address coincides with the address to which the credit company sends monthly bills. Fraudulent shoppers often ask you to ship to another address — don't do it.

- **Keep proof of shipping that can be tracked online:** Here's where those delivery-confirmation things come in handy. (See Chapter 14 to find out how you can get them for free.) For transactions greater than $250, you must get a signed proof of delivery from the shipper.

- **Ship tangible goods:** PayPal doesn't cover goods that are transmitted electronically.

- **Accept only single payments from a single account:** Don't let a buyer try to pay portions of a purchase from different e-mail addresses. Someone who is trying to pay using several accounts may be attempting to defraud you.

Other requirements change from time to time. Check PayPal's help area for updates. But know that if a transaction is eligible, Seller Protection Policy Eligible will appear on the individual Transaction Details page.

Seller's fee tiers for all accounts (including Business and Premier) are adjusted according to the prior month's transaction volume. Look at Table 13-1 for the updated PayPal fee tiers.

Table 13-1   PayPal Domestic (U.S.) Transaction Fees by Sales Tier

Monthly Sales	Fee
$0 to $3,000.00	2.9% plus $0.30 USD
$3,000.01 to $10,000.00	2.5% plus $0.30 USD
$10,000.01 to $100,000.00	2.2% plus $0.30 USD
$100,000.01 and over	1.9% plus $0.30 USD

A brilliant feature of PayPal is that you can download your sales and deposit history to your computer. Although PayPal also offers files that integrate with QuickBooks (for more on QuickBooks, see Chapter 16), the standard downloads are rich in features. Rather than importing just sales figures, you see each and every detail of your transaction — dates, names, addresses, phone numbers, amounts, and more. Even fees and taxes (if you charge sales tax) are broken down separately, making bookkeeping a breeze. The download imports into Microsoft Works and Excel.

Selling internationally through PayPal

PayPal operates in 190 markets and manages more than 133 million accounts. PayPal currently allows users to send, receive, and hold funds in 23 currencies: Canadian Dollars, Euros, British Pounds, Yen, Australian Dollars, New Zealand Dollars, Swiss Francs, Hong Kong Dollars, Singapore Dollars, Swedish Kroner, Danish Kroner, Polish Zloty, Norwegian Kroner, Hungarian Forints, Czech Koruny, Israeli Shekels, Mexican Pesos, Brazilian Real (only for Brazilian users) , Malaysian Ringgits (only for Malaysian users) , Philippine Pesos, Taiwan New Dollars, Thai Baht, and U.S. Dollars. PayPal operates locally in 21 countries, and payments from international buyers are converted to your desired currency automatically.

There is a conversion fee for accepting foreign currencies from your buyers and having them converted to U.S. dollars. Because PayPal is not a currency dealer, it must purchase foreign currencies from a bank. PayPal receives a wholesale rate (twice a day) and adds 2.5 percent above this rate to determine its retail foreign-exchange rate. This 2.5 percent is added to PayPal fees as shown in the table.

Residents in 48 new markets can now use PayPal in their local markets to send money online. These new markets include Indonesia, the Philippines, Croatia, Fiji, Vietnam, and Jordan. A complete list can be viewed at www.paypal.com/worldwide.

PayPal Fees for Receiving Payments from Non-U.S. Buyers

Monthly Sales	Price per Transaction
$0.00 to $3,000.00	3.9% plus $0.30
$3,000.01 to $10,000.00	3.5% plus $0.30
$10,000.01 to $100,000.00	3.2% plus $0.30
$100,000.00 and over	2.9% plus $0.30

Downloading your history will help you calculate income taxes and sales taxes, reconcile your accounts, predict sales trends, calculate total revenues, and perform other financial reporting tasks. It will also give you an excellent customer database. The deposits download gives you detailed information for all the deposits that you receive: payments, PayPal transaction and deposit fees, refunds, rebates, and any adjustments made to your account.

Follow these steps to download your sales and deposit histories:

1. **On your PayPal Account Overview page, hover the mouse pointer over the History tab.**

2. **From the drop-down menu that appears, click the Download History link.**

3. **Enter the time span and the file format for the information you want to view.**

4. **Click the Download History button.**

   The information appears on the screen. Or if the servers are busy, you'll receive an e-mail (usually in a minute or two) when the reports are ready.

5. **Save the file in a directory that you can access conveniently for bookkeeping.**

You can just double-click the file to open it in Excel or Microsoft Works. You now have all the information you could possibly need to apply to your bookkeeping program. This information is excellent backup in case of a tax audit. I download this data every quarter and once on December 31.

WARNING!

It is against policy (and the law) for you to charge your buyers additional funds to cover your credit card processing expense.

Registering with PayPal

If you aren't registered with PayPal yet (what's holding you up?), use the convenient Selling link on the Account tab, which is on your My eBay page. After you click the tab, you'll have the option to Sign Up for a PayPal account (as shown in Figure 13-3). If you've purchased an item through PayPal on a different eBay ID, you can link an existing PayPal account to this ID. To get more information, just click the PayPal link to arrive at the PayPal overview page; there your eBay registration information will already be filled in. You can then begin registration (it's pretty quick and simple) and sign up for a PayPal account.

Figure 13-3: If you never signed up for PayPal on your current eBay ID, you'll have the option to register for a PayPal account.

Home > My eBay > **My Account**

My eBay super-shop-a-holic (0)

| Activity | Messages(1) | **Account** |

My eBay Views | **My Account** | Close My Account

My Account
- Personal Information
- Addresses
- Communication Preferences
- Site Preferences
- Feedback
- PayPal Account
- Donation Account
- Subscriptions
- Resolution Center

How to Sell Items on eBay

① Sign up for PayPal (optional)
If you want to use PayPal to accept buyers' credit card and electronic check payments online, we recommend signing up before you list your first item for sale. Register for PayPal.

② Fill out the Sell Your Item form
The Sell Your Item form is where you'll create your eBay listing. Learn more about listing an item, or go to the Sell Your Item form.

Your PayPal Account Information *P*

New to PayPal?
Paypal makes selling on eBay safe and easy. As a buyer, Paypal speeds up your checkout and allows you to pay a seller without revealing your credit card information.

[Sign Up]

Already have a PayPal account?
Link your existing PayPal account to save time when you buy and sell items. To make things even easier, linking your PayPal account adds your PayPal addresses to your eBay address book

[Link My PayPal Account]

The convenience of PayPal integration into the eBay site really shines when your item is purchased. The auction winner just clicks a Pay Now button that pops up on your auction page immediately after the listing closes. When you list auctions, you pre-set the shipping and handling charges that appear in the shipping box at the bottom of the page. When winners click the Pay Now button (see Figure 13-4), they're taken directly to a payment page set up with your information. The process is as easy as purchasing something through Buy It Now.

Figure 13-4:
The Pay Now button appears when the buyer wins.

> **Buy It Now Confirmation**   Item number: 110615917113
>
> ✓ **Congrats, you just bought this item.**
>
> [Pay Now]   **or** visit seller's store
>
> Click **Pay Now** to confirm shipping, get total price, and arrange payment through: PayPal.
>
> You'll earn **$0.08** in **eBay Bucks**. See conditions
>
> 🛡 **eBay Buyer Protection**
> Covers your purchase price plus original shipping.
> Learn more

When a purchase is made and the payment is deposited in your PayPal account, the system holds the money until you choose how you want to withdraw it.

Because credit card and identity theft is so prevalent on the Internet — and an expensive burden to e-commerce — PayPal uses the extra security measure provided by Visa and MasterCard called CVV2. Most credit cards have 3 (or 4) additional numbers listed on the back, immediately following the regular 16-digit number. Merchants use these numbers for security or verification but aren't allowed to store them, so they're presumably protected from hackers. However, PayPal will verify your card through a procedure known as *random charge*. PayPal charges a few cents or so to your card and asks you to disclose the PIN number printed on your statement. Then PayPal knows that you control the card and didn't steal it.

Withdraw your funds from the PayPal account on a regular basis; you need that money to operate your business. Don't let it become a temporary savings account — unless you choose the PayPal interest-bearing account (check out www.PayPal.com for details). Also, any money you have in your account can be extricated for a chargeback — and chargebacks can be applied as many as 60 days after the transaction. For more about chargebacks, see the "Forget the buyer: Seller beware!" sidebar, in this chapter.

Bank debits (e-checks and instant transfers)

Despite the attached fees and a *short* waiting period, accepting a PayPal e-check or an instant transfer is a nice clean transaction because it's immediate cash in your account. After indicating a preference to pay with an e-check, a buyer must register his or her bank account with PayPal and give it the information required, as shown in Figure 13-5.

Figure 13-5:
The bank information required to register your account with PayPal.

When a buyer pays with an electronic check, it will take as many as four days to clear. An instant transfer (on the other hand) credits your account immediately — as long as the buyer has a credit card (or bank debit card) as a backup funding source — should your instant transfer fail. PayPal allows you to accept e-checks for up to $10,000 and will charge you the standard fees.

Hold this for me: escrow service

Escrow.com (eBay's official escrow service) makes it more comfortable for a buyer to proceed with transactions of more than $500. By using escrow, buyers gain peace of mind because they know the transaction will be completed securely and easily. See Figure 13-6.

Another way to assure your buyer of financial safety, especially when participating in high-dollar transactions, is to run a bonded auction. This type of service costs you far less time and money than an escrow service.

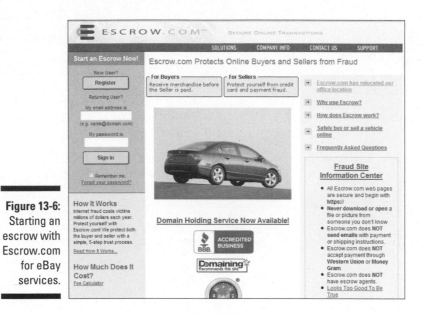

Figure 13-6:
Starting an
escrow with
Escrow.com
for eBay
services.

REMEMBER

When you want to offer escrow as a payment option in one of your sales, be sure to indicate that you're willing to accept an escrow payment in the description area of the listing page. Be sure to describe the terms clearly. Are you willing to pay all the fees? Does the buyer pay fees?

After you have a winning buyer, either you or the buyer should sign on to Escrow.com and create a transaction. If the buyer is not a registered member of the site, he or she must register with Escrow.com; registration is free.

To proceed with escrow, the buyer must send payment to Escrow.com. Escrow.com accepts all credit cards (including American Express and Discover), cashier's checks, money orders, wire transfers, and personal or business checks. A check is subject to a ten-day delay.

After the buyer makes the payment, Escrow.com asks the seller to ship the item to the buyer. When the buyer receives the merchandise, the inspection period begins promptly at 12:01 a.m. the next weekday and continues for a time previously set by the buyer and seller.

The buyer notifies Escrow.com that the merchandise is approved, and then Escrow.com releases payment to the seller. If the buyer doesn't feel that the merchandise is what he or she ordered, the buyer must return the item to the seller in its original condition, adhering to the Escrow.com shipping requirements. The buyer also must log on to the Web site to input return shipping information.

In the event of a return, the seller has the same inspection period to ensure that the item was returned in its original condition. After that is confirmed, Escrow.com will refund the buyer (less the escrow fee and, if agreed on ahead of time, the shipping fee). Either the buyer or the seller can pay the escrow fee; the two can even split the cost. But you need to decide who will pay the fee up front — and indicate this in your auction listing. The buyer is responsible for paying the escrow fee for all returns, no matter who had initially agreed to pay the fees.

In Table 13-2, I include a listing of current escrow fees. (Credit cards or PayPal payments are not accepted for payments of more than $5,000.)

Table 13-2	Escrow.com Standard Merchandise Escrow Fees
Transaction Amount	**Check or Money Order**
Up to $5,000.00	3.25% ($25.00 minimum)
$5,000.01 to $25,000.00	$162.50 plus 2% on the amount over $5,000.00
$25,0000.01 and over	.89%

Sadly, fake escrow service has become one of the most highly publicized scams on the Internet. Unscrupulous sellers set up fake escrow sites, sell a bunch of high-dollar items on eBay to unsuspecting buyers, and then direct the buyers to the faux escrow Web site to "set up their escrow." The buyers send their money (thinking the transaction is safe). After the fraudulent seller collects a bunch of money, he or she shuts down the Web site and absconds with the money! Many buyers are gun-shy of using escrow to pay for expensive items. Consider bonding your transactions to lure higher bids and confer a guarantee to the buyer.

If you're selling a vehicle, offering escrow can greatly enhance the activity of your sale. Escrow.com has a couple of useful services to encourage buyers and sellers to use their services:

- ✔ **Lien payoff service:** Guarantees that the current lien is paid off by having Escrow.com confirm current payoff amount, send title release instructions to the current lien holder and send the payoff check to the lien holder at the close of your Escrow.com transaction. Cost: $60.

- ✔ **Title transfer:** A real pain for those who buy vehicles online is getting the title transferred through their Department of Motor Vehicles. Vehicles sold within the 50 contiguous states can have their titles officially transferred and recorded for only $199.

Vehicle transactions come under a fee schedule different from that of regular merchandise. I've listed the fees in Table 13-3.

Table 13-3	Escrow.com Vehicle Transaction Fees
Transaction Amount	*Fee*
Up to $5,000	3.25% ($25.00 minimum)
$5,000.01 to $25,000	$162.50 + .26% of amount over $5,000.00
Over $25,000	0.89%

I Take Plastic: Credit Cards

As people become more comfortable with using credit cards on the Internet, credit cards become more popular for eBay payments. Plus, major credit card payment services have insured eBay payments to registered users, making credit cards safe for the buyer and easy for you. Credit card transactions are instantaneous; you don't have to wait for a piece of paper to travel cross-country.

For all this instantaneous money transfer, however, you pay a price. Whether you have your own *merchant account* (a credit card acceptance account in the name of your business) or take credit cards through a payment service (discussed previously), you pay a fee. Your fees can range from 2 to 7 percent, depending on how you plan to accept cards and which ones you accept. Unfortunately, many states have made it illegal to charge a credit card surcharge to make up this difference. You have to write off the expense of accepting credit cards as part of your business budget in the Cost of Goods Sold (COGS) — see Chapter 16 for an explanation.

The fees that brick-and-mortar stores pay for accepting credit cards are much less than those paid by online, mail, or phone orders. In most promotional material, the vendor usually quotes the "swiped card" rates. Because you won't have the buyer's card in hand to swipe, be sure to inquire with your provider for the proper rate before signing any papers.

I have to explain the downside of accepting credit cards for your online sales. To protect yourself, please be sure to check the bidders' feedback — both feedback they've received and feedback they've left — before accepting any form of credit card payment for a high-ticket item. Some buyers are chronic complainers and are rarely pleased with their purchases. They may not be satisfied with your item after it ships. In that case, they can simply call their credit card company and get credit for the payment; you'll be charged back (your account will be debited) the amount of the sale. (See the "Forget the buyer: Seller beware!" sidebar in this chapter.) PayPal protects sellers to an extent, and is a safer way to accept credit cards for your sales.

Forget the buyer: Seller beware!

When buyers dispute a sale, they can simply call PayPal or their credit card company and refuse to pay for the item. You lose the sale and possibly won't be able to retrieve your merchandise. A payment service or merchant account will then *chargeback* your account without contacting you and without negotiating. Technically, the buyer has made the purchase from the payment service — not from you — and the payment service won't defend you. I've heard of chargebacks occurring as long as six months after the transaction, although eBay says they can occur no later than two months after they sent you the first bill on which the transaction or error appeared. No one is forcing the buyer to ship the merchandise back to you. As with eBay Fraud Protection (see Chapter 3), the credit card companies skew the rules to defend the consumer. As the seller, you have to fend for yourself. See Chapter 4 on how to report fraudulent buyers. You usually have no way to verify that the shipping address is the one the credit card bills to. So, to add to your problems, the card may actually be stolen.

PayPal confirms through the Address Verification Service (AVS) that the buyer's credit card billing address matches the shipping address — and gives you the option to not accept payments from buyers whose addresses don't match. PayPal offers seller protection against spurious chargebacks under the following circumstances:

✓ Fraudulent card use

✓ False claims of nondelivery

See the section on PayPal for more details on how to be covered by seller protection.

If the issuing bank resolves a chargeback in the buyer's favor, PayPal charges you $20 if you're determined to be at fault, but will waive the fee if you meet all the requirements of the PayPal Seller Protection policy.

Your Very Own Merchant Account

If your eBay business is bringing in more than $20,000 a month, a credit card merchant account may be for you. At that level of sales, discounts kick in and your credit card processing becomes a source of savings to your business rather than an expense. Before setting up a merchant account, however, I recommend that you look at the costs carefully. I get at least one e-mail each week begging me to set up a merchant account, and each one offers lower fees than the last. But charges buried in the small print make fees hard to calculate — and even harder to compare. Even those who advertise low fees often don't deliver. Be sure to look at the entire picture before you sign a contract.

Keep in mind, too, that when you have a merchant account, your provider may choose to create a reserve account for your incoming funds. These reserves may be based on the type of merchandise you sell or your charge-back history, or just pop into existence because your provider chooses to have them. I have heard of as much as 20 percent of incoming funds being held in reserve.

The best place to begin looking for a merchant account may be your own bank, where they know you, your credit history, and your business reputation and have a stake in the success of your business. If your credit isn't up to snuff, I recommend building good credit *before* pursuing a merchant account — because your credit rating is your feedback in the offline world.

If your bank doesn't offer merchant accounts for Internet-based businesses, find a broker to evaluate your credit history and hook you up with a bank that fits your needs and business style (or join Costco as a last resort; see the following section). These brokers make their money from your application fee, from a finder's fee from the bank that you finally choose, or both.

After you get a bank, you'll be connected to a *processor,* or transaction clearinghouse. Your bank merely handles the banking; the clearinghouse is on the other end of your Internet connection when you're processing transactions, checking whether the credit card you're taking is valid and not stolen or maxed out.

The next step is setting up your *gateway,* the software (ICVerify or PCAuthorize, for example) with which you transmit charges to the clearinghouse. Some gateways use HTML Web sites and take the transactions directly on Web-based forms (Cybercash or VeriFone, among others). Web-based gateways connect your Web forms to real-time credit card processing.

In Table 13-4, I highlight various possible costs associated with setting up and maintaining a merchant account.

Table 13-4	Possible Internet Merchant Account Fees
Fee	*Average Amount*
Setup fee	$25.00 to $250.00
Monthly processing fee to bank	2.5% (1.5% to 5%)
Fee per transaction	$0.20 to $0.50
Processor's fee per transaction	$0.35 to $0.50
Internet discount rate	2% to 4%
Monthly statement fee	$9.00 to $15.00

Fee	Average Amount
Monthly minimum processing fee	$15.00 to $30.00
Gateway monthly processing fee	$20.00 to $40.00
Application fee	$50.00 to $500.00
Software purchase	$350.00 to $1,000.00
Software lease	$25.00 per month
Chargeback fee	$15.00

Remember that some merchant accounts will charge you some of these fees, and others may take a bunch of little swipes at your wallet. In the following list, I define some of the fees listed in Table 13-4:

- **Setup fee:** A one-time cost that you pay to either your bank or your broker.

- **Discount rate:** A percentage of the transaction amount (a discount from your earnings), taken off the top (along with the transaction fee) before the money is deposited into your account.

- **Transaction fee:** A fee per transaction that's paid to the bank or to your gateway for the network.

- **Gateway or processing fee:** Your fee for processing credit cards in real time, paid to the Internet gateway.

- **Application fee:** A one-time fee that goes to the broker or perhaps to the bank.

- **Monthly minimum processing fee:** If your bank's cut of your purchases doesn't add up to this amount, the bank takes it anyway. For example, if your bank charges a minimum monthly fee of $20 and you don't hit $20 in fees because your sales aren't high enough, the bank charges you the difference.

If you're comfortable with all the information in the preceding list and in Table 13-4, and you're looking for a broker, heed my advice and carefully read everything a broker offers. Be sure you aren't missing any hidden costs.

PayPal's Virtual Terminal

If you want your own merchant account and want all the benefits of PayPal, you can apply for their solution: Virtual Terminal. With Virtual Terminal, you can accept credit card payments by phone, fax, or mail. All this for an additional $30 a month over your regular PayPal fees and 0.2 percent higher transaction fees. No extras and no equipment to buy or rent. What a deal! Just log in to your PayPal Business account online at www.paypal.com/ and go to the Merchant Services tab. You will find Virtual Terminal in the Products and Services area. You must have a Business account to use the Virtual Terminal feature.

Virtual Terminal fees are based on the total amount of money you put through PayPal per month — including regular PayPal payments. The buyer's credit card charge will appear on his or her bill with the name of your business.

Costco members' credit card processing

Here's some true discount credit card processing: a one-stop merchant account *and* gateway! You can not only buy tuna fish in bulk with a Costco membership, but also obtain a reasonably priced way to handle a merchant account (check out Table 13-5) through the NOVA Network. Costco got together with Elavon, one of the nation's largest processors of credit card transactions, to offer Costco Executive members a discounted Internet credit card processing service. Costco Executive membership brings the cost of a Costco membership up from $45 to $100, but you get the benefit of receiving 2 percent back for most purchases (not including tobacco, gas, food, and some other purchases).

Monthly fees (normally $4.95 a month), as well as the $25 application fee, are waived for Costco Executive members.

Table 13-5	Costco Executive Member Internet Credit Card Processing Fees
Fee	*Amount*
Telephone order fee	1.99% plus $0.27
Internet sales fee	1.99% plus $0.27
Transaction fee to Elavon per transaction	$0.27
Monthly minimum transactions	$20.00

To get an Internet commerce account, you should already have the following in place:

✔ Products and pricing

✔ A return and refund policy

✔ An active customer-service phone number

✔ Posted delivery methods and shipment time

✔ A privacy policy stating that you will not share your customer's information with any other entity

✔ A registered domain in your name or in the name of your business

✔ A secure order page with https and lock

To begin the application process, follow these steps:

1. **Go to** www.costco.com.

2. **At the top of the home page, click the Services link.**

3. **Scroll to the Services for Your Business area and click the Merchant_ Credit Card Processing link.**

4. **Read the information and click the Apply Now link.**

5. **Type your Executive Membership number, and fill out the secure form.**

   Filling out the form online speeds up the application process.

After sending your form, you'll receive a full application package by two-day mail. A representative will also contact you by telephone.

Chapter 14

Shipping Your Items: Sending Them Fast and Saving Money

In This Chapter

▶ Examining shipping options and costs

▶ Exploring private insurance

1 think the most satisfying part of an eBay transaction is making the sale and receiving payment. After that, of course, comes the tedious process of fulfilling your orders. You shouldn't feel bad if this is the point that makes you take pause and sigh. Order fulfillment is one of the biggest challenges (and yuckiest chores) that face any mail-order or online entrepreneur. The onerous task of packing and mailing is the bane of almost all businesses.

But as an eBay businessperson, you *must* attend to these tasks, however much you'd rather not. So in Chapter 17, I detail what you need for packing (boxes, bubble pack, and so on) and some options for purchasing online postage. And in this chapter, I explain just how your items will get to their destinations, exploring your shipping options, costs, and insurance coverage along the way.

Finding the Perfect Shipping Carrier: The Big Four

When you're looking at your shipping options, you need to first determine what types of packages you'll generally be sending (small packages that weigh less than 2 pounds or large and bulky packages), and then decide how you'll package your items. Planning this before listing the item is a good idea.

Shipping really big stuff!

When it comes to shipping heavy or big stuff, you have a few options. Because I like using FedEx, I generally check FedEx Freight first. A friend of mine once purchased four large heavy-equipment tires on eBay, and there was no way he could go with a regular carrier. We called FedEx Freight, which told the seller to place the tires on a pallet and secure them. FedEx Freight picked the tires up at its location in one shipment. Shipping costs were reasonable, but the only caveat was that the shipment had to be delivered to a place of business, not a residential location. This is easy to overcome, especially if you have a friend with a retail store or a gym you go to.

A Web site called www.freightquote. com negotiates rates with several major freight forwarders and will give you a free quote on your large shipment, right on its Web site. Before attempting to sell a heavy item, you can sign on to its home page and enter the weight and dimensions of your shipment, and you'll get a free quote on the spot.

Deciding on your carrier can be the most important decision in your eBay business. You need to decide which one is more convenient for you (close to your home base, provides pickup service, gives better customer service) and which is the most economical (makes sense for your bottom line). The efficiency of your shipping is only as good as the people who service your account. If the UPS man dumps packages at your door without ringing the bell, perhaps he's not the right person to entrust with the heart and soul of your business. Maybe your letter carrier knows you by name and gives you good service; if that's the case, maybe the United States Postal Service (USPS) is the best choice for the bulk of your shipments. Many eBay sellers send packages using ground services rather than airmail or overnight, but a shipper who can give you both options may be offering you a good deal because then you don't have to deal with more than one vendor.

TIP

Keep in mind that USPS Priority Mail is considered expedited shipping by eBay. If you sell heavy items that fit in one of the USPS flat-rate boxes, you may save time and boost sales.

Settling on one main shipper to handle your shipments is important because you'll be able to have the bulk of your records on one statement or in one area. You might also need a secondary shipper (most sellers do) for special types of packages. One shipper can't be everything to every business, so having an account with more than one can be to your advantage. Also, shippers may not sign up new accounts as readily in the middle of a strike or work slowdown.

In this section, I give you the lowdown on the three major carriers — FedEx, UPS, and the USPS — so you can see which fits your requirements. For a summary of shipping costs from these four, see Table 14-1. Note that FedEx and UPS include tracking numbers for delivery confirmation. The USPS charges extra; when you purchase this service at the post office, delivery confirmation is $0.70 for Priority mail and $0.80 for Parcel Post. For info on eliminating this fee for Priority mail, print your mail electronically (see the following tip) and check out Chapter 17.

When giving the pricing for the USPS, note that I indicate Commercial Base Pricing (CBP) for Priority Mail, which is available only if you print your postage online through a USPS-approved provider. You should be good to go for these lower rates when you print through Endicia.com, stamps.com, USPS Click-N-Pay, or PayPal.

Table 14-1	Shipping Costs from Coast to Coast (Residential Delivery)				
Delivery Service	*2 lbs.*	*5 lbs.*	*10 lbs.*	*15 lbs.*	*Flat-Rate Boxes*
UPS 3-Day Select (1 to 3 days)	$19.60	$27.25	$41.60	$54.95	n/a
USPS Priority Retail (2 to 3 days)	$10.20	$18.35	$31.60	$41.65	$4.95 to $14.95
USPS Priority (CBP*) (2 to 3 days)	$9.37	$16.93	$29.57	$38.30	$10.95
USPS Priority Regional Flat Rate	$9.37	$9.37	$9.37	$9.37	15 lb max: $9.37
FedEx Home Delivery (4 days)**	$8.85	$10.51	$12.85	$16.68	n/a
UPS Ground (1 to 6 days)	$11.31	$12.77	$16.30	$21.81	n/a
USPS Media Mail*** (2 to 9 days)	$2.96	$4.13	$6.08	$8.03	n/a
USPS Parcel Post*** (2 to 7 days)	$8.28	$12.53	$16.96	$21.33	n/a

* Commercial Base Pricing includes Delivery Confirmation and is Internet electronically printed
** Includes $2.20 Residential Surcharge *** Includes Delivery Confirmation Fees

You can now prepare UPS or USPS shipping documents online through PayPal and on Web sites for the other carriers. See Chapter 17 for the ins and outs (and pros and cons) of shipping through PayPal.

When you start shipping a few dozen packages a week, you might want to check out *eBay Business All-in-One For Dummies,* by yours truly, for an in-depth analysis of the big three and their variable shipping rates.

Federal Express

Federal Express (FedEx) is world famous for its reliable service. It's the number one choice for all major companies who "Absolutely, positively have to get it there on time." FedEx also has a reputation for some of the highest costs in the business — but only to the untrained eye. FedEx acquired Roadway Package Service (RPS) and formed FedEx Ground, which has a separate division called FedEx Home Delivery that delivers to residences. For the services FedEx provides, you'll be happy to pay what you do. Read on.

FedEx Ground and Home Delivery

When FedEx's residential ground-delivery service began, its slogan was "The neighborhood-friendly service that fits the way we live, work, and shop today." Although I rarely get warm fuzzies from my package deliveries, this slogan brought meaning to the philosophy behind its service: to bring professional shipping to your home residence. FedEx Home Delivery offers low rates and a high-quality service. It is the only shipper that offers a money-back guarantee on home service. It delivers until 8:00 p.m. *and* on Saturdays, but not on Monday.

Visit the FedEx Home Delivery Web site and sign up for an account at `http://www.fedex.com/us/residential`. Even if you have a current Federal Express account, you must sign on to add the Ground service (which includes Home Delivery). Registering for Ground service is even easier than registering on eBay, so give it a shot.

To open an account, go to the FedEx New Customer page at `www.fedex.com/us/newcustomer/` and get the skinny on how to use the service. The online calculator offers the option of Home Delivery, so you don't even have to look up alternative rates and charts. And just as other shippers do, FedEx Home Delivery gives you a service schedule to let you know how long it'll take your package to arrive at its destination.

Here are a few fast facts about FedEx Ground services:

✔ You print your own labels and barcodes for your packages and track them online.

✔ FedEx Home Delivery works on a zone system based on your ZIP code and how far the package is going. Refer to the FedEx Home Delivery zone chart or get the cost online through the online calculator.

✔ Each shipment is covered for $100.00 in declared value.

✔ Residential deliveries are limited to 70-pound packages.

✔ Daily *pickup* service adds an additional weekly charge to your account.

✔ Dropping off packages at Federal Express counters incurs no additional charge.

✔ FedEx Home Delivery delivers Tuesday through Saturday until 8:00 p.m. within 1 to 5 business days.

If FedEx Ground shipping charges seem to be a great deal, they are! But you can get an even better deal if you charge your FedEx shipping to an American Express Business card (one that gives you access to the American Express Open Network). You save an additional 5 percent on all FedEx shipments when you use online shipping and place your orders online. If you have the Amex card, be sure it is officially linked so you get the discount.

FedEx Online

FedEx has one of the most intuitive online applications for shipping. The FedEx Ship Manager interface will turn your computer into a one-person shipping shop. You can generate labels for all forms of FedEx in one place. The site allows you to search for rate quotes and track packages, and it includes a shipping-notification option to send tracking information e-mails to your recipients.

Larger businesses can get the Ship Manager workstation, complete with a PC and printer. The workstation has the unique ability to choose from other carriers. Aside from FedEx Express and FedEx Ground, you can also access UPS shipping services, which allow you to rate, track, report, and ship for multiple carriers on one system.

United Parcel Service

Everyone is familiar with the big brown trucks that tool around town delivering packages hither and yon. Those trucks belong to the United Parcel Service, or UPS, whose home page is shown in Figure 14-1.

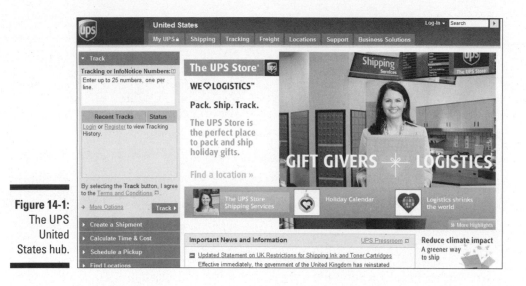

Figure 14-1:
The UPS
United
States hub.

UPS offers three levels of service, based on your shipping needs:

- **Internet account (on demand):** Print your own bar-coded labels so you can drop off packages at the UPS retail counter or store (you can also do that without an account) or give packages to a UPS driver. You can also use Internet account rates when shipping through PayPal.

- **Occasional shipper account:** Use UPS for the rare large box or heavy shipment. An occasional shipper can call UPS for a next day pickup. You have to pay an additional fee per package for the driver to pick up from you if you don't feel like lugging the package to the UPS local counter.

- **Pickup account:** When you hit the big time, you're able to get the lowest UPS rates and have a driver make daily stops to pick up your packages. Fees for a pickup account may run as much as $20.00 per week (based on the number of packages you ship each week) over the cost of your package shipping.

For big shippers, UPS offers its application program interface (API), which can be integrated into a company's home servers.

To register for UPS online, visit `http://bit.ly/registerUPS` (I shortened a very long URL for you) or go to your PayPal account. After typing your personal or business information and answering a few basic questions, *UPS* will decide what account is right for you. By registering, you can also track packages and ship online.

Here are some quick facts about UPS:

✔ Shipping with UPS requires that you pay a different rate for different zones in the country (the same as the other shippers). The cost of your package is based on its weight, your ZIP code (where the package ships from), and the addressee's ZIP code (where the package is going). To figure out your cost, use the handy eBay shipping calculator shown in Figure 14-2.

✔ The UPS Web site offers a chart that defines the shipping time for your ground shipments (remember — no weekend deliveries).

✔ Each package has a tracking number that you can input online to verify the location of a package in transit and the time of delivery.

✔ Delivery to a residence is more expensive than delivery to a commercial location.

✔ UPS delivers packages Monday through Friday.

✔ $100.00 in insurance is included with every shipment. Valuations from $100.01 to $300.00 cost $1.50, and valuations over that are an additional $0.50 per $100.00.

UNITED STATES POSTAL SERVICE.				UPS			
				UPS prices based on UPS Retail Rates.			
	Chicago	New York City	Los Angeles		Chicago	New York City	Los Angeles
USPS Priority Mail Flat Rate Envelope®	$4.90	$4.90	$4.90	UPS Ground Guaranteed in 1-5 days*	$12.17	$12.55	$9.97
USPS Priority Mail Small Flat Rate Box	$4.95	$4.95	$4.95	UPS 3 Day Select℠ Guaranteed in 3-3 days*	$20.62	$22.08	$11.45
USPS Parcel Post® Estimated delivery 2-9 days	$7.62	$8.09	$4.90	UPS 2nd Day Air® Guaranteed in 2-2 days*	$27.88	$28.97	$17.03
USPS Priority Mail® Estimated delivery 2-3 days	$8.60	$9.55	$5.00	UPS Next Day Air Saver® Guaranteed by next day*	$53.38	$55.44	$24.20
USPS Priority Mail Medium Flat Rate Box®	$10.70	$10.70	$10.70	UPS Next Day Air® Guaranteed by next day*	$58.21	$60.43	$26.80
USPS Priority Mail Large Flat Rate Box®	$14.50	$14.50	$14.50				
USPS Express Mail Flat Rate Envelope®	$18.30	$18.30	$18.30				
USPS Express Mail® Overnight to many areas	$28.50	$28.90	$17.05				
USPS Media Mail™ Estimated delivery 2-9 days (restrictions apply)	$2.77	$2.77	$2.77				

Figure 14-2: The eBay shipping calculator.

United States Postal Service

Whether you call it snail mail, POPS (plain old postal service), or whatever nickname you like, the United States Postal Service has been delivering the mail since 1775, when our first postmaster (Benjamin Franklin) took the reins. The USPS has attempted to get every piece of mail delivered to every part of our country. Check out its Web site in Figure 14-3.

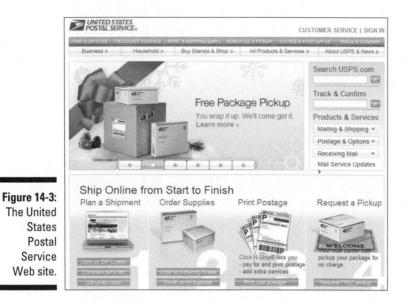

Figure 14-3: The United States Postal Service Web site.

The USPS is open to everyone. You don't have to set up an account to use its services. To get a basic idea of what you'll pay to send a package, you can access a rate calculator on the USPS Web site (www.usps.com). The post office provides many services; in this section, I go over the most popular forms of mail used by eBay sellers.

Distance and weight aren't the only measures for postal shipping fees; shape matters, too. Because the cost of handling each mail shape varies, letters, large envelopes (flats), and packages (parcels) of different sizes can incur different rates.

First Class mail

eBay sellers often forget that items that weigh 13 ounces or less can be shipped by super-speedy First Class mail at considerable savings. I send my First Class shipments in bubble-lined mailer envelopes, and they arrive swiftly. Delivery confirmation is available for First Class mail for $0.80 at the post office counter or $0.19 when you print your postage electronically.

For use of delivery confirmation, First Class mail (large envelopes, flats, and packages) must be greater than ¾-inch thick at the thickest point, unless the item is packaged in strong, rigid fiberboard or in a container that becomes rigid after the contents are enclosed and the container is sealed. The package must be able to maintain its shape throughout the mail process without collapsing.

Priority mail

The two-to-three-day Priority mail service is the most popular form of shipping for eBay packages. You can get free cartons in many sizes, stickers, and labels from the post office. (See Chapter 17 for a complete list of what the USPS supplies for your mailing needs.) You can also print postage online through PayPal, Endicia.com, or Stamps.com (again, see Chapter 17).

Priority mail rates are perfect for 1-pound packages (flat rate cross-country costs $5.20 at the post office and $4.80 when printed electronically) and 2-pound packages (from $5.20 to $10.20 or from $4.97 to $9.37 printed electronically and based on distance). There's a flat-rate Priority envelope in which you can jam as much as possible (regardless of the final weight) for $4.95 ($4.75 electronically). And you can use several sizes of flat-rate padded envelopes or boxes, load them chock-full of heavy books or whatever, and pay only $10.95 ($10.50 electronically) to $14.95 ($14.20 electronically) to get your items delivered — anywhere in the country.

In January 2011, the USPS added some new features for Flat Rate shipping. It introduced a 9-1/2-inch by 12-1/2-inch padded envelope and four Regional Flat Rate boxes available only for customers of Commercial Base Pricing (Internet postage). As you see in Table 14-2, you can save a bundle by using these new products (as long as your item fits). Regional Flat Rate boxes are charged by distance, just as regular Priority Mail.

Table 14-2	Regional Flat Rate Shipping Costs						
Box Size	Zone 1 & 2	Zone 3	Zone 4	Zone 5	Zone 6	Zone7	Zone 8
15 lb. weight limit	$4.97	$5.08	$5.58	$7.15	$7.83	$8.36	$9.37
20 lb. weight limit	$5.81	$6.88	$8.06	$10.51	$12.29	$13.12	$14.62

The Priority mail rates (including free shipping materials) are attractive until you get into the larger, heavier packages that won't fit into the flat-rate boxes. Also, if you don't print your postage online, delivery confirmation costs up to an additional $0.80. Delivery confirmation tells you only *if* the package was delivered; it doesn't trace the package along its route.

2011 is also the year for USPS to institute a new class of mail for Commercial Plus customers: Critical Mail. It's a hybrid service, more expensive than First Class, but less expensive than Priority Mail. Critical Mail provides customers with delivery confirmation and requires the usage of USPS-supplied envelopes that run $3.50 for letters and $4.25 for larger, flat-size pieces.

Media mail

To stay hip, the post office has renamed its old Book Rate to Media Mail, causing many eBay sellers to mistakenly miss out on this valuable mailing tool. The savings are immense (refer to Table 14-1). The drawback is that you must mail only books, cassettes, videos, or computer-readable media. Transit time on Media Mail can be up to three weeks, but you're likely to find the cost savings on heavy packages worth it.

Parcel Post

If you want to use USPS and have a heavy package (up to 70 pounds) that doesn't fit the requirements for Media Mail, use Parcel Post. However, USPS Parcel Post rates don't save you much when you compare them to UPS or FedEx Ground rates.

USPS Application Program Interface

If you want to print your own postage, you can use USPS Click-n-Ship, PayPal, Endicia.com, or Stamps.com — that is, unless you are a large corporation and you'd like to incorporate the post office tools into your own Web site. USPS has an API that allows your Web site to interact with USPS servers, as shown in Figure 14-4. With this software, big businesses can get delivery confirmation (among other services) at no charge and print its own barcodes. The USPS Web Tools page is at www.usps.com/webtools.

Integrating USPS APIs into a business isn't for the meek and small (like me — and maybe you?), but you can use a reliable independent service such as Endicia. com or Stamps.com. They are perfect for the e-commerce entrepreneur.

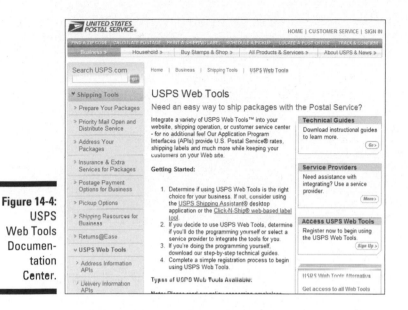

Figure 14-4:
USPS
Web Tools
Documen-
tation
Center.

Protecting Packages with Universal Parcel Insurance Coverage

If you think that printing your own postage is slick, you're gonna love Universal Parcel Insurance Coverage (U-PIC), a service that automates the post office insurance hassle. U-PIC has been in the package insurance business since 1989, mainly insuring packages for large shippers. U-PIC has expanded its business to the online auction arena, and you can insure packages that you send through USPS, UPS, FedEx, and other major carriers. If you use its insurance on USPS-shipped packages, you can save as much as 80 percent on insurance rates. If you use U-PIC, you can stop purchasing package insurance from your carriers.

The U-PIC service also enables you to print your postage through an online postage service and, if you have just a few packages, give the packages directly to your USPS mail carrier. (You don't have to stand in line to get your insurance form stamped.) If you have a ton of boxes, you'll have to drive them to the post office and shove them over the counter. No waiting in line; no hassle!

To apply for the U-PIC service, you must fill out a Request to Provide (RTP) form. Go to its Web site at www.u-pic.com and take a look around (see Figure 14-5). When you want to apply, go to http://bit.ly/eBayBusiness

and fill out the Request to Provide (RTP) form. You must answer questions about who you are, how many packages you send, how many insurance claims you've filed in the past two years, and your average value per package.

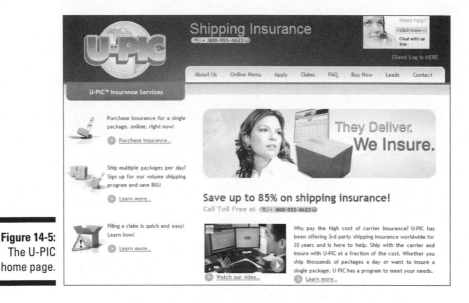

Figure 14-5:
The U-PIC
home page.

After you fill out the online form and agree to the policy (Evidence of Insurance), a U-PIC representative will contact you within 48 hours. The representative will answer your questions and help you decide which of the programs will work best for your eBay business. (I give you some details about these in just a bit.)

Your U-PIC sales representative will explain to you exactly how to declare value with U-PIC based on your present system. At the end of each shipping month, you fax, e-mail, or snail-mail your shipping reports to U-PIC.

To place a claim with U-PIC on a USPS shipment, you must do so no sooner than 30 days after the date of mailing, and you must supply the following:

- ✔ A signed letter, stating the loss or damage from the consignee
- ✔ A copy of the monthly insurance report you turned in to U-PIC reflecting the insured value
- ✔ A completed U-PIC claim form (one claim form per claim)
- ✔ A copy of the original invoice or the end of auction form

Because you're paying for private insurance, U-PIC suggests that you include in the package a copy of your insurance policy (or at the very least a note explaining that you have an insurance policy covering your shipments) so that your buyer doesn't think you're overcharging (which makes some folks a bit cranky).

Table 14-3 compares USPS and U-PIC insurance rates. UPS charges $0.75 per $100.00 package value. U-PIC charges only $0.14 per $100.00 UPS shipment value. FedEx charges $0.70 per $100.00 value with a $2.10 minimum. By using U-PIC, you can insure your FedEx packages for $0.20 per $100.00 value.

Table 14-3	USPS and U-PIC Domestic Insurance Coverage Rate Comparison	
Coverage	*USPS*	*U-PIC Standard*
$0.01 to $50.00	$1.75	$0.80
$50.01 to $100.00	$2.25	$0.80
$100.01 to $200.00	$2.75	$1.60
$200.01 to $300.00	$4.70	$2.40
$300.01 to $400.00	$5.70	$3.20

U-PIC will also insure international shipments. The cost to insure international USPS parcels is only $1.55 per $100.00, with no deductible.

If you are a high-volume shipper, you can negotiate an even lower rate with U-PIC. To reach U-PIC, call toll-free at 800-955-4623 or visit its Web site at www.u-pic.com.

Occasional shipper program

The occasional shipper program is for the person who ships less than 100 to 150 packages per month. You can pay for your insurance online using a credit card, but the rates are not as attractive as those for the standard program.

Offline standard program

The offline standard program is the service for eBay businesspeople who ship a large number of packages per month. At the end of each shipping month, you generate an insurance report and use it to calculate your premium. You can pay the premium by check or through PayPal. You can get a discount when shipping with the post office when you use a delivery confirmation.

Part IV

Your eBay Back Office

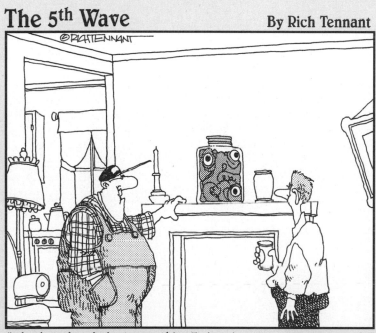

The 5th Wave   By Rich Tennant

"Oh, that there's just something I picked up as a grab bag special from the 'Everything Else' category."

In this part . . .

Do you have all your licenses? You know, those silly government-required things that allow you to run a business legally and, better yet, allow you to buy at wholesale.

Setting up your eBay business as a real business entity involves some unpleasant paperwork. Applying for licenses, organizing, and record keeping are never fun. Even though you should talk to a professional, I fill in the blanks and get you started on the right track. I also provide a handy checklist of the items you need to run your business online, such as your legal status, bookkeeping requirements, and software to automate shipping.

Chapter 15

Getting Legal: Understanding Taxes and Licenses

"*L*egal business format?" you may ask. "What's a legal business format?" I hate to be the one to tell you: You can't just say, "I'm in business," and *be* in business. When you started selling on eBay, maybe you were happy just adding a few dollars to your income. Now that the money is coming in faster, you have a few more details to attend to. Depending how far you're going to take your business, you have to worry about taxes, bookkeeping, and possible ramifications down the line.

I want to remind you that I am *not* a lawyer or an accountant. The facts I give you in this chapter are from what I've learned over the years. When you begin a formal business, it's best to involve the pros — an attorney and an enrolled agent (EA) or a certified public accountant (CPA). At the very least, visit www.nolo.com or www.legalzoom.com, both great Web sites that offer some excellent business startup advice and forms.

One of the rules in the eBay User Agreement reads ". . . you may not transfer your eBay account (including feedback) and User ID to another party *without our consent*" (emphasis mine). This means if you begin your business on eBay with another person, you'd better have some kind of agreement up front about who gets the user ID in case of a sale. And if you sell your business, the person with the original ID had best be involved actively with the new company — as the rules say, your feedback can never be transferred or sold without eBay's permission. eBay's official permission may be a long time coming or may not happen at all, and you don't want to leave these details until the last moment of signing a deal with a new owner. Otherwise, the new owner would have to start a new account on eBay with a new name — unless the principal from the old company was contractually involved and was the actual eBay member.

To my knowledge, no one has tested this rule lately, and I'll bet you don't want to be the first to face eBay's top-notch lawyers. Know that this is the rule — and plan for it.

Understanding the Types of Businesses

Businesses come in several legal forms, from a sole proprietorship all the way to a corporation. A "corporation" designation isn't as scary as it sounds. Yes, Microsoft, IBM, and eBay are corporations, but so are many individuals running much smaller businesses. Each form of business has its plusses and minuses — and costs. I go over some of the fees involved in incorporating yours later in this chapter. For now, I detail the most common types of businesses, which I encourage you to weigh carefully.

Before embarking on any new business format, be sure to consult with a certified professional in the legal and financial fields.

Sole proprietorship

If you're running your business by yourself part-time or full-time, your business is a *sole proprietorship*. (Wow — doesn't that sound official?) A sole proprietorship is the simplest form of business. Nothing is easier or cheaper. Most people use this form of business when they're starting out. Many then graduate to a more formal type of business as things get bigger.

If a husband and wife file a joint tax return, they *can* run a business as a sole proprietorship (but only one of you can be the proprietor). However, if both you *and* your spouse work equally in the business, running it as a partnership — with a written partnership agreement — is a much better idea. (See the next section, "Partnership," for more information.) A partnership protects you in case of your partner's death. In a sole proprietorship, the business ends with the death of the proprietor. If the business has been a sole proprietorship in your late spouse's name, you may be left out in the cold.

Being in business adds a few expenses, but you can deduct many of those expenses (relating to your business) from your state and federal taxes. A sole proprietorship *can* be run out of your personal checking account (although I don't advise it). The profits of your business are taxed directly as part of your own income tax, and the profits and expenses are reported on Schedule C of your tax package. As a sole proprietor, you're at risk for the business liabilities. All outstanding debts are yours — and you could lose personal assets if you default.

There's also the issue of Uncle Sam. When you're a sole proprietor, you are required to pay a self-employment tax, over and above your regular state and federal taxes. This tax covers the Social Security and Medicare taxes that are normally paid by your employer. Currently, the self-employment tax is 15.3 percent (for the first $76,200). That means the profits you make from your online enterprise get taxed additionally! Yowsers!

You *can* deduct half of your self-employment tax in figuring your adjusted gross income. This deduction affects only your income tax; it does *not* affect

- Your net earnings from self-employment
- Your dividends
- Your capital gains
- Your self-employment tax

Other legal business forms can work around this scourge. For up-to-date data on this tax, visit the IRS Web site at `www.irs.gov/businesses/small/article/0,,id=98846,00.html`.

Also, you must consider the liability of the products you sell on eBay. If you sell foodstuff, vitamins, or neutraceuticals (new-age food supplements) that make someone ill, you may be personally liable for any court-awarded damages. If someone is hurt by something you sell, you may also be personally liable as the seller of the product.

Partnership

When two or more people are involved in a business, it can be a *partnership*. A general partnership can be formed by an oral agreement. Each person in the partnership contributes capital or services, and both share in the partnership's profits and losses. The income of a partnership is taxed to both partners, based on the percentage of the business that each partner owns or upon the terms of a written agreement.

You'd better be sure that you can have a good working relationship with your partner: This type of business relationship has broken up many a friendship. Writing up a formal agreement when forming your eBay business partnership is an excellent idea. This agreement is useful in solving any disputes that may occur over time.

In your agreement, be sure to outline things such as

- Division of profits and losses
- Compensation to each of you

- ✔ Duties and responsibilities of each partner
- ✔ Restrictions of authority and spending
- ✔ How disputes should be settled
- ✔ What happens if the partnership dissolves
- ✔ What happens to the partnership in case of death or disability

One more important thing to remember: As a partner, you're jointly and severally responsible for the business liabilities and actions of the other person or people in your partnership — as well as of your own. Again, this is a personal liability arrangement. You are both personally open to any lawsuits that come your way through the business.

The partnership has to file an informational return with the IRS (Form 1065) and the state, but the profits of the partnership are taxed to the partners on their personal individual returns.

LLC (Limited Liability Company)

A *limited liability company,* or LLC, is similar to a partnership, but also has many of the characteristics of a corporation. An LLC differs from a partnership mainly in that the liabilities of the company are not passed on to the members (owners). Unless you sign a personal guarantee for debt incurred, the members are responsible only to the total amount they have invested into the company. But all members *do* have liability for the company's taxes.

You'll need to put together an operating agreement, similar to the partnership agreement. This also will help establish which members own what percentage of the company for tax purposes. Most states will require you to file Articles of Organization forms to start this type of business.

An LLC is taxed like a sole proprietorship, with the profits and losses passed on to the members' personal tax returns. An LLC may opt to pay taxes like a corporation and keep some of the profits in the company, thereby reducing the tax burden to the individual members. Although members pay the LLC's taxes, the LLC must still file Form 1065 with the IRS at the end of the year. This gives the IRS extra data to be sure that the individual members properly report their income.

More information on LLCs can be found on the Web site of my friend, Seattle accountant Stephen L. Nelson, CPA. He's the author of the bestselling books *QuickBooks For Dummies* and *Quicken For Dummies*. He also publishes *Do-It-Yourself Limited Liability Company: LLC Formation Kits*. Check out his informative (state-by-state) site at www.llcsexplained.com.

Corporation

A *corporation* has a life of its own: its own name, its own bank account, and its own tax return. A corporation is a legal entity created for the sole purpose of doing business. One of the main problems a sole proprietor faces when incorporating is realizing that he or she can't just dip into the assets of the business anytime for personal gain. Yes, a corporation can have only one owner: the shareholder(s). If you can understand (and accept) that you can't write yourself a check from your corporation unless it's for salary or for specific reimbursements of legitimate expenses, you may be able to face the responsibility of running your own corporation.

The full brunt of that nasty self-employment tax on income doesn't rear its ugly head when you have a corporation. Because you become an employee of your corporation, you pay yourself a salary. The Medicare and Social Security taxes (approximately 15 percent) are paid only on the part of your profit that you call wages. Niiiice.

You have your choice of either a C or an S corporation. Each of them has a different tax situation:

- ✔ An S corporation enables you to treat profits as distributions and pass them directly to your personal tax return.

- ✔ The C corporation files its own returns and treats you like an employee.

This is a pretty tricky area — and I suggest you consult with a professional before making a decision on which type of corporation to form.

The state in which you run your business sets up the rules for the corporations operating within its borders. You must apply to the Secretary of State for the state in which you want to incorporate. Federal taxes for corporations presently range from 15 to 35 percent, and they're generally based on your net profits. Often, employee owners of corporations use the company to shelter income from tax by dividing the income between their personal and corporate tax returns. This is frequently called *income splitting* and involves setting salaries and bonuses so that any profits left in the company at the end of its tax year will be taxed at only the 15 percent rate. It's kind of fun to see how much the big guys pay and how much you'll pay in taxes if you leave profits in a small corporation, so check out Table 15-1 for the rates.

Getting your legal documents prepared online

You just *knew* legal services would go online eventually, didn't you? If you're thinking of setting up one of the business formats described in this chapter, you might be interested in putting things together online. Real lawyers are there to help you. The platform www.legalzoom.com will handle the preparation of legal documents for business incorporation, partnerships, and more, for incredibly low prices. This online venture was developed by a group of experienced attorneys, cofounded by Robert Shapiro (yes, *that* Robert Shapiro — of O.J. fame).

These folks feature an amazing online law library that can answer many of your questions and help you make informed decisions. Documents are prepared according to how you answer online questionnaires, which are designed to cover most legal transactions. LegalZoom checks your work and then e-mails your documents to you, or mails them printed on quality acid-free paper for your signature.

You may want to also do at least a phone consultation with an attorney in your area, perhaps one who is a member of the local Chamber of Commerce.

Table 15-1   Federal Tax Rates through 2010 for C Corporations

Taxable Income	Tax Rate
$0 to $50,000	15%
$50,001 to $75,000	25%
$75,001 to $100,000	34%
$100,001 to $335,000	39%
$335,001 to $10,000,000	34%
$10,000,001 to $15,000,000	35%
$15,000,001 to $18,333,333	38%
$18,333,334 and over	35%

In small corporations, often most of the profits are paid out in tax–deductible wages and benefits. The most important benefit for a business is that any liabilities belong to the corporation. Your personal assets remain your own because they have no part in the corporation.

Taking Care of Regulatory Details

Let me give you some important words to make your life easier in the long run: Don't ignore city, county, state, and federal regulatory details. Doing so may seem to make life easier at the get-go, but if your business is successful, one day your casual attitude will catch up with you. Ignorance is no excuse. To do business in this great country, you must comply with all the rules and regulations that are set up for your protection and benefit.

Fictitious business name statement

If you plan on running your business under a name different from your own, you may have to file a *fictitious name statement* regardless of the legal format of your business. Your fictitious name (or *DBA, doing business as*) is the name under which the government and the general public know your business. In most states, every person who regularly transacts business for profit under a fictitious business name must file. Depending on where you live, you generally file this form with the county clerk. You can run a Google search for your county's clerk office to find out the exact procedures and fees for your area.

After a certain length of time after you file, your fictitious name will be published in a newspaper that has a section of fictitious names in its classified section. Usually the newspaper files with county agencies and publishes for you in one procedure.

If you have a small community or neighborhood newspaper, check with it to see whether it files fictitious name statements or DBAs. These newspapers also have the lowdown on all the licenses and certificates that you'll need for your locality. Choosing small newspapers to handle these issues for you is a smart idea because they tend to charge a lot less than big-city dailies. Plus, you get to help another small business in your area.

Business license or city tax certificate

Business licenses are the official-looking pieces of paper you see behind the cash register at local stores. Every business must have one, and depending on your local laws, you may have to have a *city license* or a *city tax registration certificate*. Yes, even if you're running a business out of your home and have no one coming to do business at your home, you may still need this. If you don't have one, the authorities may charge you a bunch of penalties if they ever find out. Skipping or avoiding this step isn't worth the risk.

To save you hanging on the phone, listening to elevator music, and being transferred and disconnected ad nauseam, I'm supplying you with the direct links to apply for your licenses (see Table 15-2). These URLs are accurate at the time of this writing, but as everybody knows, URLs change frequently. Check the following for updates: `http://business.sba.gov/register/licenses-and-permits/`.

Table 15-2   Web Sites for Business License & Startup Information

State	URL
Alabama	www.ador.state.al.us/licenses/index.html
Alaska	http://www.commerce.state.ak.us/CBP/
Arizona	http://www.azdor.gov/Business/LicensingGuide.aspx
Arkansas	http://www.dfa.arkansas.gov/offices/policyAndLegal/Documents/starting_a-new_business.pdf
California	www.calgold.ca.gov/
Colorado	http://www.colorado.gov/cs/Satellite/CO-Portal/CXP/1165693060265
Connecticut	www.ct-clic.com
Delaware	https://onestop.delaware.gov/osbrlpublic/Home.jsp
District of Columbia	http://dcra.dc.gov/DC/DCRA/For+Business/Apply+for+a+Business+License
Florida	http://www.myflorida.com/taxonomy/business/business%20licenses,%20permits%20and%20regulation/
Georgia	www.sos.state.ga.us/firststop
Guam	http://www.investguam.com/index.php?pg=license
Hawaii	http://hawaii.gov/dbedt/business/start_grow/Document.2005-10-13.4537
Idaho	http://www.state.id.us/business/
Illinois	http://www.business.illinois.gov/licenses.cfm
Indiana	http://www.state.in.us/ai/licensing/
Iowa	http://www.iowalifechanging.com/business/blic.aspx
Kansas	www.ksrevenue.org/busregistration.htm
Kentucky	http://www.thinkkentucky.com/BIC/ebpermits.aspx
Louisiana	http://www.sos.louisiana.gov/tabid/98/Default.aspx

State	URL
Maine	www.maine.gov/portal/business/licensing.html
Maryland	http://www.dat.state.md.us/sdatweb/tralicen.html
Massachusetts	http://www.mass.gov/?pageID=dorterminal&L=3&L0=Home&L1=Businesses&L2=Help+%26+Resources&sid=Ador&b=terminalcontent&f=dor_business_licpermit&csid=Ador
Michigan	http://www.michigan.gov/business/?source=MEDC
Minnesota	http://www.positivelyminnesota.com/
Mississippi	http://www.mssbdc.org/
Missouri	http://www.missouribusiness.net/sbtdc/startup.asp
Montana	http://mt.gov/business.asp
Nebraska	http://www.nebraska.gov/dynamicindex.html
Nevada	http://tax.state.nv.us/documents/TPI%2001.03%20NV%20Business%20License.pdf
New Hampshire	http://www.nh.gov/business/doingbusiness.html
New Jersey	http://www.nj.gov/njbusiness/licenses/
New Mexico	http://www.rld.state.nm.us/index.html
New York	www.tax.state.ny.us/sbc/starting_business.htm
North Carolina	http://www.nccommerce.com/en/BusinessServices/StartYourBusiness
North Dakota	www.nd.gov/businessreg/license/index.html
Ohio	http://business.ohio.gov/licensing/
Oklahoma	http://www2.okcommerce.gov/index.php?option=com_buslicense&Itemid=771
Oregon	http://licenseinfo.oregon.gov/
Pennsylvania	http://www.newpa.com/build-your-business/start/expert-assistance/center-for-entrepreneurial-assistance/index.aspx
Rhode Island	http://www.ri.gov/business/index.php?subcategory=17&linkgroup=75

(continued)

Table 15-2 (continued)

State	URL
South Carolina	www.scbos.sc.gov/
South Dakota	http://www.sdreadytowork.com/dbisd/ startup/step8.asp
Tennessee	http://www.tennesseeanytime.org/business/ professional.html
Texas	http://www.texas.gov/en/discover/Pages/ topic.aspx?topicid=/business
Utah	www.utah.gov/business/starting.html
Vermont	http://www.vermont.gov/portal/business/
Virgin Islands	http://www.usvichamber.com/business_steps. htm
Virginia	https://apps.cao.virginia.gov/IDC/index. html or http://www.virginia.gov/cms-portal3/business_4096/index.html
Washington	www.dol.wa.gov/business/licensing.html
West Virginia	http://www.business4wv.com/b4wvpublic/ default.aspx?pagename=applyforlicense
Wisconsin	http://ww2.wisconsin.gov/state/license/ app?COMMAND=gov.wi.state.cpp.license. command.LoadLicenseHome
Wyoming	http://www.wyoming.gov/business.aspx

Sales tax number

If your state has a sales tax, a *sales tax number* (the number you use when you file your sales tax statement with your state) is required before you officially sell anything. If sales tax applies, you may have to collect the appropriate sales tax for every sale that ships within the state that your business is in.

Some people also call this a *resale certificate* because when you want to purchase goods from a wholesaler within your state, you must produce this number (thereby certifying your legitimacy) so the dealer can sell you the merchandise without charging you sales tax.

To find the regulations for your state, try the following terrific site, which should have the answers to your questions: `www.taxadmin.org/fta/link/forms.html`.

Don't withhold the withholding forms

Aye, caramba. I swear it feels like the rules and regulations are never going to end, but if you have regular employees, you need to file *withholding forms* to collect the necessary taxes that you must send to the state and the IRS on behalf of your employees. You're also expected to deposit those tax dollars with the IRS and your state on the date required, which may vary from business to business. Many enterprises go down because the owners just can't seem to keep their fingers out of withheld taxes, which means the money isn't available to turn in when the taxes are due (another reason why you should have a separate bank account for your business).

If you have employees, you probably need to get the following:

- **Federal Employee Tax ID number:** File IRS form SS-4. You can apply for this number online, by going to the following: `www.irs.gov/businesses/small/article/0,,id=102767,00.html`.

  For more information, call 1-800-829-1040. For forms to fill out the old-fashioned way, call 1-800-829-3676.

- **State Employer number:** You need this for withholding taxes if your state has an income tax. Check the following site for more information: `http://www.taxadmin.org/fta/rate/tax_stru.html`.

Chapter 16

Savvy Record Keeping — Keeping the Tax Man at Bay

In This Chapter

▶ Understanding first things first: bookkeeping basics

▶ Saving your records to save your bacon

▶ Finding bookkeeping software

▶ Using QuickBooks for your bookkeeping needs

*B*ookkeeping, *bah!* You'll get no argument from me that bookkeeping can be the most dreaded and time-consuming part of your job. You may feel that you just need to add your product costs, add your gross sales, and bada-bing, you know where your business is. Sorry, not true. Did you add that roll of tape you picked up at the supermarket today? Although it cost only $1.29, it's a business expense. How about the mileage driving back and forth from the post office, garage sales, and flea markets? Those are expenses, too. I suspect that you're also not counting quite a few other "small" items just like these in your expense column.

Once I actually get into the task, I must confess that I enjoy posting my expenses and sales. It gives me the opportunity to know exactly where my business is at any given moment. Of course, I'm not using a pencil-and-paper ledger system; I use a software program that's easy enough to be *almost* fun. In this chapter, I give you the lowdown on the basics of bookkeeping, empha-size the importance of keeping records in case Uncle Sam comes calling, and explain why using QuickBooks is the smart software choice. Keep reading: This chapter is *required*.

Keeping the Books: Basics That Get You Started

Although posting bookkeeping can be boring, clicking a button to generate your tax information is a lot easier than manually going over pages of sales information on a pad of paper (or a shoebox stuffed with receipts). That's why I like to use a software program, particularly QuickBooks Pro (more about that in the section titled "QuickBooks: Making Bookkeeping Uncomplicated").

Okay, I suppose you *could* use plain ol' paper and pencil to keep your books; if that works for you, great. But even if that might work for you now, it definitely won't in the future. Entering all your information into a software program now — while your books may still be fairly simple to handle — can save you a lot of time and frustration in the future, when your eBay business has grown beyond your wildest dreams and no amount of paper can keep it all straight and organized. I discuss alternative methods of bookkeeping in the "Bookkeeping Software" section. For now, I focus on the basics of bookkeeping.

To manage your business effectively, you must keep track of *all* your expenses — down to the last roll of tape. You need to keep track of your inventory, how much you paid for the items, how much you paid in shipping, and how much you profited from your sales. If you use a van or the family car to pick up or deliver merchandise to the post office (I can load eight of the light kits I sell on eBay into my car), you should keep track of this mileage as well. When you're running a business, you should account for every penny that goes in and out.

Bookkeeping has irrefutable standards called Generally Accepted Accounting Procedures (GAAP) that are set by the Financial Accounting Standards Board. (That sounds scary to me, too.) Assets, liabilities, owner's equity, income, and expenses are standard terms used in all forms of accounting to define profit, loss, and the fiscal health of your business.

Every time you process a transaction, two things happen: One account is credited while another receives a debit (kind of like yin and yang). To get more familiar with these terms (and those in the following list), see the definitions in the chart of accounts later in this chapter (in Table 16-2) and in Appendix A (a mini-glossary I've included for your convenience). Depending on the type of account, the account's balance either increases or decreases. One account that increases while another decreases is called *double-entry accounting:*

✔ When you post an expense, the debit *increases* your expenses and *decreases* your bank account.

✔ When you purchase furniture or other assets, it *increases* your asset account and *decreases* your bank account.

✔ When you make a sale and make the deposit, it *increases* your bank account and *decreases* your accounts receivable.

✔ When you purchase inventory, it *increases* your inventory and *decreases* your bank account.

✔ When a portion of a sale includes sales tax, it *decreases* your sales account, and *increases* your sales tax account.

Manually performing double-entry accounting can be a bit taxing (no pun intended). A software program adjusts the accounts automatically when you input a transaction.

As a business owner, even if you're a sole proprietor (see Chapter 15 for information on business types), you should keep your business books separate from your personal expenses. (I recommend using a program such as Quicken to keep track of your *personal expenses* for tax time.) By isolating the business records from the personal records, you can get a snapshot of what areas of your sales are doing well and which ones aren't carrying their weight. But that isn't the only reason keeping accurate records is smart; there's the IRS to think about, too. In the next section, I explain Uncle Sam's interest in your books.

Hiring a professional to do your year-end taxes

When I say that you must hire a professional to prepare your taxes, I mean a certified public accountant (CPA) if your business format is a corporation, or an *enrolled agent (EA)* for a sole proprietorship or partnership. An EA is a tax professional who's licensed by the federal government and specializes solely in taxation and current tax laws. EAs must pass an annual two-day exam (less than one-third of the people who take the test pass it) and are required to fulfill continuing education requirements to maintain their standing. Just like a CPA or a tax attorney, EAs are authorized to appear before the IRS on your behalf in the event of an audit. Unlike a CPA or an attorney, however, EAs don't charge an arm and a leg. They're a valuable addition to your business arsenal.

Although the folks at your local "We Do Your Taxes in a Hurry Store" may be well-meaning and pleasant, they may have gone through only a six-week course in the current tax laws. This does not make them tax professionals. When business taxes are at stake, a professional with whom you have a standing relationship is the best choice. If you don't know one, ask around or call your local Chamber of Commerce.

Posting bookkeeping can be boring. At the end of the year, however, when you have a professional do your taxes, you'll be a lot happier — and your tax preparation will cost you less — if you've posted your information cleanly and in the proper order. That's why using QuickBooks is essential to running your business. (See the "QuickBooks: Making Bookkeeping Uncomplicated" section.)

Records Uncle Sam May Want to See

One of the reasons why we can have a great business environment in the United States is because we all have a partner — Uncle Sam. Our government regulates business and sets the rules for us to transact our operations. To help you get started with your business, the IRS maintains a small business Web site at www.irs.gov/businesses/small. Tax information is available for small businesses at www.business.gov/manage/taxes.

In this section, I highlight what information you need to keep and how long you should keep it (just in case you're chosen for an audit).

Supporting information

Aside from needing to know how your business is going (which is really important), the main reason to keep clear and concise records is because Uncle Sam may come knocking one day. You never know when the IRS will choose *your* number and want to examine *your* records. In the following list, I highlight some of the important pieces of *supporting information* (things that support your expenses on your end-of-year tax return):

✔ **Receipts:** Dear reader, heed this advice: Save every receipt you get. If you're out of town on a buying trip and have coffee at the airport, save that receipt — it's a deduction from your profits. Everything related to your business may be deductible, so you must save airport parking receipts, taxi receipts, receipts for a pen that you picked up on your way to a meeting, *everything.* If you don't have a receipt, you can't prove the write-off.

PayPal reports sales to Internal Revenues Service

PayPal is required to report to the IRS the total gross sales volume received by PayPal customers in the United States who

✔ Receive more than $20,000 in gross payment volume in a single year AND

✔ Receive 200 or more payments in a single year.

The reporting system applies to all payment providers you may do business with for receiving payments on various platforms. Reports begin on January 1, 2011; the first reports go to the IRS in early 2012. If your sales qualify, you will receive a 1099-K Form, either electronically or by mail, from your payment provider.

✔ **Merchandise invoices:** Saving all merchandise invoices is as important as saving all your receipts. If you want to prove that you paid $400 and not the $299 retail price for that Nintendo Wii that you sold on eBay for $500, you'd *better* have an invoice of some kind. The same idea applies to most collectibles, in which case a retail price can't be fixed. Save all invoices!

✔ **Outside contractor invoices:** If you use outside contractors — even if you pay the college kid next door to go to the post office and bank for you — you should also get an invoice from them to document exactly what service you paid for and how much you paid. This is supporting information that will save your bacon, should it ever need saving.

✔ **Business cards:** It may sound like I'm stretching things a bit, but if you use your car to look at some merchandise, pick up a business card from the vendor. If you're out of town and have a meeting with someone, take a card. Having these business cards can help substantiate your deductible comings and goings.

✔ **A daily calendar:** This is where your handheld comes in. Every time you leave your house or office on a business-related task, make note of it in your handheld. Keep as big a collection of the minutiae as you can stand. A Palm Desktop can print a monthly calendar. At the end of the year, staple the pages together and include them in your files with your substantiating information.

✔ **Credit card statements:** You're already collecting credit card receipts (although mine always seem to slip through the holes in my purse). If you have your statements, you have monthly proof of expenses. When you get your statement each month, post it into your bookkeeping program and itemize each and every charge, detailing where you spent the money and for what. (QuickBooks has a split feature that accommodates all your categories.) File these statements with your tax return at the end of the year in your year-end envelope (shoe box?).

I know that all this stuff will pile up, but that's when you go to the store and buy some plastic file-storage containers to organize it all. To check for new information and the lowdown on what you can and can't do, ask an accountant or a CPA. Also visit the IRS Tax Information for Business site at www.irs.ustreas.gov/businesses.

How long should you keep your records?

How long do you have to keep all this supporting information? I hate to tell you, but I think I've saved it all almost from day one. I must have at least ten years of paperwork in big plastic boxes and old files in the garage. But you know, I'm not too extreme; the period in which you can amend a return or in which the IRS can assess more tax is never less than three years from the date of filing — and can even be longer. As of my last visit to the IRS Web site, the information in Table 16-1 applied.

Table 16-1	How Long to Keep Your Tax Records
Circumstance	**Keep Records This Long**
You owe additional tax (if the following three points don't apply)	3 years
You didn't report all your income and what you didn't report is more than 25% of the gross income shown on your return	6 years
You file a fraudulent tax return	No limit
You don't bother to file a return	No limit
You file a claim of refund or credit after you've filed	3 years or 2 years after tax was paid (whichever is longer)
Your claim is due to a bad debt deduction	7 years
Your claim is from worthless stock	7 years
Your employment records	4 years after tax is due
You have information on assets	Life of the asset

Even though I got this information directly from the IRS Web site and literature (Publication 583, "Starting a Business and Keeping Records"), it may change in the future. You can download a PDF copy of the booklet by going to www.irs.gov/pub/irs-pdf/p583.pdf. (The download requires Adobe Acrobat Reader. If it isn't installed on your computer, you can download the software for free from the IRS Web site.) It doesn't hurt to store your information for as long as you can stand it and stay on top of any changes the IRS may implement.

Bookkeeping Software

Keeping track of your auctions is hard without software, but keeping track of the money you make without software is even harder (and more time-consuming). If using software to automate your auctions makes sense, so does using software to automate your bookkeeping. You can afford to make a mistake here and there in your own office, and maybe no one will ever know. But if you make a mistake in the books, your partner (Uncle Sam) will notice — and be quite miffed. He may even charge you a penalty or two so you'll remember not to make those mistakes again.

Those penalties aren't small, either. A 3-day-late tax deposit will cost you an additional 10 percent tax penalty. That can be an expensive lesson.

When I started my business, I used accounting ledger pads (which had just replaced the chisel-and-stone format). I soon found that I had way too many ledgers to keep track of and cross-reference. A calculator was useful, based on the assumption that I typed the correct figures to start with.

Spreadsheet software can be a boon when you're just starting out. A program such as Microsoft Office Excel is an excellent way to begin posting your business expenses and profits. The program can be set up to calculate your expenses, profits, and (I hope not too many) losses. Microsoft Works comes with several free financial-worksheet templates that you can easily adapt for an eBay small business. Also, you can find current Excel templates to get you started at office.microsoft.com. There's no need to spend any extra money on templates when you're just starting out!

With official bookkeeping software, reconciling a checkbook is a breeze. You merely click off the deposits and checks when the statement comes in. If I made a mistake originally when inputting the data, the software (comparing my balance and my bank's) lets me know. This kind of efficiency would have put Bob Cratchit out of a job!

I researched various Web sites to find which software was the best-selling and easiest to use. I had many discussions with CPAs, EAs, and bookkeepers. The software that these professionals most recommend for business is Intuit's QuickBooks. (Thank goodness that's the one I use.) QuickBooks is considered the best, which is why I devote so much of this chapter to it. Some people begin with Quicken and later move to QuickBooks when their business gets big or incorporates. My theory? Start with the best. It's not that much more expensive — on eBay, I've seen new, sealed QuickBooks Pro 2010 software for as low as $120.

QuickBooks: Making Bookkeeping Uncomplicated

QuickBooks offers several versions, from basic to enterprise-level solutions tailored to different types of businesses. QuickBooks Simple Start and QuickBooks Pro have a few significant differences. QuickBooks Pro adds job costing and expensing features, payroll, and the ability to keep track of your inventory through your sales receipts and purchases (making it a sound upgrade for eBay sellers). QuickBooks Simple Start does a darn good job, too, so check out the comparison at `quickbooks.intuit.com` and see which version is best for you. I use (and highly recommend) QuickBooks Pro, so that's the version I describe in the rest of this section.

Stephen L. Nelson wrote *QuickBooks 2010 For Dummies* (published by Wiley). His book is amazingly easy to understand. I swear that neither Steve nor my publisher gave me a nickel for recommending his book. (Heck, I even had to pay for my copy.) I recommend it simply because it answers — in plain English — just about any question you'll have about using the program for your bookkeeping needs. Spend the money and get the book. Any money spent on increasing your knowledge is money well spent (and may be a tax write-off).

I update my QuickBooks software yearly, and every year it takes me less time to perform my bookkeeping tasks (because of product improvements). If you find that you don't have time to input your bookkeeping data, you may have to hire a bookkeeper. The bonus is that professional bookkeepers already know QuickBooks, and the best part is that they can print weekly reports for you that keep you apprised of your business condition. Also, at the end of each year, QuickBooks will supply you with *all* the official reports and data your enrolled agent or certified public accountant will need to do your taxes. (Yes, you really do need an EA or a CPA; see the "Hiring a professional to do your year-end taxes" sidebar elsewhere in this chapter.) You can even send them a backup on a flash drive or a CD-ROM. See how simple bookkeeping can be?

QuickBooks integrates with PayPal

PayPal can provide your payment history in QuickBooks format. It even offers a settlement and reconciliation system download that breaks up your PayPal transactions into debits and credits. A handy feature! One warning, though: These are only financial transactions. When you use QuickBooks to its fullest, you will have your inventory in the program. When you purchase merchandise to sell, QuickBooks sets up the inventory — and deducts from it each time you input an invoice or a sales receipt. This way, your inventory receipts follow GAAP. In my *eBay Business All-in-One For Dummies*, I show you my procedures for posting your weekly (or daily) sales in QuickBooks by using sales receipts versus clogging up your program with thousands of customer listings. (This approach, by the way, received an approving nod from Stephen Nelson when I showed him my system.)

QuickBooks Pro

When you first fire up QuickBooks Pro, you have to answer a few questions to set up your account. Among the few things you need to have ready — before you even begin to mess with the software — are the following starting figures:

- ✓ **Cash balance:** This may be the amount in your business checking account (no personal money, please!) or the amount of money deposited from your eBay profits. Put these profits into a separate checking account to use for your business.

- ✓ **Accounts receivable balance:** Does anyone owe you money for some auctions? Outstanding payments make up this total.

- ✓ **Account liability balance:** Do you owe some money? Are you being invoiced for some merchandise that you haven't paid for? Total it and enter it when QuickBooks asks you.

If you're starting your business in the middle of the year, gather any previous profits and expenses that you want to include because you'll have to input this information for a complete annual set of diligently recorded books. I can guarantee that this is going to take a while. But after you've gathered together your finances, even if it takes a little sweat to set it up initially, you'll be thanking me for insisting you get organized. It just makes everything work smoother in the long run.

Firing up QuickBooks for the first time

The first thing you need to do is organize finances. Put all your expenses in one folder and sales information in another, and then you can proceed with the QuickBooks setup interview. (Relax. The interview is designed to give those with accounting phobia — and those using a bookkeeping program for the first time — a comfort level.)

QuickBooks asks you questions about your business and you fill in the (very intuitive) form. If you mess things up, you can always use the Back arrow and change what you've input. If you need help, simply click the Help button and the program will answer many of your questions. (Hey, if worst comes to worst, you can always delete the file from the QuickBooks directory and start over.)

If you're new to bookkeeping, you may want to go through the QuickBooks startup interview step by step with a tutor at your side. For more details, remember to check out *QuickBooks 2010 For Dummies* — this book can get you up to speed on almost everything you need to know about QuickBooks.

QuickBooks chart of accounts

After you've finished the setup and have successfully set yourself up in QuickBooks, the program presents a chart of accounts. Think of the *chart of accounts* as an organization system, such as file folders. It keeps all related data in the proper area. When you write a check to pay a bill, it deducts the amount from your checking account, reduces your accounts payable, and perhaps increases your asset or expense accounts.

You have a choice of giving each account a number. These numbers, a kind of bookkeeping shorthand, are standardized throughout bookkeeping; believe it or not, everybody in the industry seems to know what number goes with what item. To keep things less confusing, I like to use titles as well as numbers.

To customize your chart of accounts, follow these steps:

1. **Choose Edit⇨Preferences.**

2. **Click the Accounting icon (on the left).**

3. **Click the Company preferences tab and indicate that you'd like to use account numbers.**

   An editable chart of accounts appears. Because QuickBooks doesn't assign account numbers as a default, you'll need to edit the chart to create them.

4. **Go through your QuickBooks chart of accounts and add any missing categories.**

Learning about COGS

No, no, I'm not talking about Cogswell's Cogs (the company that George Jetson worked for); I'm talking about Cost of Goods Sold. It's a special type of expense and often varies depending on the type of business. The general definition of COGS reflects the cost of purchasing raw materials and manufacturing finished products. Some accountants look at it slightly differently in an eBay business: encompassing credit card (PayPal) fees, eBay fees, and shipping costs, making it include all direct costs of products sold and shipped to customers.

I like it this way because in the financial profit & loss statement, QuickBooks lists COGS ahead of other expense accounts. This gives me a snapshot view of the sales profitability of my eBay business without clouding things by including telephone, payroll, travel, and all the other expenses that affect the gross profits.

You may not need all these categories, and you can always add more later. In Table 16-2, I show you a chart of accounts that a CPA wrote for an eBay business.

Table 16-2	eBay Business Chart of Accounts	
Account Number	*Account Name*	*What it Represents*
1001	Checking	All revenue deposited here and all checks drawn upon this account.
1002	Money market account	Company savings account.
1100	Accounts receivable	For customers to whom you extend credit.
1201	Merchandise	COGS: Charge to cost of sales as used, or take periodic inventories and adjust at that time.
1202	Shipping supplies	Boxes, tape, labels, and so forth; charge these to cost as used or take an inventory at the end of the period and adjust to cost of sales.
1401	Office furniture & equipment	Desk, computer, telephone.
1402	Shipping equipment	Scales, tape dispensers.
1403	Vehicles	Your vehicle if it's owned by the company.
1501	Accumulated depreciation	For your accountant's use.
1601	Deposits	Security deposits on leases.
2001	Accounts payable	Amounts owed for the stuff you sell or charged expenses.
2100	Payroll liabilities	Taxes deducted from employees' checks and taxes paid by the company on employee earnings.
2200	Sales tax payable	Sales tax collected at time of sale and owed to the state.
2501	Equipment loans	Money borrowed to buy a computer or other equipment.
2502	Auto loans	When you get that hot new van for visiting your consignment clients.

(continued)

Table 16-2 *(continued)*

Account Number	Account Name	What it Represents
3000	Owner's capital	Your opening balance.
3902	Owner's draw	Your withdrawals for the current year.
4001	Merchandise sales	Revenue from sales of your products.
4002	Shipping and handling	Paid by the customer.
4009	Returns	Total dollar amount of returned merchandise.
4101	Interest income	From your investments.
4201	Other income	Income not otherwise classified.
5001	Merchandise purchases	All the merchandise you buy for eBay; you'll probably use subaccounts for individual items.
5002	Freight in	Freight and shipping charges you pay for your inventory, not for shipments to customers.
5003	Shipping	COGS: Shipping to your customers: USPS, FedEx, UPS, and so on.
5004	Shipping supplies	COGS: Boxes, labels, tape, bubble pack.
6110	Automobile expense	When you use your car for work.
6111	Gas and oil	Filling up the tank!
6112	Repairs	When your business owns the car.
6120	Bank service charges	Monthly service charges, NSF charges, and so forth.
6140	Contributions	Charity.
6142	Data services	Do you have an outside firm processing your payroll? That's a typical example of a data service.
6143	Internet service provider	What you pay to your Internet provider.
6144	Web site hosting fees	Fees paid to your hosting company.
6150	Depreciation expense	For your accountant's use.

Account Number	Account Name	What it Represents
6151	eBay fees	COGS: What you pay eBay every time you list an item and make a sale.
6152	Discounts	Fees you're charged for using eBay and accepting credit card payments; deducted from your revenue and reported to you on your eBay statement.
6153	Other auction site fees	COGS: You may want to set up subcategories for each site where you do business, such as Yahoo! or Amazon.com.
6156	PayPal fees	COGS: Processing fees paid to PayPal.
6158	Credit card merchant account fees	COGS: If you have a separate merchant account, post those fees here.
6160	Dues	If you join an organization that charges membership fees (relating to your business).
6161	Magazines and periodicals	Books and magazines that help you run and expand your business.
6170	Equipment rental	Postage meter, occasional van.
6180	Insurance	Policies that cover your merchandise or your office.
6185	Liability insurance	Insurance that covers you if someone slips and falls at your place of business (can also be put under Insurance).
6190	Disability insurance	Insurance that will pay you if you become temporarily or permanently disabled and can't perform your work.
6191	Health insurance	If provided for yourself, you may be required to provide it to employees.
6200	Interest expense	Credit interest and interest on loans.
6220	Loan interest	When you borrow from the bank.
6230	Licenses and permits	State and city licenses.
6240	Miscellaneous	Whatever doesn't go anyplace else in this table.
6250	Postage and delivery	Stamps used in your regular business.
6251	Endicia.com fees	COGS: Fees for your eBay business postage service.

(continued)

Table 16-2 *(continued)*

Account Number	Account Name	What it Represents
6260	Printing	Your business cards, correspondence stationery, and so on.
6265	Filing fees	Fees paid to file legal documents.
6270	Professional fees	Fees paid to consultants.
6280	Legal fees	If you have to pay a lawyer.
6650	Accounting and bookkeeping	Bookkeeper, CPA, or EA.
6290	Rent	Office, warehouse, and so on.
6300	Repairs	Can be the major category for the following subcategories.
6310	Building repairs	Repairs to the building where you operate your business.
6320	Computer repairs	What you pay the person who sets up your wireless network.
6330	Equipment repairs	When the copier or phone needs fixing.
6340	Telephone	Regular telephone, FAX lines.
6350	Travel and entertainment	Business-related travel, business meals.
6360	Entertainment	When you take eBay's CEO out to dinner to benefit your eBay business. (Just keep it clearly business-related, okay?)
6370	Meals	Meals while traveling for your business.
6390	Utilities	Major heading for the following two subcategories.
6391	Electricity and gas	Electricity and gas.
6392	Water	Water.
6560	Payroll expenses	Wages paid to others.
6770	Supplies	Office supplies.
6772	Computer	Computer and supplies.
6780	Marketing	Advertising or promotional items you purchase to give away.
6790	Office	Miscellaneous office expenses, such as bottled water delivery.

Account Number	Account Name	What it Represents
6820	Taxes	Major category for the following four subcategories.
6830	Federal	Federal taxes.
6840	Local	Local taxes.
6850	Property	Property taxes.
6860	State	State taxes.

QuickBooks on the Web

If you want to handle everything on the Web, use the QuickBooks online service. The online QuickBooks program offers fewer features than the Pro version, but if your accounting needs are simple, it may be right for you. Before you decide, however, consider that while your accounting needs may be simple now, they may not be so simple later.

Intuit pricing starts at $12.95 a month for the service, which is comparable to buying the QuickBooks Pro version — but at least you can continue to use purchased software for more than one year. The online version also requires you to have a broadband connection to the Internet so you're always online (dial-up connections need not apply). The online edition doesn't include integrated payroll, purchase orders, online banking, and bill payments.

Chapter 17

Building an eBay Back Office

*T*he more items you sell, the more confusing things can get. As you build your eBay business, the little side table you use for storing eBay merchandise isn't going to work. You have to start thinking industrial. Even part-time sellers can benefit by adding a few professional touches to their business areas.

In this chapter, I emphasize the importance of setting up and organizing your *back office* — essentially the daily, practical, behind-the-scenes details that keep your business running. Organization will save you huge amounts of time when it comes to fulfilling your orders. I cover everything from stacking your stock to keeping inventory to indispensable packing materials and online postage services. Organization will be your byword. Dive right in. The sooner you read this chapter, the sooner you can build your eBay back office and get down to business.

The Warehouse: Organizing Your Space

Whether you plan to sell large items or small items, you need space for storing them. As you make savvy purchases, maintaining an item's mint condition will be one of your greatest challenges. Organized storage is an art in itself, so in this section I cover the details of what you'll need to safeguard your precious stock

Shelving your profits

Before you stock the shelves, it helps to have some! You also need a place to put the shelves: your garage, a spare room, or somewhere else. You have a choice between two basic kinds of shelves:

- ✔ **Plastic:** If you're just starting out, you can always go to the local closet-and-linen supply store to buy inexpensive plastic shelves. They're light and cheap — but they'll buckle in time, rendering them useless.

- ✔ **Steel:** If you want to do it right the first time, buy steel shelving. The most versatile steel shelving is the wire kind (versus solid-steel shelves), which is lighter and allows air to circulate around your items. Steel wire shelving assembles easily; I put mine together without help. They come with leveling feet or four-inch casters, so you can move the unit if necessary. Installing the casters is up to you. You can combine steel wire shelving units to create a full wall of shelves. Each shelf safely holds as much as 500 pounds of merchandise.

  Search eBay for **shelving** (**steel**, **plastic**) to find sellers offering this kind of industrial shelving. The main problem with ordering this product online is that the shipping usually costs more than the shelving.

To save you time, dear reader, I researched the subject and found some readily available, reasonably priced shelves. Just go to Target or Costco and look for steel-wire four-shelf commercial shelving, sold in 36- and 48-inch-wide units. Each shelf will hold up to 500 pounds. These shelves are available also on the Costco Web site, but you have to pay for shipping.

Box 'em or bag 'em?

Packing your items for storage can be a challenge. As long as you're picking up your shelving (see preceding section), pick up some plastic bags in snack, sandwich, quart, and gallon sizes. The snack baggies are perfect for storing the smallest of items. When items are stored in plastic, they can't pick up any smells or become musty before you sell them. The plastic also protects the items from rubbing against each other and causing possible scratches. If you package them one item to a bag, you can then just lift one off the shelf and put it directly into a shipping box when the sale is made. Also, when you ship the item, the plastic protection may save the package from a rainy day.

Your bags of items will have to go into boxes for storage on the shelves. Clear plastic storage boxes, the kind you often find at superstores, are great for bulky items. They're usually 26 inches long — so before you buy these big plastic containers, be sure they'll fit on your shelving easily, and that you'll have easy access to your items. Using cardboard, office-type file-storage boxes from an office supply store is another option. These cardboard boxes are 10 x 12 x 16 inches, which is a nice size for storing medium size products. At around $1 each, they're the most economical choice. The downside is that you can't see through cardboard boxes; if your label falls off, you have to take the box off the shelf and open it to check its contents. Smaller see-through plastic boxes with various compartments, such as the kind home-improvement stores carry for storing tools, work great for storing very small items.

When using these large plastic bins, it's always a good idea to tape a pad of Post-it notes on the end of the box so you can quickly identify the contents. You *can* use regular sticky labels, but changing them will leave large amounts of paper residue over time, and your storage will look sloppy and icky.

Inventory: Keeping Track of What You Have and Where You Keep It

Savvy eBay sellers have different methods of handling inventory. They use everything from spiral-bound notebooks to sophisticated software programs. Although computerized inventory tracking can simplify this task, starting with a plain ol' handwritten ledger is fine, too. Choose whichever works best for you, but keep in mind that as your eBay business grows, a software program that tracks inventory for you may become necessary. If you use QuickBooks for your bookkeeping, note that this all-in-one software will also keep track of your inventory (every time you post your purchases and sales).

Ledger systems won't accommodate the burgeoning records of a company that has a warehouse full of stock, but they'll work nicely in a beginning eBay sales environment. Many sellers tape sheets of paper to their boxes to identify them by number and refer to those numbers in a simple Excel spreadsheet for selling purposes. Excel spreadsheets are perfect for keeping track of your sales as well, but if you're using a management service or software, you don't need both for physical inventory. As you get to the point of running a bigger business, however, you have to keep Uncle Sam happy with a periodic dollars-and-cents accounting of your inventory, so keep your inventory records in a standardized program such as QuickBooks (discussed in Chapter 16). In Chapter 9, I detail a variety of auction-management software options and Web sites, many of which include features for tracking physical inventory.

Planning: The key to good organization

When it was time for me to put my eBay merchandise in order, I was still busy with my regular job, so I hired people to organize my eBay area. This decision turned out to be one massive mistake. They organized everything and put all my items in boxes — but didn't label the boxes to indicate what was stored in each. Also, the boxes weren't placed in a way that was intuitive for me to assemble my outgoing packages quickly. It took me months to recover.

A bit of advice: Think things out and plan where you'll put everything. Organize your items by theme, type, or size. In my eBay business area, I have books in one area, DVDs in another, photographic equipment on shelves, and so on. If you try to "organize" before planning where everything goes, you might end up with "organized" disorganization.

You may also want to use Excel spreadsheets for your downloaded PayPal statements, to hold information you're waiting to transfer to your bookkeeping program or merely for archival purposes at the end of the year.

The Shipping Department: Packin' It Up

If you've read *eBay For Dummies,* you know all about the various ways to pack your items. I hope you've become an expert! In this section, I review some of the things you must have for a complete, smooth-running shipping department, such as cleaning supplies and packing materials. The *handling fee* portion of your shipping charges pays for these kinds of items. Don't run low on them — and pay attention to how you store them. They must be kept in a clean environment.

Packaging clean-up

Be sure that the items you send out are in tip-top shape. Here are a few everyday chemicals that can help you gild the lily:

- **WD-40:** This decades-old lubricant works incredibly well at getting price stickers off plastic and glass without damaging the product. The plastic on a toy box may begin to look scratchy and nasty, even when stored in a clean environment. A quick wipe with a paper towel containing a dash of WD-40 will make it shine like new. WD-40 also works well for untangling jewelry chains and shining up metallic objects. (It also removes ink and crayon marks from many items.)

✔ **Goo Gone:** Goo Gone works miracles in cleaning up gooey sticker residue from nonporous items.

✔ **un-du:** This amazing liquid easily removes stickers from cardboard, plastic, fabrics, and more without causing damage. It comes packaged with a patented miniscraper top that you can use in any of your sticker-cleaning projects.

Okay, you can use lighter fluid to clean an item if you have to, but it's considerably more dangerous and may damage your item.

Packing materials

To make sure that your items will arrive at their destinations in one piece, you'll want to keep the following supplies on hand at all times:

✔ **Bubble wrap:** A clean, putty product that comes in rolls (see Figure 17-1), bubble wrap is available in several sizes. Depending on your product, you may have to carry two sizes of bubble wrap to protect your goods properly. Bubble wrap can be expensive, but check out vendors at eBay; you'll find quite a lot of them (and possibly a deal). The best part about bubble wrap is that it's highly recyclable, and the packing material that comes in with your merchandise orders can be reused on your outgoing items.

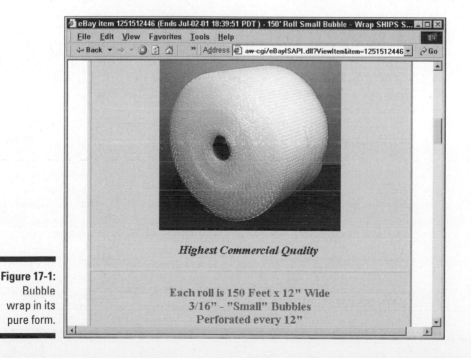

Figure 17-1:
Bubble wrap in its pure form.

Removing musty odors from apparel items

Clothing can often pick up odors that you just don't notice. I once bought a designer dress on eBay from a seller who had the typical disclaimer in her description: "No stains, holes, repairs, or odors. Comes from a smoke-free, pet-free home." Unfortunately, the minute I opened the box I could smell the musty odor of an item that had been stored for a long time.

To prevent that icky storage odor, keep a package of Dryel fabric care system around. This is a safe do-it-yourself dry-cleaning product. Just toss your eBay clothing items in the patented Dryel bag with the special sheet and toss the bag in the dryer (per the instructions on the box). Your garment will come out smelling clean — and will hang up wrinkle-free. For more information, visit the Dryel Web site at `www.Dryel.com`.

✔ **Styrofoam packing peanuts:** Why they call them "peanuts," I'll never know — I guess somebody thought they look like peanuts. Nonetheless, Styrofoam peanuts protect just about everything you ship. Storing them is the tricky part. I store mine by putting them into 33-gallon drawstring plastic trash bags and then I hang the bags on cup hooks (available at the hardware store) around the walls and rafters of my garage. When packing your items with peanuts, be sure that you place the item carefully and use enough peanuts to fill the box *completely*; leaving any airspace defeats the point of using the peanuts in the first place. (Don't go short in the land of plenty.)

✔ **Plastic bags:** Buy plastic bags in bulk to save money. Make sure you buy various sizes and use them for both shipping and storing. Even large kitchen or trash bags are good for wrapping up posters and large items before shipping; the plastic protects the item from inclement weather by waterproofing it.

✔ **Two- or three-inch shipping tape:** You'll need clear tape for finishing up packages. You'll also need the clear tape to place over address labels to protect them from scrapes and rain. I once received a package with an address label completely soaked with rain and barely legible. Don't risk a lost package for want of a few inches of tape.

✔ **Bubble mailer envelopes:** If you send items that fit nicely into bubble-lined envelopes, use them (see Figure 17-2). This type of envelope — with paper on the outside and bubble wrap on the inside — is perfect for mailing small items or clothing using First Class or Priority mail. The envelopes are available in quantity by the case (an economical choice) and don't take up much storage space. Table 17-1 shows you the industry-standard sizes of bubble mailer envelopes and their suggested uses. To get a real-world idea of how these mailers fit your items, bring the items to a local office superstore and buy one each of several different sizes of envelopes before ordering.

Figure 17-2:
Bubble-
wrap-lined
mailer
envelopes
for sale on
eDay.

Table 17-1   Standard Bubble Mailer Sizes

Size	Measurements	Suggested Items
#000	4" x 8"	Collector trading cards, jewelry, computer diskettes, coins
#00	5" x 10"	Postcards, paper ephemera
#0	6" x 10"	Doll clothes, CDs, DVDs, Xbox or PS2 games
#1	7¼" x 12"	Cardboard sleeve VHS tapes, jewel-cased CDs, DVD sets
#2	8½" x 12"	Clamshell VHS tapes, books
#3	8½" x 14½"	Toys, clothing, stuffed animals
#4	9½" x 14½"	Small books, trade paperbacks
#5	10½" x 16"	Hardcover books, dolls
#6	12½" x 19"	Clothing, soft boxed items
#7	14¼" x 20"	Much larger packaged items, framed items, and plaques

Packaging — the heart of the matter

Depending on the size of the item you sell, you can purchase boxes in bulk at reliable sources. Because you have a resale number (see Chapter 15), look in your local Yellow Pages for wholesale boxes. (You still have to pay tax, but the resale number identifies you as a business — and that often can get you a lower price.) Try to purchase from a manufacturer that specializes in business to business (B2B) sales. Some box companies specialize in selling to the occasional box user. Knowing the size that you need enables you to buy by the case lot.

You can save big money if your items fit into boxes that the post office supplies without charge (that's *free*, my friends) and you plan on using Priority Mail. The USPS will give you all the boxes and mailing envelopes you need for free, and it offers plenty of sizes. See handy Table 17-2 for available sizes.

Table 17-2	Free Priority Mail Packaging	
Size	*Description*	*Minimum Quantity*
8⅝" x 5⅝" x 1⅝"	Small Flat Rate Box	10
11 18" x 3 3/8" x 13 5/8"	Medium Flat Rate Box FRB2	10
11" x 8.5" x 5.5"	Medium Flat Rate Box FRB1	10
12" x 12" x 5 1/2"	Large Flat Rate Box	10
10 1/8" x 7 1/8" x 5"	Regional Rate Top Load A1*	10
12 1/4" x 10 1/2" x 5 1/2"	Regional Rate Top Load B1**	10
13 1/16" x 11 1/16" x 2 1/2"	Regional Rate Side Load A1*	10
16 1/4" x 14 1/2" x 3"	Regional Rate Side Load B2**	10
9¼" x 6¼" x 2"	Large Video Box 1096LX	10
11½" x 13⅛" x 2⅜"	Medium O-1097	10
12½ x 15½" x 3"	Large O-1095	10
12.125" x 13.375" x 2.75"	Medium O-1092	10
6" x 38"	Triangle Tube 14F	10
6" x 25"	Triangle Tube 1098S	10
7" x 7" x 6"	Small Square Cube BOX4	10

Size	Description	Minimum Quantity
12" x 12" x 8"	Square Cube BOX7	10
11⅞" x 3⅜" x 13⅝"	Flat Rate Rectangular Box FRB2	20
11" x 8.5" x 5.5"	Flat Rate Medium Box FRB1	20
7.5" x 5.125" x 14.375"	Shoe Box	10
11.625" x 15.125"	Tyvek Envelope EP14	10
6" x 10"	Cardboard Envelope 14B	10
10" x 7"	Gift Card Mailer	5
12½" x 9½"	Flat Rate Cardboard Envelope 14-F	10
5" x 10"	Cardboard Window Envelope	1

* Maximum weight 15 lbs.

** Maximum weight 20 lbs.

Go to `http://shop.usps.com/` and then click the For Mailing/Shipping link (see Figure 17-3). Scroll down near the bottom of the page and click the Priority Mail link to order your boxes, labels, forms, and just about anything else you'll need for shipping your items by Priority Mail. Be sure to order a month or so in advance to make sure you'll have what you need when you need it.

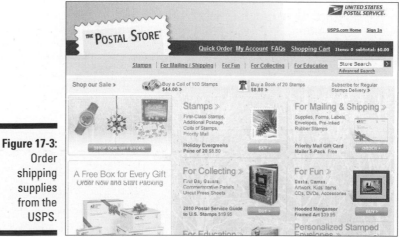

Figure 17-3:
Order shipping supplies from the USPS.

The Mail Room: Sendin' It Out

In August of 1999, the United States Postal Service announced a new service: information-based indicia (IBI). Targeted for the small office/home office (SOHO) market, IBI is USPS-certified postage that you can print on envelopes and sticker labels right from your PC. In this section, I give you the lowdown on the main Internet postage vendors: Endicia.com, Stamps.com, and PayPal.

I'm a savvy consumer and businesswoman. I don't believe in paying for extras, nor do I believe in being a victim of hidden charges. The online postage arena — while providing helpful tools that make running your eBay business easier — is fraught with bargains, deals, and introductory offers. I urge you to read these offers carefully so you know what you're getting yourself into: Evaluate how much it will cost you to start and to maintain an ongoing relationship with the company. Although you may initially get some free hardware and pay a low introductory rate, the fine print might tell you that you've agreed to pay unreasonably high prices six months down the line. I always double-check pricing before getting into anything, and I urge you to do the same.

Your old pal the United States Postal Service has Web tools that enable you to print postage and delivery confirmations online. One caveat: This is a no-frills online service, and you often get what you pay for. Keep in mind that you can't print the labels on a label printer. You must print to regular 8½ x 11 paper. For more details, go to `www.usps.com/clicknship`.

Printing labels on your printer is convenient until you start sending out a dozen packages at a time — then cutting the paper and taping the label gets a bit too time-consuming. I highly recommend that you do yourself a favor and get a label printer. Yes, they can be expensive, but you can find some great deals on eBay. I bought my heavy-duty, professional Eltron Zebra 2844 thermal label printer on eBay for one-fourth the retail price. (Search eBay for **zebra 2844**.) It's saved me countless hours. I also have a Dymo 450 XL that's lightweight and makes a very good label printer for beginners.

Free USPS package pickup

Yes! Some things *are* free! If you print electronic postage through one of the vendors mentioned in this chapter, you can go the United States Post Office Web site at `http://carrier-pickup.usps.com` and request free pickup for your items (as long as you have at least one Priority Mail package). If you misplace the URL, go to the Post Office main page and type **carrier pickup** in the search box. You can request a next-day pickup as late as 2:00 a.m.

If you're asking yourself why I haven't included a certain world-famous, popular postage-meter service in this book, you have a good question. Purchasing and printing online postage is just about the *de facto* standard in the online selling industry. Postage meters not only eat up your profits in fees, but the ink is *sooo* expensive. Inkjet ink is expensive enough (I know I don't have to tell *you* that), so if you're going to print your labels on paper, try to use a laser printer and put clear tape over the address. That's another reason why I love that Zebra label printer. No ink! It's thermal and prints over and over without ever needing ink.

Printing online postage with handy software

In the early days of online commerce, I had to scour the Internet to find places to conveniently print my shipping postage. Previous editions of this book listed each service individually, but now I examine how the current services can save you time and money. Online postage labels have a unique look. Figure 17-4 shows you a typical online 4 x 6 postage label printed from Endicia's DAZzle software.

Figure 17-4:
A custom label instantly printed on my thermal printer.

Printing your postage the twenty-first century way makes life a lot simpler:

✔ **Online postage purchases:** With a click of your mouse, you can purchase postage instantly — either by using your credit card or by direct debit from your checking account. You can register your preferences when you sign up with Endicia.com.

- **Hidden postage:** A *stealth indicia* (also known as the postage-paid indicia) is an awesome tool for the eBay seller. By using this feature, your customer will not see the exact amount of postage that you paid. This allows you to add reasonable shipping and handling costs to your invoice and not inflame buyers when they see final costs on the label.

- **Free delivery confirmations on Priority mail:** Delivery confirmations may be printed for First Class, Parcel Post, and Media Mail. Priority Mail delivery confirmation is free (that's right — no more $0.70 each) when you print postage online. (First Class delivery confirmation is only $0.19 cents online versus $0.80 cents at the post office counter.)

- **Address validation:** Before printing any postage, the software contacts the USPS database of every valid mailing address in the United States. This Address Matching System (AMS) is updated monthly.

- **ZIP code check:** The software runs a check on your addresses and corrects any ZIP code errors you've made.

- **Addition of the extra four digits to your addressee's ZIP code:** This nifty feature helps ensure swift delivery while freeing you of the hassle of having to look up the extra digits.

- **Packages are ready for the letter carrier pickup:** After you've used the online services, you have all your mail ready to go. No more socializing in the Post Office lines!

As you can see, the benefits hugely outweigh any possible service costs. The two major players that cater to online sellers are Endicia.com and Stamps. com. I give you a bit of background on both.

Endicia.com

At the beginning of PC graphics in the early '90s, I attended a cutting-edge industry trade show. I had a successful graphics and advertising business, so I was interested in the latest and greatest innovations to bring my business off the light table and onto my computer. In a smallish booth were a couple of guys peddling new software to enable artists to design direct-mail pieces from the desktop. Wow! What an innovation! Their inexpensive software even let you produce your own bar-coding for the post office. I fell in love with that software and used it throughout my graphics career.

Today's Endicia Internet Postage is based on DAZzle, its award-winning mail-piece design tool that lets you design envelopes, postcards, and labels with color graphics, logos, pictures, text messages, and rubber stamps. You can print your mailing label with postage and delivery confirmation on anything from plain paper (tape it on with clear tape) to fancy 4 x 6 self-adhesive labels in a label printer (you just choose a label template from its extensive list).

DAZzle, combined with its patented Dial-A-Zip, became the basis for today's version of the software, which is distributed to all Endicia.com customers. There isn't a more robust mailing program on the market.

Its service also makes international mailings a breeze. From Anniston, Alabama, to Bulawayo, Zimbabwe, the DAZzle software not only prints postage but also lists all your shipping options and applicable rates. For international mailing, it will also advise you as to any prohibitions (for example, no prison-made goods can be mailed to Botswana), restrictions, necessary customs forms, and areas served within the country.

A nifty thing that I love about Endicia is that you can highlight the buyer's name and address from an e-mail or from your PayPal history, click Copy, and the data is transferred automatically to the DAZzle software and plunked down in the address field. No pasting needed.

Endicia offers its own private (third-party) package insurance. It also supports U-PIC (one of the first private package insurers catering to online sellers). The insurance cost is charged to you automatically. Or, in the case of U-PIC, you can send your monthly insurance logs electronically to U-PIC at the end of the month — a service that's integrated into the DAZzle software. That way, there's no need to print insurance logs to mail.

If you're using an auction-management service or software, Endicia integrates directly with the most popular. Visit www.endicia.com/endicia-usa/Site/integratedpartners.cfm for the current list.

All the features just listed come with Endicia's standard plan. Its premium plan adds customizable e-mail, enhanced online transaction reports and statistics, business reply mail, return shipping labels (prepaid so your customer won't have to pay for the return), and stealth indicias.

With all this, you'd think the service would be expensive, but it's not. The standard plan is $9.95 a month, and the premium plan is $15.95 a month. For a free 60-day trial just for my readers (and a super package deal on a thermal label printer), go to www.endicia.com/coolebaytools.

Stamps.com

Stamps.com purchased 31 Internet postage patents from e-stamp, making its services a combination of the best of both sites. (I was a big fan of e-stamp, but it discontinued its online postage service late in 2000.) Many eBay sellers moved their postage business over to Stamps.com, which is shown in Figure 17-5.

Stamps.com works with software that you probably use every day, integrating itself into many programs, such as Microsoft Word, Outlook, and other Office applications; Corel WordPerfect; Palm Desktop; and Quicken.

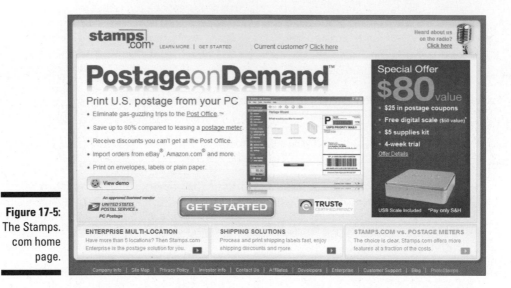

Figure 17-5:
The Stamps.com home page.

Stamps.com offers all the standard features of an online postage service, and purchasing postage is as easy as going to www.stamps.com and clicking your mouse. With Stamps.com, you don't *need* any extra fancy equipment, although most introductory deals come with a free 5-pound-maximum scale. Serious users should get a better quality postage scale from a seller on eBay or through an office supply store.

To find the Stamps.com introductory deal of the month, visit its Web site. It charges a flat rate of $15.99 per month. The site regularly offers sign-up bonuses that include as much as $25.00 free postage.

Because Office Depot, Staples, and OfficeMax deliver any order over $50.00 free the next day, any of them would be a great place to get paper and labels. Better buys on scales, though, can be found on eBay, especially if you search for **postage scale**. I use a super-small, 13-pound-maximum scale that I bought on eBay for only $29.95, complete with a 5-year warranty.

Figuring out the best solution for your business

Before deciding which service is the one for you, check out the current fees and features offered by each. Following are some of the specialized features you might want to look for:

✔ **Mac compatibility:** If you use a Mac in your daily business, you need to be sure that your postage vendor has easy-to-use Mac-compatible software that performs all the features that the service offers on the PC platform.

✔ **Print customs forms for international mail:** Printing postage for international mail isn't enough. You must be able to print the associated customs forms that go with each package and their particular level of service.

✔ **Mailpiece design:** It's nice to be able to add your own logo or even slightly customize a label (within postal guidelines).

✔ **Use your printer to print envelopes:** If your printer allows it, you can even print logo-designed envelopes along with bar-coded addresses, your return address, and postage. This saves quite a bit in label costs.

✔ **Third-party insurance:** Save time and money using a private postal insurance company (get the lowdown on this money saver in Chapter 14). Software that automatically integrates this feature is worth its weight in gold.

✔ **Integrated package tracking:** It's nice to have all your shipping data in one place, and a sophisticated mailing system will allow you to simply click a button or link to discover whether your package has been delivered.

✔ **Hard-drive records of shipping:** Software that permits you to keep your shipping records on your own computer gives you a way to check records even if the server on the Internet is down.

Postage online through PayPal

PayPal continues to add great features for sellers. Now you can not only buy postage or ship with UPS through PayPal but also print labels on your own printer. If you ship lots of items and use a different service for printing your shipping data (such as the other services mentioned in this chapter), PayPal allows you to input the tracking information on the site even if you've printed your delivery confirmations with postage elsewhere. Here's the drill:

1. **Look for and click the Add Tracking Info link.**

   A page appears, ready to receive the information.

2. **Input the tracking or delivery-confirmation information from USPS, UPS, or whichever shipping company you're using, as shown in Figure 17-6.**

PayPal sends an e-mail to your buyer with that information and updates the record on your My eBay page: The transaction moves from Awaiting Shipment in Selling Manager to Paid and Shipped.

Figure 17-6: Input your tracking information, and PayPal sends an e-mail to your buyer.

The information you added appears in three places: the record of your PayPal transaction list, the buyer's transaction list in his or her account, as shown in Figure 17-7, and on the My eBay page. (You can check whether the package has progressed by clicking the Track link on the Transaction list.)

Figure 17-7: The tracking information becomes part of the sales record on PayPal.

PayPal shipping services work great when you're just starting out in your eBay business, but once you get rolling, you need a mailing service that includes e-mail and recordkeeping, such as Endicia or Stamps.com. When you process your shipping (UPS or USPS) through PayPal, the shipping amount is deducted from your PayPal (sales revenue) balance. This is an important issue.

If you're starting a business in earnest, you need to keep track of your online expenses separately (see Chapter 16). Allowing PayPal to deduct your shipping costs from your incoming revenue creates a bookkeeping nightmare. You need to have exact figures for expense and income — and it really helps keep confusion to a minimum when your deposits (withdrawals from your PayPal account to your bank) match your sales receipts. If you want to ship through PayPal, be sure you withdraw your sales amount from your checking account *before* you process your shipping. That way, your shipping can be charged to your business credit card for easier tracking.

To purchase postage and print your label for a specific purchase, click the Print Shipping Label button next to the payment record in your PayPal account overview, as shown in Figure 17-8. You'll be taken through a step-by-step process for paying for your shipping and printing the appropriate label on your printer.

Figure 17-8:
You can buy postage and print a label for a specific purchase.

	Date		Type	Name/Email	Payment status	Details	Order status/Actions	Gross	Fee	Net amount
	Nov 22, 2010		Payment From		Completed	Details	Shipped, Track	$7.99	-$0.50	$7.49 USD
	Nov 21, 2010		Payment From		Completed	Details	Shipped, Track	$7.99	-$0.50	$7.49 USD
	Nov 21, 2010		Payment From		Completed	Details	Shipped, Track	$230.00	-$6.05	$223.95 USD
	Nov 20, 2010		Payment From		Completed	Details	Shipped,	$42.98	-$1.37	$41.61 USD
	Nov 18, 2010		Payment From		Completed	Details				$47.96 USD
	Nov 15, 2010		Payment From		Completed	Details	Shipped, Issue refund	$296.33	-$7.71	$288.62 USD
	Nov 14, 2010		Payment From		Completed	Details	Shipped, Track	$92.50	-$2.61	$89.89 USD
	Nov 14, 2010		Payment From		Completed	Details	Shipped, Issue refund	$109.75	-$3.04	$106.71 USD

Payments received - Oct 24, 2010 to Nov 22, 2010

Displaying 20 results per page — Next ▶

Move to Recent Activity   What's this   Payment status glossary

USPS Tracking No.
4200202191019690103866671405596

Part V

The Part of Tens

The 5th Wave   By Rich Tennant

"It worked, honey! I'm connected to the network!"

In this part . . .

Not everyone is a top-rated eBay all-star — or even a PowerSeller — but those are good goals. For your inspiration, I've included profiles on some interesting people — from all walks of life — who've turned eBay into a profitable enterprise, some working only part time. These are not people in big companies. Instead, they're people like us, working hard to expand their income through a business on eBay. In the second chapter, I provide information on moving merchandise that you think you might never sell.

Chapter 18

Ten (or So) Sellers Who've Made the Jump from Hobby to Profits

In This Chapter

▶ People who make their living selling at eBay . . .

▶ . . . and love it!

1 love hearing stories about how much people like eBay. I enjoy it even more when I hear that they're doing something that they get pleasure from while earning a good living. One of the best parts of writing and teaching about eBay is talking to the hundreds of sellers who attend my seminars and send me e-mails. I get the opportunity to bounce ideas around with them and find out about the creative ways they spend their time at eBay.

I thought you might like to know more about some of the people at eBay, too, so I interviewed them; it was so much fun getting to know about each of them. They have different backgrounds and lifestyles — but they all have one thing in common: eBay!

In favor of highlighting some of the regular folks at eBay, I dispensed with the customary writer thing (you know, finding the largest PowerSellers at eBay to interview). No one is a success overnight, and the people I discuss in this chapter certainly have been plugging away at eBay, increasing their businesses, and becoming successful. I dug through some old feedbacks (all the way back to 1997) and contacted sellers to see how they're doing these days. Here I present their stories (and their advice).

Beachcombers!

Member since December 2002; feedback: 7703; positive feedback: 99.4%

eBay store: `stores.ebay.com/Beachcombers-Bazaar`

Beachcombers! eBay store (see Figure 18-1) came into my search when I was looking for some reasonably priced holiday gifts. I've shopped with them continuously since. The store is run by Jody Rogers and her other half, Asad Bangash.

Figure 18-1:
Beach-
combers
Bazaar
eBay Store.

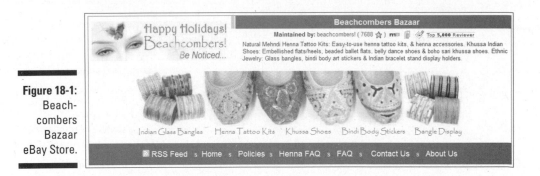

Asad started on eBay by selling car parts for his previous employer. He was successful, and after he got addicted to making a profit, he suggested to Jody that they clean out their house in Ohio and sell things on eBay. After their house emptied out, they went to neighbors' houses. Then Jody and Asad decided to move to Florida. Rather than getting new jobs, they decided to go into eBay full-time.

Jody loved Indian glass bangles and khussa shoes, and thought that mehndi (Indian temporary tattoos) were a fun idea. She looked around for sources and started selling these products on eBay. Now Jody even designs them for the American market — making popular handmade khussa shoes — they're beautiful, and in sizes that fit the larger U.S. foot. Funny thing, she's also sold them to people in India who can't get shoes to fit larger feet! And the glass bangles they sell are custom made, available only in limited quantities.

They're strong on customer service; they offer a full return policy and have a toll-free incoming number. They include complete instructions with their mehndi kits. They've also come up with unique ways to get repeat business, such as the bangle-of-the-month club: The recipient gets a handmade bangle stand and Indian glass bangles for the first shipment and then gets a new bangle set every month for the duration of the membership. There is also a Build-A-Bangle line, where you create and design your own bracelet set.

They started with Turbo Lister and now use Channel Advisor.

 Jody agrees with what I've been saying since 1998: Success in an eBay business means selling what you know and enjoy. Mailing out merchandise every day that doesn't make you happy won't make for a happy, profitable business in the long run.

Bubblefast

Member since May 1999; feedback: more than 50,000; positive feedback: 100%

eBay store: `stores.ebay.com/Bubblefast`

I first met the Bubblefast "family" when I needed to move my mother's things from Florida to California. When I got the price quote from the moving company for rolls of cushioning, it was so high I nearly fell over! I knew that I could find a better price on eBay — and I did. Bubblefast prices were 50 percent less than the moving company had quoted, and it shipped the wrap directly to my mom's house so that I could meet it there to wrap her valuables.

The Bubblefast business began with Robin and her husband Alan. Their first transaction on eBay took place in early 1999, when Alan bought a Macintosh computer. When it came to finally selling, Alan figured that all eBay sellers would need shipping supplies. At first, they sold just one product — a 150-foot roll of ³⁄₁₆" (small size) bubble cushioning. Now they sell more than 10,000 products in a variety of categories — such as bubble cushioning, bubble bags, bubble mailers, foam rolls, boxes, corrugated mailers, poly bags, labels, and sealing tape (see Figure 18-2).

Figure 18-2:
Bubblefast
eBay Store.

bubbleFAST!

Bubblefast
Maintained by: bubblefast (49704 ☆) ○ top-rated m⁹⁹ 🛡
Shipping Supplies: Bubble & Corrugated Mailers, Wrap, Anti Static, Bubble Out Bags, Foam Rolls and Pouches, Boxes, Tape, Labels, CD & LP Mailers, Bookfolds, Packing Peanuts, Air Pillows, Poly & Zipper Bags, No Bend. You can also visit our Virtual Garage Sale.

Alan passed away in 2001, and Robin and her family carried on the business. On the bright side, Robin remarried in 2003, and now (with a combined family) there are even more indentured employees. All the kids — Michelle (26), Jenny (23), Steven (17), and Sara (15) — have put in their fair share of hours helping out. When Robin and Mark recently traveled to California for a long weekend, Steven and Jenny were able to come in and do all the shipping so the business didn't miss a beat. A seller with many repeat customers (more than 50,000 positives — remember that repeat customers help build businesses!), Bubblefast decided to branch out with additional distribution centers now in California and Toronto. To serve the increasing demand for earth-friendly shipping supplies, it has launched a new line of eco-friendly "green" shipping supplies. In an effort to "pay it forward," Mark and Robin are using Giving Works to donate a portion of their eBay sales to causes like the Susan G. Komen for the Cure — Chicagoland Area Affiliate and Global Green USA. They use Turbo Lister for listing their items. They ship anywhere from 100 to 200 orders a day. The family has customers from around the world who buy from their auctions, eBay Store, and Web site (www.bubblefast. com). Last year, the business grossed $650,000. The profit margin on the Bubblefast products is low, so they have to make it up in volume.

eBay has totally changed this family's lives. Alan used to say "Our family is together all the time now; we've learned to pull together for a common goal." It's still true today with the family business he started.

The Le Vine family's tip for eBay sellers: "If you want to create a thriving eBay business and are willing to put the time and energy into it, the possibilities are endless. With a minimal investment of money, you have the potential to reach the world! Treat every customer like you want to be treated. After all this time, the customer is still always right."

Dan's Train Depot

Member since January 1999; feedback: more than 74,000; positive feedback: 100%

eBay store: stores.ebay.com/Dans-Train-Depot

Dan Glasure started selling comic books on eBay. Then he sold LEGOs, and they did well. But his real passion was model trains (and his wife was tired of a living room full of LEGOs), so he branched out (see Figure 18-3). He found a train collection for sale in a local newspaper. He and his father checked out the collection and were wowed by the price; $27,000! Their innate sales sense said that this was still a good deal, so dad put a second mortgage on the house and they took the plunge.

He sold trains out of his office at home, and the spare bedroom was the packing facility. The family quickly learned the importance of going above and beyond in packaging the precious trains carefully.

He did well on the trains — and continued purchasing collections locally. Then he branched out again, buying six brass model trains — having no idea what they were — and then selling them for about $600 each on eBay. Getting even braver, he purchased a large brass train collection for $45,000. Now brass trains make up the largest percentage of sales (www.brasstrains.com).

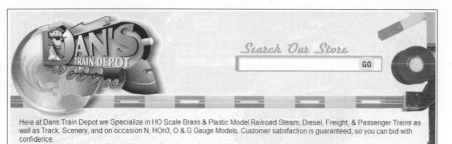

Figure 18-3:
Dan's Train
Depot eBay
Store.

Here at Dans Train Depot we Specialize in HO Scale Brass & Plastic Model Railroad Steam, Diesel, Freight, & Passenger Trains as well as Track, Scenery, and on occasion N, HOn3, O & G Gauge Models. Customer satisfaction is guaranteed, so you can bid with confidence.

Dan's father passed away in 2000. His employees and his mom still keep up the great service. They still buy out estates, hobby shops, and large collections, so you never know what treasures they'll find and put up for sale on eBay. He recently spent more than a million dollars on one collection! Sales continue to grow each year and are on track (yes, pun intended) for 4 million in sales this year.

Dan's tip for eBay sellers: "Watch your cash flow. Treat your business professionally. Keep your profits separate so that you can make it through the slow times."

3rdPowerOutlet

Member since December 1999; feedback: more than 84,000; positive feedback: 99.5%

eBay store: `stores.ebay.com/ 3rdpoweroutlet`

John Lawson started to get serious selling on eBay because of the lousy economic downturn. He found himself in a tough position, trying to flip a house and not having it work out. He thought about eBay and began to sell his collection of used technical books from his library.

He had quite a collection of books — he was an IT guy who had worked for Accenture. He and his partner John (yes, I know — John and John) work together in the business. John (Lawson) does the marketing, listing, and customer support; partner John handles order fulfillment.

After the books began to run out, they sold "free after rebate" items. (That's like going to Staples and discovering that they have a deal going that gives you a free pack of DVDs when you make a purchase). Then one day they saw Eminem wearing a do-rag on the MTV awards and figured everybody would want one. They sought out a supplier and the business was born (see Figure 18-4).

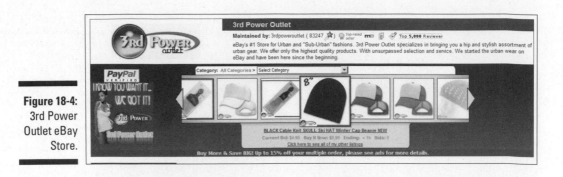

Figure 18-4: 3rd Power Outlet eBay Store.

John reinvested his profits into more merchandise and subscribes to the "God-given law that work is required for success." As the physicists say, "work = force × distance," so fxd = w — another way of saying that if you don't put the work in, you get nowhere.

If you're putting the work in but still getting nowhere, take a closer look at your business and see how you might make it more a vehicle and less a hamster wheel. For example, John saves time by printing postage with Endicia. Check out his site at `3rdpoweroutlet.com`.

Give good service through quality fulfillment. Your customers must be satisfied the moment they open the box.

GalleryNow

Member since June 1999; feedback: more than 6,200; positive feedback: 100%

eBay store: `stores.ebay.com/GalleryNow`

Stephen Kline has been an artist for more than 35 years. He's a self-representing artist who runs his own eBay store. He designed the State of Florida's "State of the Arts" license plate, and his work has been exhibited worldwide, featured in "Art in America" and by the American Kennel Club.

Kline's eBay store (see Figure 18-5) specializes in offering his signature dog and animal art along with his renowned paintings. It all started one Christmas, when he sent out a Santa lithograph drawn with the words "Season's Greetings." When the next Christmas rolled around, many friends had framed and displayed the art as part of their holiday celebration. So he decided to try a dog drawing that incorporated the breed's name. When he placed the art on eBay, the response was overwhelming. He sells pictures of more than 100 breeds now, along with other charming animal images that his buyers love. He has sold to every state in the union and more than 20 countries around the world.

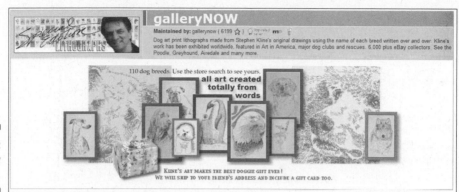

Figure 18-5:
Gallery Now
eBay Store.

Stephen personally operates all functions of his eBay store, with marketing support from his wife Kris. He's hands-on all the way, from packing all the art (guaranteeing a safe delivery) to answering all e-mail requests, questions, and comments.

He lists manually with his own template.

Stephen's tip for sellers: "Make sure that you treat the customer like gold. Good feedback will be the key to success in your business." Stephen also follows my advice by sending a note along with every order, assuring all his customers that he appreciates their business.

McMahanPhoto

Member since June 2002; feedback: more than 14,000; positive feedback: 99.9%

eBay store: `stores.ebay.com/Robert-McMahan-Photography`

Robert McMahan was (and is) a talented freelance New York photographer. Originally from Los Angeles, he began shooting pictures in 1991. Since 2001, he has concentrated most of his work in the area of journalism. He continues to build a body of travel, scenic, and holiday images, which lead to many photographs for sale. As with many other people living in New York on September 11, 2001, his life was changed by the events of that day. Heading down to the twin towers with his camera, Robert caught a now-famous photo of firefighters entering the smoke and dust of the collapsed World Trade Center. The image is named "Walk of Courage."

Photography is his passion, "be it on the street capturing the often-overlooked moments of everyday life, or in the lab producing the most stunning print possible." That's what Robert sells on eBay (see Figure 18-6). He sells quality photographs from both the Robert McMahan Collection and his RMP Archive Collections, producing high-quality prints of some of the greatest documentary photos ever taken.

Figure 18-6:
McMahan
Photo eBay
Store.

He stocks more than 5,000 historic and documentary photographs by hundreds of photographers, as well as photographic greeting cards and note cards. (I bought a set of his stunning holiday cards.) His customers include museums, archives, galleries, publishers, collectors, and interior decorators. All his prints, unless otherwise noted, are glossy, chemically processed lab photographs. He's proud of the prints and says they are the sharpest, brightest, most stunning photos available anywhere.

Robert also runs his own Web site at www.mcmahanphoto.com.

Melrose_Stamp

Member since March 1998; feedback: more than 25,000; positive feedback: 100%

eBay store: stores.ebay.com/ Melrose-Stamp-Co

A while back, I needed a rubber stamp or two for my business and didn't have time to go out to a printing store and place an order. I thought that surely someone on eBay must sell custom rubber stamps! I was right. That's when I met Jeff Stannard of Melrose Stamp Company. He specializes in self-inking custom rubber stamps and also sells stock design stamps.

Jeff was an assistant in a New York State economic development agency when he started his part-time business on eBay. Being around entrepreneurs gave him the inspiration he needed to quit his job and take his part-time sales to the next level.

He's had his eBay store since 2001 (see Figure 18-7) and works the business with his wife, Donna, and his Mom, Diane. His biggest sale came from a Chamber of Commerce in South Carolina. It ordered 65 custom stamps to use for a promotional day, where various merchants stamp a customer's card to indicate that the customer visited the store.

Figure 18-7:
Melrose
Stamp eBay
Store.

eBay has changed Jeff's life. No longer a 9-to-5er, he works more than 60 hours a week. All his life he wanted to run his own business. "My business model would fail if it were locally based only. With eBay, I'm living my dream and selling my products globally. It's a life of independence, free from the corporate rat race!"

In mid-2010, Jeff opened his own site. The decision did not come easily — but the Web site allowed greater flexibility and broader exposure. "I found that my business customers in recent years were becoming more comfortable sourcing office supplies not from platform sites like Amazon or eBay — or big-box sites — but rather from a niche site like mine, which ranks high on Google — where I fill the gap for hard-to-find selections."

What tips can Jeff offer for the eBay seller looking to make the jump? "Start a site early and ramp it up long before you need it. Your eBay repeat customers will follow you to your new Web store, especially if you offer PayPal. Keep item descriptions brief, with simple text and as little extra HTML code as possible — Google and Bing like these e-commerce pages the best. Last, maintain a vibrant storefront that can intensively cater to a specific customer segment." Jeff says, "It used to be other eBay sellers as my bread and butter — now I target office workers shopping with the boss's credit card."

Jeff's advice to new eBay sellers? "Invest time to create a business plan. A business plan will help you identify your strengths and weaknesses, threats and opportunities. Build into the plan a set of financial projections as well; this will help you to clearly identify investment and working capital needs. Treat your eBay operation as a real, sustainable business and you will go far!"

Perpetual Vogue

Member since April 2002; feedback: more than 6,500; positive feedback: 100%

eBay store: `stores.ebay.com/Perpetual-Vogue`

Looking around eBay for some unique items, I ran across Clarissa Parashar's eBay store, Perpetual Vogue (see Figure 18-8). Clarissa, a native Southern

Californian, has developed a store with a style of its own. The store specializes in rock 'n' roll, musician, tattoo design, biker, and streetwear apparel and accessories.

Figure 18-8:
Perpetual
Vogue eBay
Store.

> **Perpetual Vogue**
> **Maintained by:** perpetual-vogue (6492 ☆) m   Top 5,000 Reviewer
> Tattoo Apparel, Lucky 13, Musician Stage Wear, Anama, DOCTRINE, Casualties of Summer, Self Idol Shirts, Fifth Culture, Mission Clothing, Fender Shirts, Rock House, Jimmy Valentine, Perpetual Vogue Brand, Indigo Star, Se7en Deadly, Red Chapter, Jimi Hendrix Shirts, Belt Buckles and Accessories.
>
> **Be sure to add us to your favorites list.**
>
> Please NOTE: We have separate listings for different sizes. We may at times only have one size listed on eBay. Feel free to contact us to request that we list your size in an item you like. Our contact information is on our ABOUT ME Page and on our item pages. For the quickest response please contact us directly using the email address listed on our About Me Page or Listings.

Clarissa discovered eBay as a buyer and found it to be a fabulous marketplace for finding great items. After six months, she thought she'd like to become a seller. That timing coincided with the first eBay Live Convention in Anaheim, California, which she attended. She was inspired to take a chance on an eBay business. (She attended my class, too!) Her eBay business took off — and she opened an eBay Store to further expand her sales. Although Clarissa runs the business, she gets quite a bit of help from her family. Her husband often serves as the model for menswear. Her mom is retired, but has lots of energy and helps when new shipments come in — unpacking items, inventorying sizes, and folding the items away into their bins.

This shrewd business lady increases sales through marketing. Clarissa promotes through a page on Facebook www.Facebook.com/TattooApparel, keeps in touch with customers on Twitter, and sends out a regular newsletter to her customers. Two years after she started sales on eBay, she opened her own Web site, www.tattooapparel.com later expanding and adding sites — www.PerpetualVogue.com and www.RockerJewelry.com. The retail bug really bit her, and she just opened a retail store in LaHabra, California.

Clarissa bonds her transactions through BuySAFE so that her customers receive a *surety bond* on their purchases — a guarantee of performance. "This takes the risk out of shopping online for my customers. The customer pays nothing for this added benefit. It is paid for by me, as I feel the most important thing I as a merchant can do is to give the customers confidence so they have the freedom to shop online without worry."

Chapter 19

Ten Other Places to Move Your Merchandise

*W*hen a corner of your eBay merchandise area becomes the graveyard of unsold stuff (at some point it will — believe me), whatcha gonna do? Inevitably, you'll find yourself holding on to some merchandise that you feel may never scrape together a profit, and you'll become sick of looking at it. (Besides, you undoubtedly have *some* cash tied up in it.) Whether you have hundreds of salad spinners that are suddenly appearing in multiple auctions or you jumped on the opportunity to buy a truckload (literally) of bargain-priced cat-scratching posts, you have to make room for this stuff immediately or sell it fast.

Every business has a problem with excess inventory, so don't feel bad about it. You can't expect to bat a thousand every time you select a product to sell. The key is getting rid of excess merchandise while losing minimal amounts on your investment. None of your merchandise is trash — I hope — so someone out there will want it and will pay *something* for it. If not, you can always donate it and take a tax write-off. In this chapter, I highlight the top ten ways to move that superfluous merchandise and still save your investment.

Donate to Charitable Organizations

Charitable donations are my favorite way of unloading unwanted items. Not only are you doing something good for someone else but your donation may be a 100 percent business write-off. My community — no doubt yours, too — has many private schools, churches, and synagogues. What these places all have in common are putting on fundraisers (auctions, raffles, tournaments, bingo) and welcoming donations. You have to give the best stuff to your schools or churches — especially if your item will be some sort of prize. Some organizations even make up gift baskets of varied items to put together a higher-value prize. Charities will often gratefully take boxes of miscellaneous stuff (think Salvation Army and Goodwill).

Classy gifting

Something I like to do is put together little gift baskets for charity auctions. I'll take a bunch of female-related, male-related, or kids' items and put them in a basket on a base of shredded Sunday comics. I keep a roll of clear cellophane on hand to wrap the entire thing. I then top it off with a nice big bow. It's always an appreciated donation and when wrapped up this way, it always gets a higher price at bazaars or silent auctions.

Online charities

One of my favorite Web sites, `MissionFish.com` (see Figure 19-1), joined with eBay to organize eBay Giving Works. MissionFish helps nonprofit organizations support their missions by teaching them to fish and to build their own fisheries (to paraphrase the parable). Select your charity from the more than 10,000 on its approved list, and MissionFish does the rest. See Chapter 2 for more on charity auctions on eBay.

When an item sells, you (the donor) are responsible for shipping the item. You must use a shipping company that supplies a tracking number, which you submit to eBay Giving Works. (In addition to the item, the entire cost of shipping is tax-deductible.) After the winner receives the item, all proceeds are sent from MissionFish to the designated nonprofit. You then receive a thank-you letter as proof of your gift for IRS tax purposes. You'll have a write-off, and you'll feel good about what you did to help others.

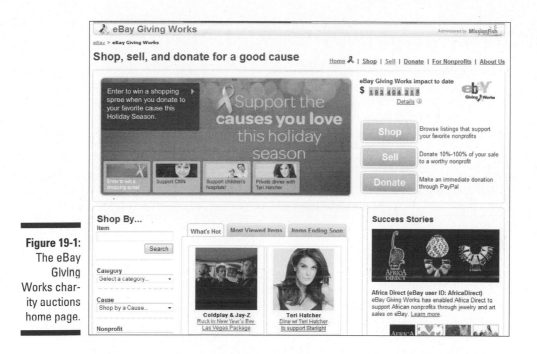

Figure 19-1:
The eBay
Giving
Works char-
ity auctions
home page.

eBay Giving Works (through MissionFish) has raised more than $194 million to date for nonprofits. Many sellers have found that by participating in this program and contributing a portion of their sales to a charity, they've increased their bids and final sale prices. This merchandising model makes a lot of sense because it helps your other listings as well. By donating your proceeds (or a portion of them) to a charity, you build an image of being a caring business on eBay rather than just another seller. Remember these facts:

✔ Listings stand out with a Giving Works ribbon icon.

✔ Your chosen nonprofit's mission statement is on every listing that benefits it.

✔ Each donation is tax-deductible (MissionFish provides the receipt for you).

✔ The eBay fee credit policy rewards your generosity.

Many other charities accept *gifts-in-kind,* items that are new or gently used that they resell to raise funds. I've brought excess eBay inventory to the American Cancer Society's Discovery Shop, and it has been very gracious about the donations. Now it also sells on eBay (aside from its many retail locations) under its own user ID.

Have a Garage Sale

Garage sales draw big crowds when promoted properly, and you'll be surprised at the amount of stuff you'll unload. An especially good time to have a garage sale is late fall or early winter — just in time for the holidays. (Before it freezes!)

Because you've probably been to a bunch of garage sales but maybe haven't *given* one in a long time, here are a few reminders:

- ✔ **Plan the sale at least three weeks in advance:** Decide on the weekend of your sale well beforehand and be sure to set a specific opening time. If you welcome *early birds* (people who like to show up at 6:00 or 7:00 a.m.), be sure to put that in your ad and flyers.

- ✔ **Invite neighbors to participate:** The more the merrier, right? Also, the bigger the sale, the more customers you're likely to entice. Everyone can drum up at least a few items for a garage sale.

- ✔ **Gather and price items to go in the sale:** After you set a date, immediately start putting things aside and pricing them with sticky tags. This way, you won't have to scramble the day before to find things.

- ✔ **Place a classified ad:** Call your local newspaper a week before the sale and ask the friendly people in the classified department when the best time is to run an ad. Take their advice — they know what they're talking about! Think also about putting an ad in eBay's classifieds. They've devised some locally oriented classifieds, and you can find your community's ads at www.ebayclassifieds.com.

- ✔ **Make flyers to post around the neighborhood:** Fire up your computer and make a flyer; include your address, a map, the date, and the starting time. Be sure to mention special items that you've thrown into the sale to bring 'em in — and mention also that many items are new. If two or three families are participating in the sale, mention that, too. If you have small throwaway types of items, include the line "Prices start at 25 cents." Hang the flyers in conspicuous places around your neighborhood.

- ✔ **Post large signs on nearby corners:** The day before the sale, put up *large* posters advertising the sale. (You can pick up 22 x 28 poster board from an art store or office supply store.) When you make the posters, use thick black shipping markers on brightly colored boards. Use few words, including only the basic details — for example: "Garage Sale June 22–24, 8:00 a.m., Tons of Stuff, 1234 Extra Cash Blvd." Also make a sign to hang at the sale location "Sale Continues Tomorrow. New Items Will Be Added!"

- **Clean up any dusty or dirty items:** If you want someone to buy an item for a good price, you have to make it look good.

- **Gather supplies:** Get lots of change; make sure you have plenty of tens, fives, a ton of singles, and several rolls of coins. Get a calculator for each person who will be taking money. Set aside a box to use as the cash box. (Cigar boxes work nicely.) Collect all the supermarket shopping bags that you can for those with multiple purchases.

- **Hang helium balloons to draw attention to your signs:** The day of the sale, go to the busiest corner near your sale and tie some helium balloons to your sign — that's sure to attract attention. Do the same thing at the corner near your sale and also at the curb of the sale.

- **Display everything in an orderly fashion:** Pull out your old card tables and arrange items so that people can easily see what's there; a literal pile of junk will turn them off. Hang clothes on a temporary rack (or use a clothesline on the day of the sale).

- **Get ready to negotiate:** Talk to people when they approach, use your selling talents, and *make that sale!*

At the end of your sale, be sure to take down the signs you've plastered all over the neighborhood. It's the nice thing to do.

Rent a Table at the Local Flea Market

Local *swap meets* or *flea markets* (regularly scheduled events where you can rent space for a token fee and sell your wares) can be a great place to meet other eBay sellers. But whatever you do, don't mention that you sell on eBay. Let the customers think that you're a rube and that they can get the best of you. Offer great deals; give 'em a discount if they buy a ton of stuff. In one important way, a flea market is just like a garage sale (see the preceding section): You can move lots of merchandise here.

Don't forget to try to unload your goods to other sellers; perhaps they can do with a little extra inventory. Check the classifieds of local newspapers for swap meets, which occur once a month in some towns.

If you have a weekly Farmer's Market in your area, check it out. This might be a great place to buy a table for a few hours — especially if you're selling related (culinary or home) items.

Consign Merchandise to the Local Antique Mall

An *antique mall* is a retail store that's often run by several people who take your merchandise on consignment. You can probably find a few in your area. Your items are sold in the store (good for you), and the store owners take a commission on each sale (good for them). They take your items, tag them with your own identifying tag, and display them for sale. Antique malls usually see an enormous amount of foot traffic, and this may be as close to having a traditional retail store as you'll ever get.

Take a Booth at a Community Event

Where I live, the local business community often holds special events: street fairs, Fourth of July extravaganzas, pumpkin festivals, and more. As a vendor, you can buy a booth at such events to peddle your wares. For seasonal events, purchasing a bunch of holiday-related items to make your table match the festivities is a savvy marketing idea. Your excess eBay inventory will just be part of the display — and a big part of your sales. You might even consider donating a percentage of your sales to a local nonprofit to help boost traffic.

If the event is in the evening, purchase a few hundred glow-in-the-dark bracelets on eBay (you can often get 100 for $20). The kids love them and will drag their parents to your booth. Be creative and think of other ways to make your booth stand out. Support your community, have a barrel of fun, and make some money!

Resell to Sellers on eBay

Sell your items to other eBay sellers. Hee-hee, only kidding (maybe not). Maybe another seller (your competition) is selling the same items but is doing a better job getting those items moved. If so, offer to sell your stock to that seller. It's a win-win situation. Perhaps some of the stuff you have may appeal to the locals in your community (some of whom probably sell on eBay).

Package up your items into related lots that will appeal to sellers who are looking for merchandise online. Take a tip from the successful eBay seller who often combines many lost packages into single lots to sell on eBay: the Post Office Mail Recovery Center. If you're overstocked with stuffed animals, put together a lot of a dozen. If you don't have a dozen of any one item, make packages of related items that will appeal to a certain type of seller.

Be sure to use the words *liquidation, wholesale,* or *resale* (or all three) in your title. A world of savvy sellers is out there looking for items to sell. Maybe another seller can move the items later or in a different venue.

Note that eBay has Wholesale subcategories for almost every sort of merchandise.

Visit a Local Auctioneer

Yes, when I say you should visit a local auctioneer, I mean a real live auctioneer — one who holds live auctions at real auction houses that real people attend. Many people enjoy going to live auctions. (I recommend that you go occasionally to acquire unique items to resell on eBay.) Shopping at auctions can be addictive (duh), and live auctions attract an elite group of knowledgeable buyers.

The basic idea is to bring your stuff to an auctioneer, who then auctions off lots for you. Good auctioneers, such as those at the Los Angeles Bonhams & Butterfields (www.bonhams.com), can get a crowd going, bidding far more than an item was expected to sell for. If you're interested in having an auction house sell your merchandise, look for a How to Sell or appraisal section on its Web site.

Here are a few facts about real live auctioneers and some pointers to keep in mind when looking for one:

✔ **Make sure that the auction house you choose is licensed to hold auctions in your state and is insured and bonded.** You don't want to leave your fine merchandise with someone who will pack up and disappear with your stuff before the auction.

✔ **Get the details before agreeing to the consignment.** Many auction houses give you at least 75 percent of the final hammer price. Before you consign your items, ask the auctioneer's representative about the details, such as

   • When will the auction be held?

   • How often are the auctions held?

   • Have you sold items like this before? If so, how much have they sold for in the past?

   • Will there be a printed catalog for the sale, and will my piece be shown in it?

> Get the terms and conditions in writing and have the rep walk you through every point so that you thoroughly understand each one.

✔ **Search the Internet.** Type *licensed auctions* and see what you come up with; it can't hurt.

✔ **Contact local auctioneers.** If your items are of good quality, a local auction house may be interested in taking them on consignment.

Find Specialty Auction Sites

If you have some specialized items that just don't sell very well on eBay, you might look for a different venue. Although eBay is the best all-purpose selling site in the world, you may have an item that only a specialist in the field can appreciate.

For example, I've seen some fine works of art not sell on eBay. But don't fret, you'll find many other places online where you can sell these items. For example, I searched Yahoo! for *art auctions.* Under the Web Results heading, I found more than 6 million Web sites that auction artwork. You might want to refine your search with your telephone area code so you find auction locations in your immediate area.

You may find an online auctioneer who specializes in the particular item you have for sale, something too esoteric for the eBay crowd. I've found some incredible bargains for myself on elegant new sunglasses made by a company in Italy called Persol, a company world famous for crystal lenses and ultra-fine quality. The super-famous wear these sunglasses: Robert De Niro, Tom Cruise, Donald Trump, Sharon Stone, Mel Gibson, and Cindy Crawford. These sunglasses normally retail from $150–$300 a pair, but you can sometimes find them on eBay for as low as $40. Unless you're buying them dirt-cheap, you're not making your profits on eBay. Maybe the crowd just doesn't know about them, but they sell well elsewhere.

Try Alternative Online Selling Venues

It's no secret that there are plenty of places you can sell on the Internet. There are auctions and fixed-price venues. Here are a couple of my favorites:

✔ **Amazon.com:** When you go to a page on Amazon for an item that you have for sale, you'll see (on the right side below the buying choices) a small line that reads: *Have one to sell?* It's followed by a button: *Sell* *yours here*. Click that button and you're taken to a page where you can list your item for sale. Amazon shows you the prices that the item is currently being offered for on the site; that way, you can make a clear judgment as to how to set your own price. Fees can be pretty steep at Amazon for small sellers, so be sure to check the fine print before you list an item for sale.

✔ **Etsy.com**: If you're an artist or make your items, Etsy is a very crafty place to sell. The site has been growing quietly over the years — and is a favorite of those who seek unique and creative items from all over the world. To list an item on Etsy, it's only going to cost you $0.20 per item for a listing that can last up to four months. When your item sells, there's a 3.5 percent transaction fee on the final sale price.

✔ **Bonanza** (formerly Bonanzle): If you want to sell your merchandise in a place that gives its users the warm fuzzies, you might just try Bonanza. It's a marketplace just like eBay, but it's more generally community-oriented. It's not as picky as eBay is about brand-new merchandise, and has the attitude that an item that's "a little loved" is okay. The fees are very reasonable; as a matter of fact, listing is free. If your item sells for up to $10, the final fee is $0.50. If it sells for $50, you'll only be charged $1.

Sell Everything on eBay for a $.99 Opening Bid . . .

. . . and take what you get.

Appendix A

eBay Business Glossary

1099: An end-of-year form that you file with the IRS to record your payments to outside contractors. A 1099 must be filed for anyone to whom you pay more than $600 in a calendar year.

1099K: IRS form sent to you from payment providers like PayPal if your total sales fall within prescribed parameters. You file this with your business' taxes.

About Me: The free Web page given to every eBay user. An excellent promotional tool.

absentee bid: A bid that an auction-house employee places on a lot (or lots) — up to a maximum amount that you designate — in your absence. When you want to participate in a live auction but can't attend it physically, you can arrange to have the auction house place absentee bids for you.

accounts payable: The amount your business owes to vendors and office supply stores, your credit card charges, and the like. This includes any money your business owes.

accounts receivable: The money people owe you, such as the checks and money orders you're expecting in the mail and the money sitting in your PayPal account that you haven't transferred to your checking account.

announcements pages: eBay pages where you get all the latest eBay information. Be sure to check these pages periodically. If you follow the Announcements link, which is at the bottom of the eBay home page (or the first link in the Community drop-down menu in the Navigation bar), you end up at the Community announcements page at announcements.ebay.com/. If you're wondering whether it's your computer's problem or an eBay problem when the search engine isn't working, check out the System Status Announcements Board at www2.ebay.com/aw/announce.shtml.

as is/where is: An item that comes with no warranty, implied or otherwise, speaking to the merchantability of the product.

bid increment: The minimum amount that a bid must advance, based on the auction's high bid.

bid retraction: A cancelled auction bid. Retractions can occur only under extreme circumstances (such as when you type the wrong numerals).

bid shielding: An illegal process wherein two bidders work together to defraud a seller out of high bids by retracting a bid at the last minute and granting a confederate's low bid the win. Not as much of an issue anymore due to eBay's new bid-retraction policy; *see also* bid retraction.

bonding: A surety bond can be issued by a third party (usually an insurance company) to guarantee a seller's performance in a transaction.

card not present: Credit card services use this term to describe transactions that typically happen over the Internet or by mail order. It means that the seller hasn't seen the actual card. This is the opposite of *swiped,* where the seller had possession of the card.

caveat emptor: Latin for *let the buyer beware.* If you see this posted anywhere, proceed cautiously — you're responsible for the outcome of any transaction in which you take part.

chargeback: When someone calls his or her credit card company and refuses to pay for a transaction. The credit card company will credit the card in question and make you pay back the amount.

consignment: When someone hands over merchandise to you to sell, which you then auction on eBay. You make a little commission, and the other person sells something without the hassle. Become an eBay Trading Assistant to get more leads in this area (`http://pages.ebay.com/tahub/index.html`).

cookie: A small text file that may be left on your computer to personalize your experience on a particular Web site. When you sign on to eBay and check the box to remain signed on, a cookie is placed on your computer that keeps your user ID and password active for the next 24 hours.

corporation: A separate entity set up to do business.

CPA: Certified Public Accountant. Someone who has been educated in accounting and has passed a certification test. CPAs are at the top of the accounting professional heap.

CTR: Click-through rate. It's a ratio of the times a visitor clicks a Web ad, versus those who view and don't click through.

DBA: Doing business as. These letters appear next to the common name of a business entity, sole proprietorship, partnership, or corporation that conducts business under a fictitious name.

DOA: Dead on arrival. The product you purchased doesn't work from the moment you opened the package.

DUNS number: Data Universal Numbering System number. An identification number issued to businesses from a database maintained by the great and powerful Dun and Bradstreet. These numbers are issued to allow your business to register with more than 50 global, industry, and trade associations, including the United Nations, the U.S. Federal Government, the Australian Government, and the European Commission. My business has had a DUNS number for years. You can get yours at no charge by logging on to the Dun and Bradstreet Web site at `https://eupdate.dnb.com/requestoptions.asp`.

EA: Enrolled agent. Enrolled agents are the only tax professionals tested by the IRS on their knowledge of tax law and regulations. They specialize in taxes, not in corporate accounting. They (like CPAs) are required by the IRS to take Continuing Professional Education and are governed by Treasury Circular 230 in their practice before the IRS.

EIN: Employer identification number. If you run your business as a partnership or a corporation, you need an EIN number from the IRS. If you're a sole proprietor, your Social Security Number is your EIN because you file all your business on your personal tax return.

entrepreneur: That's you! An entrepreneur is someone who takes the financial risk to start a business. Even if you're buying and reselling garage-sale items, you're still an entrepreneur.

FOB: Free on board. When you begin purchasing large lots of merchandise to sell, you'll encounter this term. The FOB location technically means the place where the seller delivers the goods. If the price you're quoted is FOB Chicago, you're responsible for all shipping costs to get the goods from Chicago to your home city.

FTP: File transfer protocol. The protocol used to transfer files (such as images) from one server to another.

GMS: Gross Merchandise Sales. The total receipts from your sales without deducting expenses.

hammer fee: A fee that the auction house charges at a live auction. Be sure to read the information package *before* you bid on an item in a live auction. Hammer fees usually add 10–15 percent to the amount of your bid.

HTF: Hard to find. An abbreviation that commonly appears in eBay auction titles to describe items that are, uh, hard to find.

invoice: A bill that outlines the items in a specific transaction, who the item is sold to, and all costs involved.

ISBN number: International Standard Book Number. Just like a car's VIN or the UPC on a can of beans, the ISBN identifies a book by a universal number.

keystone: In the brick-and-mortar retailing world, 100 percent markup. A product *sells for keystone* if it sells for twice the wholesale price. Products that you can sell at keystone are very nice to find.

LLC: Limited liability corporation. A form of corporation that's a little less formal than a regular C corporation. This type of corporation has become popular in the e-commerce world.

mannequin: A representation of the human form made of wood, fiberglass, or plastic. Essential for modeling clothing for your eBay apparel sales.

MIB: Mint in box. Okay, the item inside the box is mint, but the box could be in just about any shape, even looking like an 18-wheeler ran over it.

MIMB: Mint in mint box. Not only is the item in mint condition, but it's in a perfect box as well.

mint: An item in perfect condition is described as *mint*. This is truly a subjective opinion, usually based on individual standards.

MSRP: Manufacturer's suggested retail price. The price the manufacturer would really love to get, but hardly anybody actually pays.

NARU: Not a registered user. A user of eBay or other online community who has been suspended for any number of reasons.

OOP: Out of print. When a book or CD is being published, it usually has its own lifetime in the manufacturing process. When it is no longer being made, it's out of print.

provenance: The story behind an item, including who owned it and where it came from. If you have an interesting provenance for one of your items, be sure to put it in the auction description because it adds value to the item.

QuickBooks: A top-of-the-heap accounting program that helps you keep your records straight.

register: Similar to a checkbook account listing, a register goes up and down depending on the amount of flow in an account balance.

ROI: Return on investment. A figure expressed as a percentage that stands for your net profit after taxes and your own equity.

STR: Sell-through rate. The percentage of your successful listings over a prescribed period of time, usually a month.

sniping: The act (or fine art) of bidding at the very last possible second of an auction. You can do this manually or you can subscribe to any number of services that can do it for you in the last six seconds of an auction.

sole proprietorship: A business that's owned by only one person. The profits and losses are recorded on that person's personal tax return.

split transaction: A transaction that you must assign to more than one category. If you pay a credit card bill and a portion of that bill went to purchase merchandise, a portion to gas for business-related outings, and yet another portion to eBay fees, you must post each amount to its own category.

tax deduction: An expenditure on your part that represents a normal and necessary expense for your business. Before you get carried away and assume that *every* penny you spend is a write-off (deduction), check with your tax professional to outline exactly what is and what isn't legit to deduct.

TOS: Terms of service. eBay has a TOS agreement; check it out at `pages.ebay.com/help/policies/user-agreement.html`.

W-9: A form that must be filled out by any outside contractor you pay for services. This form includes the contractor's Social Security number and address. Your outside contractors must give you an invoice for each payment that you make to them. You use the information from this form to issue your 1099s at the end of the year. *See also* 1099.

wholesale: Products sold to retailers (that's you) at a price above the manufacturer's cost, allowing for a mark-up to retail. I hope you buy most of your merchandise at wholesale. Stores such as Costco or Sam's Club sell items in bulk at prices marginally over wholesale. To buy at true wholesale, you must get a resale number from your state that certifies you as a business.

Appendix B

The Hows and Whys of a Home Network

• •

*W*hat is a network? Well, these days it doesn't mean a TV channel: A *network* is a way to connect computers so they can communicate with each other — as if they were one giant computer with different terminals. The best part is that a network enables all those computers to share a single high-speed Internet connection, as well as share printers, smartphones, and other peripherals. By setting up a computer network, you can delegate tasks; one computer might run bookkeeping, another might run a graphics server, and others might be used as personal PCs for different users. From each networked computer, it's possible to access programs and files on all other networked computers.

Today's technologies allow you to perform this same miracle on the *home network.* You can connect as many computers as you like, and run your business from anywhere in your home — you can even hook up your laptop from the bedroom if you don't feel like getting out of bed.

Now for the *whys* of a home network. A network is a convenient way to run a business. All big companies use them, and so should you. You can print your postage, for example, on one printer from any computer in your home or office. You can extend your DSL line or Internet cable connection so you can use it anywhere in your home — as well as in your office.

In a network, you can set certain directories in each computer to be *shared.* That way, other computers on the network can access those directories. You can also password-protect certain files and directories to prevent others — your children or your employees — from accessing them.

I devote the rest of this appendix to a quick-and-dirty discussion of home networks installed on Windows-based PCs. I give you a lesson on what I know works for most people. (Hey, if it doesn't work, don't e-mail me — head back to the store and get your money back!)

At this point, I want to remind you that I'm not a techno-whiz (just like I'm not a lawyer or an accountant). For more information about anything you'd think to ask about home networking, I defer to Danny Briere and Pat Hurley, authors of *Wireless Home Networking For Dummies,* 4th Edition (published by Wiley).

What I know about home networks, I've found out the hard way — from the school of hard knocks. A lot of research went into this appendix as well, so humor me and read on.

Variations of a Home Network

Basically, you have a choice of three types of home networks: Ethernet, powerline, and wireless. See Table B-1 for a quick rundown of some pros and cons of each.

Table B-1	Network Pros and Cons	
Type	**Pros**	**Cons**
Traditional Ethernet	Fast, cheap, and easy to set up.	Computers and printers must be hardwired; cables run everywhere.
Powerline	Fast; your home is already prewired with outlets.	Electrical interference may degrade the signal.
Wireless network	Pretty fast; wireless (no ugly cords to deal with).	Expensive; may not be reliable because of interference from home electrical devices.

Many people still use an Ethernet connection to hardwire the network's main (desktop) computer to connect to a wireless router. If you have an office, it's nice to know that Ethernet cabling will work over 300-foot distances. You can then connect laptops (and desktops) throughout the house via wireless and powerline.

The wireless network is the hot ticket and highly touted by the world in general these days. However, in a home office setting, the wireless signal may experience interference because many networks run with the same 2.4 GHz technology as some home wireless telephones. I have a wireless network and it works great. My primary network hookup is via Ethernet. But it's actually a hybrid, combining Ethernet, powerline, and wireless.

With broadband over powerline, you get high-speed Internet directly into your home electrical system. Just plug in your powerline boxes (more on that later) and you're up and running!

All networks need the following two devices:

- ✔ **Router:** A router allows you to share a single Internet IP address among multiple computers. A router does exactly what its name implies; it routes signals and data to the different computers on your network. If you have one computer, the router can act as a firewall or even a network device leading to a print server (a gizmo that attaches to your router and allows you to print directly to a printer without having another computer on).

- ✔ **Modem:** You need a modem for an Internet connection. You get one from your cable or phone company and plug it into an outlet with cable (just like your TV) or into a special phone jack if you have DSL. The modem connects to your router with an Ethernet cable.

If you have broadband, you don't even need to have a main computer turned on to access the connection anywhere in the house. If you keep a printer turned on (and have a print server), you can also connect that to your router and print from your laptop in another room — right through the network.

Hooking up with wireless

Wireless networking — also known as WiFi or, to the more technically inclined, IEEE 802.11 — is the hot technology for all kinds of networks. It's an impressive system when it works, with no cables or connectors to bog you down.

If you're worried about your next-door neighbor hacking into your computer through your wireless connection, stop worrying. Wireless networks are protected by their own brand of security, called Wired Equivalent Privacy (WEP). WEP encrypts your wireless transmissions and prevents others from getting into your network. Another flavor of security is WPA (Wi-Fi protected access), which is even more secure. Although super-hackers have cracked this system, it's the best currently available for the home office user.

To link your laptop or desktop to a wireless network with WEP (or WPA) encryption, you have to enter a key code from the wireless access point. Just enter it into your wireless card software on every computer (or system-based software program) that uses the network, and you should be good to go.

You may get confused when you see the different types of wireless available. Here's the lowdown on the variations:

- **802.11a:** This wireless format works really well — fast with good connectivity. It's also very expensive. This format is used when you have to connect a large group, such as at a convention center or in a dormitory. It delivers data at speeds as high as 54 Mbps (megabits per second). It runs at the 5GHz band (hence its nickname, WiFi5), so it doesn't have any competition for bandwidth with wireless phones or microwave ovens.

- **802.11b:** My laptop has a built-in 802.11b connection, so I can log on to the popular hotspots in Starbucks and airports. It's the most common wireless type, and it's used on the most platforms. It travels over the 2.4GHz band. The 802.11b version is slower than the 802.11a version, transferring data at only 11 Mbps.

    The lower frequency of 2.4 GHz drains less power from laptops and other portable devices, so laptop batteries will last longer. Also, 2.4GHz signals travel farther and can work through walls and floors more effectively than 5GHz signals.

- **802.11g:** This flavor is based on the 2.4GHz band. It speeds data up to a possible 54 Mbps, and it's backward-compatible with 802.11b service.

- **802.11n:** The latest, fastest form of wireless, 802.11n is a dual frequency that works through multiple input/multiple output (MIMO) technology. It travels farther and faster than any of the other formats — I'm using it now as I write this, and it's amazing!

Installing your wireless network isn't a gut-wrenching experience, either (although it can be if the signal doesn't reach where you want it). You hook up your computer (a laptop works best) to the wireless access point (the gizmo with the antenna that broadcasts your signal throughout your home or office) to perform some setup tasks such as choosing your channel and setting up your WEP (or WPA) code. (The wireless access point comes with its own instructions.)

After you complete the setup and turn on your wireless access point, you have a WiFi hotspot in your home or office. Typically, a hotspot provides coverage for about 100 feet in all directions, although walls and floors cut down on the range.

Here are some simplified steps on configuring your network:

1. **Run a cable from your cable connection, or a phone cord from your DSL line, to your modem.**

2. **Connect one Ethernet cable from your modem to your router.**

3. **Connect one Ethernet cable to your wireless access point.**

Take a look at the network diagram from Netgear in Figure B-1.

Notebook PC with
802.11b Wireless
PC Card

Desktop PC with
802.11g Wireless
USB Adapter

Internet

802.11g Wireless
Access Point

Figure B-1:
A typical
home
wireless
network.

Cable/DSL
Modem

Firewall
Router

Desktop PC with
802.11g Wireless
PCI Adapter

Extending wireless with powerline

An ingenious invention, a *powerline wireless extender* uses your existing home powerlines to carry your network and your high-speed Internet connection. You access the network by plugging a powerline adapter wired to your router into an electrical outlet on the wall. Then another little box can be placed farther away in your home to broadcast an additional wireless signal. Standard powerline networks have been around for a while; this is the second round of technological advances for them.

I have a powerline wireless extender, so I can bring my network out to the garage and to far points in my home.

Hooking up a wireless powerline extender is so easy that it's a bit disappointing — you'll wonder why it isn't more complicated. Most installations work immediately right out of the box. Hooking up the wireless/powerline network goes like this:

1. **The high-speed connection comes in through your DSL or cable line.**

2. **Plug the cable line (or phoneline for DSL) into your modem.**

3. **Connect one "in" Ethernet cable from your modem to a router.**

4. **Connect the "out" Ethernet cable to the wireless powerline extender.**

5. **Plug the wireless powerline extender into a convenient wall outlet.**

6. **Plug the wireless powerline receiver box into a convenient wall outlet wherever you want to extend the signal.**

That's it!

Index

● *G* ●

• N •

• O •

Apple & Macs

iPad For Dummies
978-0-470-58027-1

iPhone For Dummies,
4th Edition
978-0-470-87870-5

MacBook For Dummies, 3rd
Edition
978-0-470-76918-8

Mac OS X Snow Leopard For
Dummies
978-0-470-43543-4

Business

Bookkeeping For Dummies
978-0-7645-9848-7

Job Interviews
For Dummies,
3rd Edition
978-0-470-17748-8

Resumes For Dummies,
5th Edition
978-0-470-08037-5

Starting an
Online Business
For Dummies,
6th Edition
978-0-470-60210-2

Stock Investing
For Dummies,
3rd Edition
978-0-470-40114-9

Successful
Time Management
For Dummies
978-0-470-29034-7

Computer Hardware

BlackBerry
For Dummies,
4th Edition
978-0-470-60700-8

Computers For Seniors
For Dummies,
2nd Edition
978-0-470-53483-0

PCs For Dummies,
Windows
7 Edition
978-0-470-46542-4

Laptops For Dummies,
4th Edition
978-0-470-57829-2

Cooking & Entertaining

Cooking Basics
For Dummies,
3rd Edition
978-0-7645-7206-7

Wine For Dummies,
4th Edition
978-0-470-04579-4

Diet & Nutrition

Dieting For Dummies,
2nd Edition
978-0-7645-4149-0

Nutrition For Dummies,
4th Edition
978-0-471-79868-2

Weight Training
For Dummies,
3rd Edition
978-0-471-76845-6

Digital Photography

Digital SLR Cameras &
Photography For Dummies,
3rd Edition
978-0-470-46606-3

Photoshop Elements 8
For Dummies
978-0-470-52967-6

Gardening

Gardening Basics
For Dummies
978-0-470-03749-2

Organic Gardening
For Dummies,
2nd Edition
978-0-470-43067-5

Green/Sustainable

Raising Chickens
For Dummies
978-0-470-46544-8

Green Cleaning
For Dummies
978-0-470-39106-8

Health

Diabetes For Dummies,
3rd Edition
978-0-470-27086-8

Food Allergies
For Dummies
978-0-470-09584-3

Living Gluten-Free
For Dummies,
2nd Edition
978-0-470-58589-4

Hobbies/General

Chess For Dummies,
2nd Edition
978-0-7645-8404-6

Drawing
Cartoons & Comics
For Dummies
978-0-470-42683-8

Knitting For Dummies,
2nd Edition
978-0-470-28747-7

Organizing
For Dummies
978-0-7645-5300-4

Su Doku For Dummies
978-0-470-01892-7

Home Improvement

Home Maintenance
For Dummies,
2nd Edition
978-0-470-43063-7

Home Theater
For Dummies,
3rd Edition
978-0-470-41189-6

Living the
Country Lifestyle
All-in-One
For Dummies
978-0-470-43061-3

Solar Power Your Home
For Dummies,
2nd Edition
978-0-470-59678-4